Girlfriend on the Rocks

One Woman's Transformative Adventure
with Glaciers, Rocks and Love

Cheryl Berry

Cheryl Berry Presents
PETALUMA, CALIFORNIA

Cheryl Berry Presents
Petaluma, California
cherylberrypresents.com
email: cheryl@cherylberrypresents.com

Author's note:
This is a true story. Much of it was painful to write and challenging to explore. I have therefore changed the names of all persons except my family, girlfriends, and the Peters clan who have all graciously allowed me to celebrate them in print.

Ordering Information:
Quantity sales. Special discounts are available on quantity purchases by corporations, associations, and others. For details, contact the "Special Sales Department" at the address above.

Girlfriend on the Rocks/ Cheryl Berry. -- 1st ed.
ISBN 978-0-9908163-0-0

Library of Congress Control Number: 2014952822

Dedicated to
rock lovers everywhere

Acknowledgements

Audrey who encouraged me, heard my musings on the article I wanted to write for my rescue rangers and first declared, "It's a book!"

Aliza who let me look over her shoulder as she read each weekly chapter of my first draft

Diana Krista who loved me enough to make me hear what the manuscript needed to move from, as she put it, a "Sierra Club Reader to a Bestseller."

Linda Howard and Linda Jay, my wonderfully compassionate and supportive editors.

My sister Marcia who not only orchestrated my care, then helped filled me in on parts of the story where I wasn't present.

Dave and Kelley who continue to remind me of the heart of the book and the power of its message, and Ken who has championed me throughout.

To members of the Redwood Chapter of the California Writer's Club and the Bay Area Independent Publishers Association for bringing me the education and support to turn my dreams into a reality.

And to Ruth, the book midwife, for helping me birth this, my first.

Table of Contents

Where Am I?

WHATEVER WAS LEFT of my consciousness was blissfully suspended, surrounded by the inky black void. It felt like a soft embrace from the darkened stillness, like the most satisfying of subtle caresses, and filled my being with a deep and profound sense of peace.

Then, some part of me knew: this is my entrance into the afterlife.

What I can only describe as my etheric body had the memory of just having passed through some invisible portal where time itself seemed to flow over my skin. I detected this movement, since the space around me was now exerting a slightly different density against my soul-body. On this side of that portal, I found myself floating freely within the vast emptiness.

As my awareness gained a small measure of focus, I felt I was expanding into a supreme state of serenity that was not of the material world I had once known. I basked in peacefulness and sublime pleasure while untethered from my body, unencumbered even by the mental constructs of my mind within the dark and endless void. Without any connection to my physical body, I enjoyed the weightless sensation as I floated around ecstatically in an endless sea of bliss.

Soon, tiny bits of emotional memory and various images started to come together from the outer edges of space. I saw lighted flashes of memory, like physical objects dropping out of the darkened expanse. Ideas about how I had arrived at this state started to gently coalesce as individual fragments were grouped into larger thought forms.

Ah, yes, I was hiking in the mountains of Colorado on vacation. I had lost my footing at the top of the glacier and careened down the steep, icy slope before I slammed into the rocks. Well, if I didn't feel anything after *that* impact, then I *must* be dead.

Even as I tried to orient my awareness within this timeless expanse, the thought that I might be dead made sense. There's no way I could have survived after crashing into those rocks so fast. This idea seemed to enhance my peace and satisfaction as I entered this new realm where I explored the burgeoning awareness of my death.

Dying was actually pretty easy, I mused. That's funny, considering all the years I had suffered from depression and yearned for this very moment of relief. A long time ago, I ached to find a permanent way to escape my grief and emotional pain after Mom died. To that end, I spent a lot of time musing about how I could kill myself. How curious that those rocks had just provided me with the release I had fantasized about so much. I marveled at the relative ease of this painless transition. Who knew it could happen so fast, especially after such a glorious day hiking up the mountain and over to this glacier?

In the sweet bliss of my experience, I could almost see simple thoughts gather and take form before they'd gently drift away. I watched as a new thought floated in, this time in the form of a question. *When will I see the light?* I felt a thrill of excitement to think that I would soon find myself entering the tunnel of light. I had read about people who had passed to the other side and encountered loved ones who greeted them on the way. *Who will*

I see? I wondered in anticipation. *Will it be Grandma or Mom?* I'd love to see Mom, I thought. It's been almost 20 years since she was on earth. My eagerness and delight grew at the prospect. I want to see the light. *Where is the light?*

I continued to wait, anticipating that someone would soon come for me. But there was no light. No one coming to guide me into the tunnel.

As I waited, I began to explore my new and peaceful reality. I watched as another thought arose out of the stillness: *Can I still feel my body?* I decided I wanted to test this idea. So I gathered the energy necessary to create a command to blink my eyes. But after successfully opening and closing my eyes, everything around me was still dark, quiet and peaceful. *Are my eyes really open if nothing has changed and all I see is black?* Wondering if I could feel my body, I then asked my fingers to move, generating a slight ripple in my expanded quietude. Then another idea arose. *Can I move my hand up to feel if my eyes are really open?* I issued the thought, and my arm seemed to be moving slowly toward my face. But instead of my eyes, my fingers felt the edge of my sunglasses. And my nose felt the glasses pushing up against it. Puzzled by this unexpected sensory feedback, I slowly lifted my sunglasses and finally saw the light. But it wasn't the one leading me into eternity. It was the light of day, a clear blue sky.

Oh, wow, I *am* alive.

I instantly recoiled from that thought.

Oh, no. This can't be good.

I closed my eyes against the insistent pull from the physical world. Grieving the sudden loss of peace, I dreaded the implications that flooded in at the thought of being alive.

I did not want to deal with the reality of what might have happened to my body after hitting those rocks. I opened my eyes again, blinked a few times, and then slowly looked down at the sunglasses, which were caked with snow. Oh, so that's why I could only see the blackness. But what about the peace? The floating? The serenity? The portal of energy I had passed through?

The yearning to go back to the three-dimensional world was growing stronger, yet I was still reluctant to respond to the demands of living.

A morbid sense of curiosity pushed at me to take an inventory of my body. If life had won out over death, I wanted to find out what parts of my body still worked.

Am I paralyzed? After slamming into the rocks at such a high speed, I had to confront that possibility. With a keen sense of trepidation, I cautiously lifted my head and shoulders like a corpse rising from the grave. *Not paralyzed,* I thought with relief.

Good. That's a start.

***

Krista, my girlfriend, put down her tea and interrupted my story. "Where was Doug when this happened?" she asked.

I shook my head and tried to bring myself back from recounting my experience.

"Doug?" I replied distractedly. "He was still somewhere back up on the glacier."

Krista knew that Doug had seduced me into this vacation with the idea that we could have fun as we climbed the icy expanses. She had heard about the ups and downs of our relationship over the past two years and still didn't quite understand what drove me to follow him into the wilderness.

"So were you still lying on the snow?"

"No, I was on the rocks," I moved my hand across my front to show how my momentum had carried me several feet beyond the glacier's edge.

That would be Andrews Glacier in Rocky Mountain National Park, where Doug and I had spent the day climbing and hiking at 12,000 feet. The glacier was at the top of a steep gorge lined with jagged grey boulders as far as the eye could see. The massive icy sheet was covered with a thin layer of snow as it descended into a V-shaped gorge between the towering walls of chiseled granite rising up on either side. We were far above the tree line, even at the bottom of the glacier, so this was a rocky paradise with huge blocks of stone impeding the full view down the entire valley. The wind was much calmer at the bottom of the glacier than when we were exposed on the open plateau.

***

Back on the glacier, Doug, the man I trusted, had navigated the ice and scrambled over the rocks to be at my side. He had taken this route before and was the *experienced* climber to lead us on what was supposed to be my first day hike on a glacier. He had planned our route and instructed me on my equipment and technique with an attention to detail worthy of the brilliant engineer that he is. As I followed him deeper into the wilderness on the few climbing weekends we had shared, Doug was more than generous and patient with his instruction and support. He was not the kind of man to display strong emotion himself and had never been comfortable when I shed tears. But when he came to my side, and squatted down, his eyes were wide as saucers, and filled with disbelief.

"You're alive! Cheryl! Oh, my God! Are you okay? I saw you hit," he gasped, "I thought you died."

His mouth, which before had covered me in kisses, was now pulled taut with fear. His brow was furrowed as tightly as his eyes, which had recently looked at me with love, but were now frantically scanning my body, trying to analyze the situation.

Only after I turned my head to look at him did I notice that my chest had started rapidly heaving up and down and that my breath was escaping my lips in quick, ragged bursts. Then the shuddering started, my whole body shaking uncontrollably as the effects of shock set in.

"What did you hurt?" he asked, bringing me into focus with those beautiful blue eyes.

Good question, I thought. I wanted to think about the rest of my body, but my head felt like it was filled with lead and moved very slowly. I was just starting to accept the idea of having arms and legs again. I opened my mouth to respond, but my teeth were chattering hard, and no words came out. I was shaking so violently, I was afraid that I'd bite through my tongue if I tried to talk. I opened my mouth repeatedly, trying to coordinate my breathing to form intelligible sounds. It took several attempts before I could finally spit out a response. "M-m-my r-r-right f-f-foot."

Yes, I was alive, but my mind was altered and my entire body was now shaking horribly. *Can't I just blink and start this day again?*

My eyes looked to the right and slowly I dragged my head to follow them. I started taking in the extreme desolation of my surroundings. Everything around had the dull grey shading of rocks and boulders as far as the eye could see. No trees. No plants. Just rocks. My mind slipped into a repetitive loop, demanding over and over again, "Where's my 'do-over'? Don't I get a 'do-over'?" I closed my eyes hard and willed the situation to change. A childhood television memory of Jeannie blinking her eyes to get Major Nelson out of trouble inspired me. So I blinked for my "do-over." But nothing happened. I blinked again, harder. After several ever more increasingly hard blinks, nothing around me had changed. I was desolate. I could not turn the clock back, escape the crash and avoid this whole situation. No, I was still injured, hyperventilating and in shock, miles from a trail, and had no one but Doug to help me.

Also, I didn't have the luxury of calling 911 and sitting back to wait for a paramedic to come. I closed my eyes and thought, how wonderful it would be to simply lie down and allow myself to die. That seemed infinitely better than the pain and fear that was starting to consume me. *If I didn't get a "do-over," couldn't I at least be left here to die?* I willed myself to return to that dark and peaceful realm. Death as an escape had been so tantalizingly close.

But all that was to no avail. I opened my eyes and looked down at my shaking body. I was not dead; it seemed I could not will myself to die. Death was no longer the easy escape. Darn, darn, darn. No "do-over," can't die. My mind was fixated on these options, as if sheer force of will could cause a change in my circumstances. As much as I loathed the idea, I knew I was going to have to deal with the painful ruin that was now my life. My heart was beating so fast, I thought it would leap out of my chest. My breath was going in and out too hard and too fast. God only knows what's broken. What a mess! Oh, my God! What will I do?

I turned and saw Doug's face, pressed close to mine. He was looking at me wide-eyed and ashen, as though he were in shock himself. Okay, he's no help, I decided. So my mind kept searching for what I could do. I knew I would have to stop shaking and hyperventilating if I was going to get out of this alive. A peaceful death was no longer an option. My goal was now to avoid even more pain and the prospect of slowly freezing to death.

7

A barrage of thoughts started flying around inside my head; the swirl was almost dizzying. I had to sort through it to capture anything useful. *What about taking Arnica?* I thought. Yeah, that homeopathic pill would help with an injury. But it was back in the tent. Well, that's no help. Jeez, I've got to stop shaking! What can I do?

Then another idea popped up: the Emotional Freedom Technique. Could tapping really alter my breathing and shaking?

Luckily, I had tapped those points many times before. "Please, please, please," I prayed, "help me do it right." My fingers were fluttering wildly as they searched for the right locations to tap on my hands and around my face. I could only stutter the phrases in unsteady bursts as I stated my intention to calm myself down. My hands were so unsteady I was worried that the technique wouldn't be effective.

Doug was looking at me as if I'd gone crazy, stuttering and tapping myself. But I didn't know what else I could do to help me return to some normal level of functionality. When I was done, I thought, wow, my shaking and chattering has dropped by 70 percent! Doug looked dumbfounded. "Wow. How'd you do that? You've stopped shaking, and your breathing is more normal."

I was amazed at the transformation myself. But I waved him off, unable to form an intelligible response from the scattered thoughts that continued to ricochet around the insides of my head.

Now that I was shaking less, we both turned to address what was wrong with my foot.

"Can I take off your boot to check your foot?" he asked. I nodded to him and he unlaced the boot before gently pulling it off my foot. We both saw how swollen my right ankle had become. With one hand on my calf, he gently held the arch of my foot up and moved it so my toes went in a small circle. I felt an eerie grinding sensation, as if there were gravel in my ankle, and then a searing pain shot up my leg. "Stop!" I cried, as my leg recoiled from the intensity.

Doug stood there, tall and lean, looking down at my foot. Towering above me at 6'4", he cut a striking silhouette against the barren landscape.

"It's probably just a sprain," he enthused. "I sprained my ankle once. It got big and swollen like this," he offered, trying to sound positive. I was desperate to hear some good news, so I went along and accepted his assessment. A sprain wasn't so bad and was a small ray of hope that things might work out after all. He carefully slid the boot back onto my foot.

"Let's see," he reflected. "If you can put some weight on it, then I can help you down the mountain." Towering above me, Doug crouched down, wrapped his arm around my waist and helped me stand on my left foot. I lowered my right boot gently onto the ground.

"NO!" I gasped, jerking my leg back up. It felt like a bolt of lightning shooting up my leg, even when I applied the slightest bit of pressure.

He eased me back down, and I sat there, hanging my head in defeat. If I could not walk, there was no hope for me to get down the mountain. Now I would surely die. But this time I would be cold and it would be a slow and painful death.

In the quiet and stillness of the canyon, I was very present to my consciousness as it slowly started to move away from me. Crowded out by the injury, shock and pain, I felt as if I was watching my soul make a steady retreat from my body. Then I felt something else rise up. A primitive force had emerged from some place deep inside me and started to galvanize every resource I had. It fed into my thoughts and fueled my will to survive, then moved through me and seized control of my limbs. Rapidly taking command, the force turned all of my attention and energy to these simple edicts: Preserve your body. Get to safety. Seek out help.

I now was clear that I had to get down this mountain. If I didn't, I would surely die.

Doug returned from hiking back up the mountain a ways to see if his cell phone would connect. "No signal," he reported as he shoved his useless cell phone back into his pocket.

"I could go for help, but I don't want to leave you here," he said, looking down at me. "And I can't carry you through this stuff," his voice rising, sweeping his hand toward the floor of the canyon, crowded with jagged boulders. "I just can't," he spat out in desperation. Then, ever the pragmatic engineer, Doug started listing our non-options all over again. "It's so late in the day, no one will be coming up the canyon, and we haven't seen anyone else for hours. We're at 12,000 feet and I can't reach the rangers on my cell. I can't carry you..."

As I heard his words, a cruel realization slowly came to me. All around me, rock, rock and more rock—nothing but rock as far as the eye could see. I had come to the mountains because of my love of rocks. That painful irony cut a sharp and bitter path to my heart. Now the only thing that stood between me and any hope for survival was this endless sea of huge, magnificent rocks.

I continued to sit there, staring at all the boulders through the heavy fog that had settled inside of my head. Doug continued on, offering up his litany of non-options, but his words only seemed to hover in the air above me. As much as he tried to shape a plan for my safety, the words only fell to the ground beside me before blowing away in a gust of wind. In that moment, my desperate hope for rescue also vanished.

The Long Shot

SHIVERING FROM COLD and in shock, sitting at the edge of the glacier, a barrage of ideas moved through my mind, bouncing around, then disappeared as quickly as they had come. I couldn't walk. Doug was strong, but he couldn't carry me over these rocks.

What else could I do? I slowly scanned the canyon, rimmed with high walls. There were no forms of life: no trees, bushes or plants. There were only rocks all around me—a few larger boulders and the huge, grey monolith stones that were two stories high. The rocks got me into this mess, but offered no help in getting me out of it.

Each time I looked at a different rock, it was like my eyes had to move slowly through a dense cloud of Jell-O before I could bring my focus to a new scene. Then it was another moment or two before I could truly comprehend what I was looking at. My mental process was stripped down and simplified, as my life was now unfolding in slow motion.

When my eyes eventually focused on the jagged rocks I was sitting on, I contemplated my body. My teeth were still chattering as I finally stared at my open palms.

I considered my body as if it was an assortment of tools at my disposal. I disregarded my right leg because of the pain in my foot, and then moved on. What could I still do? My right leg wouldn't work, but the left leg did, and so did both my arms. Those three limbs were going to have to be enough. Yet I was facing long odds, to be sure.

Doug was still pacing around, voicing the options of leaving me alone or staying the night. I was clear that neither of those options were acceptable to me. So I decided that if no one else could save me, then I would have to rescue myself. It was up to me to get myself to safety. It was a pathetic long shot at best, but I had no other choice; my life was on the line. If I was going to survive, I would have to crawl by myself out of that canyon.

Doug was unaware of my decision as I continued to explore what my body could do.

As I sat there, I carefully placed my hands, palms down, on the rocks on either side of me. The rocks were cold and hard, but stable. Next I turned to focus on straightening my left leg. I willed it to unbend and stretched it out, placing my left boot on a rock further away from me. This can work, I kept telling myself.

I wondered if I could trust these three limbs to support me. I shifted some of my weight onto each point to test if my body was strong enough and if the rocks would hold still. I locked my elbows, and slowly lifted the weight of my torso. I held my breath as my hips gently rose up and off the rock. I was suspended only briefly before I carefully eased my body forward a bit, toward my left foot. I let out a breath of relief when I realized that I had done it. I had moved myself forward! My makeshift tripod worked!

My right foot protested at the movement, so I added lifting my right leg to this process. Buoyed by my success, I tried it again, placing my hands and left foot on other rocks and gently swinging my butt forward for a second time. *I can do this*, I thought, *I'm not totally helpless.* I wasn't concerned about my slow pace, the impossible terrain, or the tremendous distance that lay ahead of me. For me, the bodily experience of actually moving myself forward was nothing short of a miracle. *I could get myself to safety,* I thought, *maybe I won't die tonight.* So I continued on, like a drunken crab picking its way through an impossible field of boulders.

Although I was just thinking about how to coordinate the proper placement and sequence of these motions, it was exhausting labor. As I looked ahead, there was not even a semblance of a trail, but I kept moving. At this elevation, the canyon seemed utterly impenetrable. I was crawling over jagged rocks that looked like a field of cinderblocks. What I saw around me was a valley full of tremendous boulders, rockfall and snowfields. Huge, two-story boulders blocked the view further down the valley, so I had no idea what kind of terrain lay ahead.

"What are you doing?" Doug asked, bewildered to see me moving. "Getting down the mountain," I grunted back, my eyes still focused on where I could place my hands next.

He must not have had a better idea, because he went ahead of me with the pack. He looked around, set it down and scrambled back up to me, panting from the effort, then pointed toward the pack and said, "Go that way." I continued to scoot my butt one rock at a time, veering to the left, making my way around the huge chunks of the mountain that were in front of me.

I inched along, while Doug chose the best route for me. I crawled over and around the rocks, and he would go ahead and come back each time to see if he could help me in some way. I would shake him off and continue to concentrate on the effort it took to lift my body and move it ahead very slowly from stone to stone.

Eventually we came to a more level area closer to the edge of the canyon wall. "Let's see if I can carry you over this," he said.

There was a dirt path that was smooth and flat. He helped me to stand up and balance on my left leg; then he bent down and I crawled onto his back. He could only carry me for a short distance before my weight and the lack of oxygen forced him to stop and rest. We continued on like this for about 30 minutes.

After setting me back on the ground, he pointed to a large bloodstain on my right thigh, and came over to inspect it more closely. "There's no tear in the pant leg, so you weren't cut," he concluded. "How could there be so much blood?" I could not see the stain myself, as it was mostly towards the back of my mid-thigh. Then he quickly offered, "You're in your period. Maybe it's just from that." I had to concentrate just to keep my balance while I hauled my eyes around to see more of it for myself. The stain was four to five inches across. The deep blood red contrasted against my light tan hiking pants and the size of the stain surprised me. It just didn't make any sense.

***

Krista chimed in, "You're right, Cheryl! It doesn't make sense. You don't bleed over on your thigh!"

"I know, but you've got to give him some credit," I replied. "To a guy, it's a very logical thought. It didn't matter to him that the blood was way over on the outside of my thigh."

"I didn't feel anything specific going on in my leg," I continued. "Even though I was out of it," I said, drawing circles by my head. "I knew that so much blood could not come so suddenly from my monthly flow. But I couldn't take the idea any farther than that. My mind was still thick and barely functioning from shock. Every thought felt like a heavy weight I had to lift, and there was no way I could hold two competing thoughts up for comparison."

"Didn't you want to look and see, since you knew it wasn't the blood from your moon?"

"Sure, there was a little voice inside that said, 'You should see where that blood stain came from.' But I didn't have the energy or strength to say that aloud, let alone act on it."

Krista was still incredulous. "But Doug was such an experienced climber. Didn't he at least have a first aid kit, or care enough to want to check your leg?" Krista wasn't the first (or last) person to challenge me on Doug's neglectful behavior.

"You'd have to ask him yourself," I conceded, shaking my head. "I didn't have the presence of mind to think about that. After he drew his own conclusions about where the blood had come from," I affirmed, "he didn't pursue it any further." And I had dismissed any more concern about my leg as quickly as Doug had.

***

The question of what to do next continued to hang between Doug and me. Since I didn't have the strength to contradict his idea about the blood's source, I conceded that there was nothing more I could do about it. So I focused what remained of my energy and attention back to navigating the next section of the canyon.

As I physically moved down the canyon, the heaviness in my head lessened slightly and I could change my visual focus more easily. The rhythm of placing my hands on the rocks and lifting myself over them became easier and increased my confidence in being able to carry on.

The rocks were cold and sharp against my hands and bottom. Even when I'd look up, I saw only more gray and buff rock rising up from the canyon floor. We were still far above the tree line and there were not even stunted bushes to break up the desolate view. But I was content with the singular fact that my body was still functional and capable of negotiating the rugged terrain.

15

We continued down, alternating with me crab-crawling over the rocks and Doug carrying me on his back over the short stretches of flattened dirt. When he carried me, I kept an eye out for high enough boulders that he could set me down on easily. Doug was still covering the distance twice. First with the pack, selecting the route, then coming back to carry me or guiding me to crawl through the next maze of rocks and boulders. He could only stand there and watch me as I painstakingly picked my way through the jagged rockfall that filled my path. I would carefully lift my right foot away from banging into anything. Sometimes I had to squeeze through narrow passages between the towering monoliths. Clear, flat ground was a rarity and should have been seen as a promising sign, but climbing up onto Doug's back was a painful struggle.

He would hitch me up higher on his back and I had to bite back cries of pain as every movement shook my foot. As he held my legs around his waist, I could feel a sharp tearing pain in my right thigh. After he set me down, I noticed a dark red circle on the toe of my right boot. A drop of blood. My blood. I was bleeding enough for it to drip down my leg!

Under normal circumstances, that would be a huge warning sign to take action to stop the bleeding. But, still suffering from the effects of shock and having my brain sloshed from crashing into the rocks, this fact barely entered my consciousness as an abstract thought. It concerned a bodily process, but seemed not to be connected to me. It was just of transient curiosity before I had to refocus and hunker down to crawl my way through the next tangle of boulders.

Moving forward required my total concentration. I focused on the positive action of getting down the mountain, with the hope that I might actually survive. But even with all the effort it took to keep moving ahead, I couldn't escape the lethal implications of the discovery of my mysterious bleeding. That had only increased my fears and felt like cold cement around my body.

Yet curiously, I also felt very detached, as though I was watching a movie, that someone else's life was at stake. As muddled as my head felt, I was clear that any chance for survival depended upon me staying conscious, focused and moving steadily down the mountain.

Doug and I continued our slow descent down the canyon for over an hour. Periodically he would give me regular weather forecasts. "The clouds don't look like rain," he predicted in his analytical monotone. "There is usually a rain shower in the afternoon when the clouds gather over these mountain ranges. I've been watching for them all afternoon. They can come on fast. You never can tell."

Doug's ongoing conversation with himself came to me as a gentle mantra. His words buzzed through my mind in a constant hum. "It's getting darker," he brooded, "and there's still three miles to go 'til we reach the trail head."

Then we came upon a thick field of waist-high boulders. "There's no way around these," Doug advised. "You'll have to climb through them." The boulders left only narrow spaces between them, and covered the canyon floor. Navigating these boulders would be tough; my body rebelled. I hung my head and closed my eyes, overwhelmed. I paused to rest and gather some strength for the task before me.

"We're not making fast enough progress to get you to safety before sundown," Doug said. He paused and reflected a moment. "We've got to do something," he finally said in desperation. The tone of his voice finally broke through the constant buzz of his words as I heard him state our options. "We could stay here until the morning, then I could go for help, or I could leave you here and go look for someone."

"I will not stay on this mountain tonight!" The words flew out of my mouth before I could even think. I feared that a night on the mountain would surely be the end of me. I had dismissed

17

these options before in favor of moving forward, but I knew that after having crawled for some time, we'd now have to try something else. I knew that I could not just stop and wait. I had to keep moving. I had to get someplace else where it was warm and safe and dry.

Doug explained the other option. "If I head down by myself, there may or may not be someone on the trail this late in the day," he said, looking up at the evening shadows as they started to creep down the ridge.

Yes, we did have to decide, but I realized that Doug would not choose to leave me on his own. He was waiting for me to make that choice.

Neither of Doug's ideas sounded good to me. These were heady decisions and I felt overwhelmed at the implications of the wrong choice. I considered what it would be like to stay the night in that cold place. I had a very strong feeling that I would die. A long, cold death was not appealing to me. But if I let Doug go and look for help, even though I would be left alone in the wilderness, it would give me a better chance for survival. I knew I was forced to make a choice. Doug was looking at me, waiting. With a sharp pang of defeat, I finally said, "You should go look for help."

"But I don't want to leave you here all alone," he protested.

"I don't want you to leave, either." My voice rose in fear. "But you've gotta go. It's our best chance."

I was standing on my one good leg, propped up between two waist-high boulders, doing my best to sound confident in this new plan. I didn't like being forced to make the decision. It was all I could do to keep a brave face and hide my terror at being left alone. Still, I knew that I could deal with that situation far better than the prospect of dying here.

With the decision made, I switched my focus from dealing with the rocks to orienting my thoughts toward this new plan. But Doug was ahead of me. "I'll leave you the pack," he said, verifying its contents. "It has some water, the trail bars, and my snow pants. You can use them and my fleece to keep warm."

"Leave the pack up there," I pointed to a level spot thirty feet in front of me, "where you'll be able to find me again," I said, my voice rising again in fear. "Then I can continue to work my way toward it." I wanted something to occupy me after he left, and getting through those boulders to the pack would be plenty distracting.

He looked around and spotted an opening through the rocks, quickly moved the pack to that high place thirty feet ahead of me, then checked its visibility from below.

I figured that his chances of running into someone on the trail were pretty slim. "Call out for help," I said, my heart beating faster in my chest, "Your voice will carry further than your feet will."

Doug seemed to ignore my words and continued positioning the pack. "Promise me that you'll call out. Shout out for help as you go down. Doug, will you do that? Say you will. Please?"

"Okay, okay, I will," he finally said. "I just don't know how long it will take me to find someone," he cautioned. "But if I don't find help, I'll be back to you within three hours," he emphasized, pointing to his watch.

"How will you find your way back?" I asked anxiously. "Don't worry, I've got my head lamp," he said, pointing to his forehead. He flashed the lamp on and off as if to give me confidence in his mission.

I saw the gravity of this decision etched in worry lines around his eyes. His shoulders strained under an unseen weight. My life was, literally, in his hands.

"I'll come back as soon as I can," he said firmly, looking at me across the boulders as if he could fill me with hope and strength just by the mere promise of his return.

"I love you." Doug's final words were issued with such ferocity, almost like a declaration that things would be all right. What I actually heard was, "Trust me. You'll be fine. Hang in there."

My response was just as impassioned. "I love you, too." That was my feeble attempt to convey confidence and somehow convince him that I would be okay while he was gone.

In that moment, fear, love and bravado formed a strong yet invisible bond between us. I drank long and deep from that moment to savor the experience and the comfort of his presence. He was leaving me alone in the wilderness. *Dear God,* I thought, *if I keep looking at him, I won't have to face the terrifying unknown beyond his departure.*

A barrage of feelings and thoughts ricocheted through my mind, clamoring for some means of expression. My head was filled with a dizzying swirl of images and conversations. I flashed back to all the preparations for, and promises about, this trip. The history of our entire relationship was condensed into this very moment. And even if I had been able to organize all of my thoughts into a coherent whole, that wouldn't change the facts. I had been injured and was forced to make this horrific choice.

I pushed myself to stand up straighter between the rocks. I wanted to show him that I would be okay on my own, and hoped fervently that I believed that myself.

He shifted uneasily, looked down at his feet, then back up at me. The silence was heavy with the implications of his departure. I was saying goodbye to Doug, who was my only help, protection and comfort. I held his gaze and willed his safe return with all my heart. When I could stand it no longer, I broke the spell.

"Go!"

He looked down the gorge, then back at me, promising, "I will be back." Then he turned and disappeared through the rocks.

A Love Story Begins

HOW DID I END UP desperate, alone and injured in the wilds of Colorado?

I can trace the origins of this trip all the way back to my first love affair. It was 1974 and I was in the fourth grade, at summer camp, where pet rocks were all the rage. So at craft time, it was no surprise that we were encouraged to pick a rock that we would paint and take home with us. My rock was painted with watercolors in a translucent shade of red, with a purple stripe across the middle. The girls in my cabin decided that our rocks needed to be named, so I blindly chose random letters from the alphabet to create a name for mine: Anibator.

I delighted in the way the curve of her back fit in my palm (yes, my rock even had a gender). She had a notch for my fingers when they wrapped around her sides, and a flat bottom, so she looked like she belonged there on my desk. I also enjoyed the simple pleasure of feeling her cool weight resting in my hand. She was beautiful, solid, and all mine.

I was instructed that proper care of my new pet rock included holding and talking to her. I don't know if those craft counselors were "on" anything (this was the 1970s, after all), but they said I should talk to my pet rock, and so I did. As a child of the '70s, I had read books about people who talked to plants, so I figured, why not talk to a rock?

Anibator turned out to be too big to carry with me all the time, so I began finding some of her smaller brethren. That's when I developed the habit of having a rock in my pocket that I could reach in and hold onto whenever I wanted a little comfort. Through the years I've made it a point to look for beautiful, smooth or unusual rocks to carry with me. Other rocks I would group together and place in tall clear vases to display them around my home.

Staunching the Tide

It was on my 30th birthday that I found my first real triangular rock. I couldn't believe that such a perfect triangle could be found in nature. She was thick and tall and pointy, an isosceles triangle for you geometry fans. I decided then and there that if I was going to live in Lake County, California, an area rich in rock-filled creeks, I had better specialize in the rocks I collected; otherwise I would surely be buried with all of the beloved friends I was likely to bring home. I thought that specializing in triangles would stem their flow into my life. It probably did staunch the tide a bit, but I was amazed at how many triangular rocks there were. I would come home from a creek stroll with my shorts falling off my hips from the weight of all of the new triangles I had pocketed. Over time I noticed other special rocks and gathered them in little rock families amidst my collections: small, round pastel-colored rocks from the creeks, and round and oval black stones from the beach. Friends would proudly bring me triangular rocks they had found and be amazed when I showed them the extent of my own collection.

The hot summers would dry the creeks near my house, so for many months of the year I could actually walk through these canals. They were filled with miles and miles of water-rounded rocks. I often sought refuge in those creek beds. I'd sit down in the middle of a creek bed and check out the local talent of rock, noticing the different colors and shapes that were endemic to different areas. It always calmed me down and even provided comfort, even if it was not comfortable to actually be sitting *on* them. "Thanks for being here for me," I'd say. "Thanks for being my family." I could always count on the rocks to hold a space for me as I sorted out my heart and mind when I was upset or feeling a little blue.

My Collections

Moving to Mt. Shasta, my rock friends changed from the water-rounded creek variety to angular rockfall. I would take a canvas bag to the roadside turnouts and identify the triangles easily, pressed flat into the dirt. My collection grew so fast from these outings that I started to have rock management issues. I needed to separate the rocks into different piles before I could start arranging them. I actually went so far as to buy a beautiful wooden multi-drawer cabinet to keep them sorted: right triangles and obtuse ones here, my scalenes and isosceles there. I really hated to shut the rocks away, but it was the easiest way to keep them organized until I was ready to start arranging them. That's when I'd sit on my grandma's green wool rug and arrange them into elaborate French curves and spirals all across the floor. I could sit there for hours on cold winter nights and "play" with my rocks. Once again, my rock friends kept me company and provided me with immense pleasure as I created designs and mandalas all across the floor.

"Wow, these are amazing," friends would say, picking their way carefully across my living room floor. One friend was admiring a small intricate arrangement I had done, a simple starburst that pleased my eyes with a balance of color, shape and design.

"You're doing white magic, Cheryl," he said.

I blanched at his comment. I wasn't comfortable with his implications of my intent.

"White magic?" I asked. "No way!"

"White magic is just when you place order on natural objects," he said reassuringly. Well, if that was the case, then I was indeed doing white magic. All I knew was that I was having tremendous fun while creating beauty with my rocks.

Sweat Lodge Stones

I really felt I had finally found the people who understood me during my first sweat lodge in Shasta. As the heated rocks were transferred from the fire into the lodge, they were blessed and welcomed as our grandfathers. The native elders introduced them as ancient beings that had a profound wisdom to share with us in the heat. I was thrilled to know that I was not alone in my experience of a personal relationship with rocks.

Letting Go

When I left Mount Shasta, one of the hardest things I had to do was return the vast majority of my triangles to the forest. I still think about them, all piled up together under a tree. Over the years I had started to collect very small triangles, in my next attempt to lessen the impact of rocks on my living space. I let go of the larger triangles (some up to 16 inches high) but I was able to keep and pack up the countless smaller triangles, with ¼" to 1" sides, which I could more easily arrange on clear glass platters in my home.

Big Rock Love

Up until my first visit to Yosemite Valley at age 42, I had only laid upon or held rocks in my hand. But my relationship with rocks changed after visiting my friend Carol at her home inside of Yosemite National Park. That's when I found that the rocks in the Valley were big enough to hold me. One day we were climbing on Sentinel Dome. It is situated on the edge of Yosemite Valley and provides spectacular 360° views around the park from atop its huge granite expanse. The dome's cap was slowly breaking apart, like a peeled onion, with layers of the rock breaking off in slightly curved, yet substantial chunks.

I snuck away from the crowd and settled myself down inside one of these massive cracks in the dome's surface. No longer just lying atop a rock, I was now securely wedged inside of it. It made me feel wonderfully safe and protected. It was such a new experience to feel so powerfully embraced by this massive granite being. I felt like I had come home. I could have stayed there all day, basking in its strength and the stillness. Shortly after, I felt a little sheepish when I found that Carol had been looking for me while I was happily tucked away inside the granite. Finally on that first visit to Yosemite, I felt as if I had found my long lost family.

But the biggest surprise came later that week.

Carol and I were hiking down a narrow rocky passage between Nevada Falls and Liberty Dome. We had to go single-file because the stairway cut into the rock was only a few feet wide. I looked up to see a smooth, solid rock wall that rose high overhead on each side. As I walked through, I slowed down and felt my entire body ensconced, as if I was being held inside an earthly womb. I strained my neck upward, trying to comprehend the beauty of this extraordinary passage. Looking up, I saw only rock. Above. Rock. Below. Rock. All around, rock, rock and more rock. Moving through the passageway, I felt as though I was entering deeper and deeper into something very ancient, something sacred. As the granite surrounded me in its soft embrace, I felt transported and couldn't imagine ever wanting to leave this hallowed place. Something deep inside me stirred and I felt as though my very soul was being caressed by this intimate connection with the rock. My heart opened and it was as if a lifetime of love for rocks was pouring back into me all at once.

I was overwhelmed and perplexed, as my mind could not process all of the energy that was moving through me. It was an intoxicating call, as if a siren's song was beckoning me towards some exquisite place I could not see. I felt naked — and utterly vulnerable — standing there looking dopey-eyed up at the rock. Luckily, no one was coming down the path to find me in that state, because my head was blank and I was at a loss to explain what had happened. How had I become so moved by simply entering into this passageway? I tried to put one foot in front of the other so I could continue stumbling down the path, although still slightly disoriented. It took an incredible effort to draw my body away from the passageway. I wanted to stay, but how would I explain this experience to Carol?

What was pulling me? How could being around rocks affect me so deeply? Not quite understanding what had just happened to me, I tried to clear my head as quickly as I could and continue down the trail to catch up with her. I did not speak of this experience to anyone because I did not understand it myself, and I was still embarrassed for feeling so vulnerable in a public place.

***

"Wow, Cheryl, I knew you loved rocks, but that takes 'rock love' to a whole new level!" Krista said, giving me a knowing look.

I blushed. "I know. I felt that you all would consider me crazy if I talked about it. You're the first one I've dared share this with."

"Well, it sure helps explain your desire to be in the mountains."

"Yeah. It was truly a magical week for me."

***

In addition to my connections with the rocks, Carol had instructed me in the art of wildflowering, or how to identify the colorful springtime offerings beside the trail. I was familiar with looking down to find rocks and now she had trained my eyes to search for the small splashes of color tucked between them. In return, I taught Carol to look up more and have a greater appreciation for the grandeur of the towering granite beings in the Valley. Carol had witnessed firsthand my passion for the rocks, as I took endless pictures and repeatedly hugged the rocks whenever I could.

So, as I shared my desire to experience more, she gave me some advice. "If you really want to see the biggest rock formations, you need to go to the 'high country.'" With that in mind, I went to the visitors' center to see about accessing that part of the park, but I wasn't a camper who could hike in by myself, and the guided trips were all booked up.

It was with a very heavy heart that I left Yosemite and drove back to Petaluma. The only solace was the riot of color by the roadsides, where I was moderately successful at identifying some of the wildflowers. Carol will be proud of me, I thought, craning my neck for a better view.

Into the Wilds

BACK HOME IN PETALUMA, my boyfriend Doug heard me going on and on about how much I wanted to see the rock formations in Yosemite's high country. "If you're serious about going," Doug suggested, "I could take you there. We could backpack."

"Really?" I was stunned at the suggestion. I had always considered myself a civilized city girl, born in Detroit and reared in its placid suburban landscape. Sure, I liked to hike, but backpacking? Me? It seemed like such an outlandish thought. "Do you think I could?"

"If you really want to experience the high country—sure, it could be fun," he mused. "I've never been to Yosemite."

It was an intoxicating yet terrifying thought. Not just a camping trip, but backpacking. Oh, boy. Heading out into the wilds with only what I could carry on my back. Was I up for it? I had never even been camping. It was such a big mystery to me; I couldn't even imagine what it would be like.

Doug had climbed and backpacked all over the U.S. He had boxes and boxes of pictures of himself and his brother on top of this or that mountain. "I can't remember the name of this one," he said, after I'd asked him about a snapshot he showed me once. I couldn't believe that he had been on so many mountaineering adventures that he couldn't even remember the name of a particular peak.

"Don't worry, Cheryl. I'll take good care of you," Doug promised me, "I know how you love those big rocks. You'll love it out there."

The news of my first backpacking trip sent ripples of curiosity through the office. "You're going to do *what?*" my co-workers asked in disbelief.

"My boyfriend has promised to keep me safe," I reassured them.

"Maybe you'll see a bear," Carol suggested excitedly. She was always thrilled to see a bear on her many wildflower hikes in Yosemite. *Thanks, Carol,* I thought, *I'll just add "bears" to my growing list of fears about heading into the wilderness.* It's one thing to see a bear from the safety of your car, and quite another thing to have a bear rummaging through your tent. As excited as I was about my impending adventure, I was still quite nervous.

Doug had given me a list of what I would need for the trip and we went shopping at REI for what I didn't already have. He planned out our food and we pored over the map at night. Doug did his best to answer the myriad of questions I had about backpacking. We put all of our food into small plastic bags, which we stuffed into our bear-proof canister. The smooth barrel could only be opened with the turn of a screwdriver or a nickel, something the canister's designers presumed a bear would not be able to do.

It was a Friday afternoon in early September, eleven months before my glacier climb, when Doug and I arrived in Yosemite for my first backpacking trip.

The first night we camped by Sunrise Lakes. Doug set the food that wouldn't fit into the bear canister away from our campsite. If I had been concerned that a bear *might* stop by, with this new plan I was now completely convinced that one *would* stop by.

I'm generally a light sleeper and was already nervous about spending the night out in the woods, on the hard ground, with only a thin little sleeping pad beneath me. Unable to sleep, my mind envisioned bears stopping by for our extra food. Throughout the night, with each little rustle or noise, my eyes would fly open and my heart would race. Each time I had to slow my breathing back down before huddling deeper into my sleeping bag, listening for the telltale sounds of an ursine marauder coming to storm our tent. If it had been up to my powers of imagination, we surely would have had a steady stream of bears parading through our camp all night long.

The next day, we hiked as far as the Cathedral Lakes. After setting up camp and having dinner, we sipped tea while sitting on the granite slabs next to the lake and watched the golden light caress the nearby peaks as the sun dropped lower in the sky.

"This is really heaven," I said. "That's a gorgeous shoulder there next to the peak. Looks like it would be a lot of fun to climb around on."

"You did very well today. We covered another five miles," Doug nodded, satisfied with the day's progress.

"And I'm exhausted," I said, "I sure hope I sleep better tonight."

"I never sleep well my first night out," he said reassuringly. "Most people don't. You'll sleep better tonight," he added confidently.

I settled in for the night, wearing my long underwear and wool socks. The lower elevation next to the lake made the air much colder than the night before. Still not warm enough, I put on my hat and pulled my 25°-rated mummy bag tight around my face until only my nose stuck out. Unable to sleep in the cold, I spent the night curled up in my bag and watched the glow of the moon through the roof of the tent, tracking its movement as it slowly glided on its path across the sky.

When the morning sunlight finally touched the top of our tent, I sat up. "What's this?" I asked, scratching at the white film on the wall. My fingernail came back cold and wet. "Ice! There is ICE in our tent! It FROZE in here last night!"

"The condensation from our breath collects on the tent walls and then freezes," Doug informed me calmly. "Don't worry; it will dry out quickly. The sun will heat the tent up soon."

"*Ice*," I murmured to myself. No wonder I was cold last night.

That second morning, it seemed like Doug was waiting on me hand and foot. He went down to the lake to pump the water through the filter. He heated up each individual cup of water in his JetBoil to make me tea, and cooked my oatmeal for me. He was doing his best to keep me as happy as possible after my less-than-comfortable night. Not that I complained. Well, okay, just that once, about the ice in the tent.

"I guess that rocky glen radiated a lot of heat for us the first night," Doug mused. Good thing, too, because if I had frozen like that my first night I'd have probably turned right around and never looked back.

As we packed up our tent, a pair of backpackers came by, scanning the area. "If you're looking for a good camping spot, we're leaving this one," Doug offered to the young couple.

"Thanks," the guy said. They put their packs down and started to pull out their climbing ropes and helmets. "Are you going to climb Cathedral Peak?" Doug asked enthusiastically. "Yeah, there are lots of different routes up," the backpacker answered.

I saw two sets of helmets and harnesses and knew that she was going to climb with him.

"Have you been climbing long?" I asked, directing my question to the young woman.

"He's been climbing for three years," she answered. Then she added shyly, "I've only been climbing for one year." I understood that dynamic. I had already donned a climbing harness while being suspended by ropes in Doug's garage, and learned a few knots while he gave me a quick lesson in trusting my weight to the ropes.

I got a hopeful look from Doug, along with the scary suspicion that I was looking at *my* future. "We could come back here and climb Cathedral," he said, pointing enthusiastically at the peak. I had mentioned that it would be nice to spend some time playing around it so I could get closer to the rocks. But climb the peak itself?

I gave him a tentative smile, but didn't dare encourage him in these plans. I couldn't imagine how we would haul the heavy ropes and harnesses on top of all our other backpacking gear. As if reading my mind, Doug said, "Of course, I would carry the ropes." *Oh no*, I thought, *what will he get me into next?* I've barely survived two nights out here and now he wants to drag me up Cathedral Peak on a climbing trip.

"Yeah, well," I hedged, "we'll see," I said, looking at the ground, exhausted at the mere thought of such an expedition.

"Have a great climb." Doug shouted, waving back at the couple as we started off towards the trail. "You know," he said, turning back to me, "it could be a lot of fun."

"Yeah," I deadpanned. "Fun." Please, I prayed, just let him forget the whole idea.

The pack always feels overwhelming when I first put it on and have to shoulder that extra weight. But after a while, I would grow accustomed to having my center of gravity shifted higher and be more comfortable in managing its heft. The hip belt is a thick foam pad, but I still found that my shoulders and hipbones were tender from the past two days. I was starting to fuss with a shoulder strap when Doug came over. "Is it seated okay?" He was checking the position of the pack on my body.

"Yeah, it's just rubbing on my hipbones," I lifted up my shirt and showed him how red my protruding hipbones were.

"Well, you are a skinny thing," he said, beaming. Seeing my frown, he quickly added, "but strong, definitely strong," as I punched him mockingly. "Here, let's see if adjusting it higher helps."

As we continued our trek back, the trail started to slope down. I had done well enough climbing uphill with a pack, but going downhill was another matter entirely. "My knees are starting to hurt," I said, bracing myself against a tree and reaching down to rub my right knee.

"Want some ibuprofen?" he offered. I shook him off at first, but a short time later I was more open. "Yeah, I guess I'd better take something." But my knees were still screaming at me after I took the pills. Each step I took produced intense pain. I stopped to rest frequently, which slowed Doug down.

"Want me to take your pack?" he offered. "No," I replied indignantly. How could he carry both our packs? *What a silly suggestion*, I thought. "I just need to rest a bit."

After several stops, Doug finally said, "Here, use my trekking poles." He took the straps off his wrists and held the poles out to me. "They'll help with your knees." Now I understood why most everyone we passed on our way down had poles. I took them, but didn't understand how my hand would go through the loop at the handle until Doug showed me. The poles telescoped out in three sections of metal tubing, with a small black disk flaring out near the pointed metal tip. Doug had them folded up in his pack, so I first saw him using the poles on this downhill section.

It took a lot of concentration to coordinate my feet and the poles. All of a sudden I was walking as if I had four feet and had to pay close attention to where each one would go. "This is a lot harder than I thought it would be," I said quietly.

Doug was following me, watching my form while I used the poles. "No," Doug corrected, "you're doing it again. I told you you're supposed to put your weight on the *opposite* foot from the pole." I bit back an unkind response to his incessant suggestions, not that I was ungrateful for his concern. Even though he corrected me, oftentimes I just couldn't get it right.

At this point in the trip, all the chocolate in the world could not make up for the depth of my exhaustion, frustration and pain. And now, I had failed Trekking Poles 101. I spotted a big log next to the trail, plopped my weary body down and started to shake my head slowly, finally accepting defeat. I was bent forward and my shoulders were shaking; tears started to fall. *I am a complete and total failure,* I thought. *I can't do anything right.* I squeezed my eyes tight against the shame of it all.

Doug approached cautiously and stood there, looking down at me. "Want me to take your pack?" "No," I said stubbornly, still looking down at the ground. "You can't carry both," I snuffled.

As if to prove me wrong, he reached forward and slowly unbuckled the pack from my hips, pulled it gently from my shoulders and heaved it up onto his shoulders. Would my shame never end? Now Doug was going to carry BOTH our packs. "It's only about a half-mile more," he said, against my protest. "I can take it that far." He started down the trail.

How would I ever show my face in public? I was sure that word would get out that Doug had to carry my pack for me and I would never live it down. I was sure that Doug would never want to go camping with me again after this. What had become of me? After a few minutes of self-flagellation, I pulled the tattered remains of my pride up off that log and continued behind him down the trail.

Relieved of the heavy pack, I practically floated the rest of the way down. I could also move more quickly. Then I saw Doug ahead of me, seemingly unburdened by the extra pack he was now carrying. *How does he do it?* I wondered, looking at his easy gait although he had the weight of both packs. Guys are just built differently, I concluded, shaking my head.

When I finally arrived at the trailhead, Doug was there. He gave me a big hug.

"You did it!" he said.

"But I couldn't carry my pack," I whined back at him, still feeling a strong sense of defeat.

"Yes, but look at all you did," he said, his hands braced on my shoulders, forcing me to listen to him. "You spent two nights in the wilderness by yourself, Cheryl. You carried a pack for over seven miles at elevation. Are you kidding? You did great!" he said.

"I did?" I asked looking up, still skeptical.

"Yeah. This was your first time out—just a little trouble with your knees at the end. So what? You can get yourself some trekking poles for next time."

I considered his suggestion as we took off our boots and socks and soaked our feet in the cool stream. Trekking poles.... Next time.

"So you'd go backpacking with me again?" I asked, still uncertain.

"Yeah, Cheryl, I would. You're a real trooper."

I still couldn't believe what I was hearing. Doug would be willing to take me out into the wilderness again? His assessment stunned me. I thought about it and realized that he was probably right. I had stuck it out. I had survived my initiation. I could proudly call myself a backpacker. But, that being said, would I want to do it again?

Well, it turns out that backpacking is kind of like what they say childbirth is like. You only remember the good stuff.

Encouraged at the thought that Doug would take me back up into the high country, I started preparing my list. I was going to need to build up much more strength in my legs, get some trekking poles and find a much warmer sleeping bag.

I researched hiking poles online and, after wading through the dizzying array of choices of pole metal, handle types and tips, I ultimately chose the pole that promised me some degree of shock absorption. I figured they must have developed that type for a reason and, at my age, my joints could certainly use all the help they could get. I looked at zero-degree sleeping bags for months, trying to find one with poly fill instead of down. I had learned that down doesn't keep you warm if it gets wet.

That fall, I hired a personal fitness trainer to help me build up my leg strength and ended up with a leg, arms and abs workout I could fit in during my breaks at work. I had gotten my taste of the high country and had lived to tell the tale. Someday I would go back; next time I would be prepared.

The Wait

HERE I AM in the wilds of Colorado. Alone. Injured.

I looked around and watched as the gorge seemed to grow ever larger around me. My body seemed to shrink ever smaller against its enormity and I lost my sense of scale.

Before I fell, I would have seen this canyon as filled with a magnificent display of towering strength. I had never before experienced the raw power of such an elemental place, with its sheer cliffs and soaring monoliths! These kinds of rock formations had always evoked a profound visceral response from my body that kept calling me back. I was continually pulled into the wilderness so I could drink deeply of their wild and savage beauty.

For years I had sought the largest rock formations on hikes so I could bask in their awesome presence, caress their cool surfaces and delight in their strength. Their permanence and stability had always been a balm to me. When I reclined atop a massive slab, I could feel it patiently supporting not only my body, but holding the concerns that drove me to seek their comfort in the first place. These ancient beings were always there for me — through the seasons, through the years. I appreciated how they always shared that strength with me so freely whenever I came to be with them. There had been so many beautiful and peaceful times that I had spent with them over the years.

In my weakened state, the boulders now seemed to crowd around me. They were like a menacing threat. No longer safe or comforted, I was a prisoner under their guard. They felt cold, impassive — even stubborn — as I fought my way through them.

I had wasted a lot of my energy in my display of confidence for Doug and coming to terms with his departure. Now that I was alone, what little remained of my body's energy seemed to be flowing down my legs and draining out the bottoms of my feet.

The emptiness I felt was profound, and I knew I needed to distract myself. I returned my focus to getting over to Doug's pack, still a few yards ahead of me. I was like a flamingo standing there on my one good leg, with my right leg bent, keeping my right foot from contacting anything. Propped up at the edge of these waist-high boulders, I placed my hands on top of them and began lifting myself up to gently ease myself through them. It was as if someone had just set the gravity meter on HIGH, as it became more and more difficult to even lift an arm or move a leg. My efforts to move my limbs were like that dream where your legs are spinning around and your arms are pumping madly, and you look around and feel a sensation that turns your stomach. Because, despite all of your effort, you're not going anywhere.

I looked at my palms; they were red and scuffed. The skin was angry from bearing my weight over so many rock surfaces. How much more could my hands take? *I can do this*, I told myself, and took several deep breaths. I had to gather every last bit of energy and pour it into navigating through this maze of boulders. I turned my hips to squeeze myself through sideways before I could place my left foot forward. Sometimes the rocks were very close together and my boot would be wedged and get caught. "Oh, man!" I cried. I hated that I would have to squander my energy by pressing down even harder with my arms to extricate my wedged boot. When the left boot popped free, my suddenly elevated body would cause my right leg to swing forward. My right foot would then painfully bang against the rock. "Can't anything be easy?" I implored, looking up at the sky. But the sky was big and empty.

There was no one to hear me, no one around to care. I had called out to my angels for help before I had crashed into the rocks. Now standing alone amongst the boulders, I couldn't even imagine the angels being anywhere close. I shook my fist skyward as I cursed God for leaving me alone in such a desperate state. But my cries were swallowed up by the enormity of the canyon. I didn't believe that even God could hear me. I had never felt so completely abandoned in all my life.

I closed my eyes and shook my head angrily against the futility, against the absurd reality of my situation. My chin dropped to my chest; I was exhausted. My shoulders were weary, my leg ached and my foot throbbed. Looking around, I saw that I was now stuck in the middle of these boulders and still had more challenging yards to go. I took several deep breaths, trying to clear my head. I knew I had to keep moving. I couldn't stay here wedged in between the rocks. *Keep your focus on getting through the rocks*, I told myself. *Don't dwell on the fact that you're alone. Don't panic.* The activity kept me from thinking about what might happen, now that it was just me, alone in the wilderness.

The painful irony of the situation floated somewhere in the recesses of my mind. This could have been a glorious rocky playground for me. A special place where I could climb and touch and wrap my arms around each and every boulder. Now it was a cruel maze to torture me, where winning would be painful and losing could mean death.

I finally extricated myself from the sea of rocks, lowered my body to the ground and scooted on my butt over to Doug's pack. It was lying on the level ground, a few yards away. I rooted through it, looking for anything useful. I pulled out

Doug's fleece and added this layer over my own jacket. His Gore-Tex leggings were big, so I laid them beside me and rocked back and forth on my hips to ease them underneath me for some measure of protection against the cold ground. *Well, I said to myself, at least it's something.* The earth had been steadily pulling the heat away from my body, and I could feel myself starting to chill. Now that I wasn't moving, it would be harder to keep myself warm. My pants were still wet from both the snow and that mysterious flow of blood down my thigh.

Where did the blood come from? There was no rip or tear in my pants. My thoughts on the subject were brief, as I didn't have the energy to try to figure out what had happened to produce such a stain. Then I noticed another drop of blood on my boot. The blood is still dripping down my leg! I was sitting in my own blood. I closed my eyes to steady myself as my head swam with this realization. I could bundle up against the cold rocks and the nighttime air, but I couldn't get away from the cold and wet of sitting in my own blood.

I shuddered again, the movement making my foot ache. *What's going on with my foot?* It was tender, swollen and aching. Utterly useless. I thought about how many steps I had taken climbing all the way up that glacier and across the tundra. But now, I couldn't take even one more step. I can't even walk out of this canyon. I had no choice but to sit and wait and hope that Doug could find someone to come and help me to safety.

I forced myself to drink some water, glad that Doug had left it for me. I watched my hands shake as I fumbled to unwrap a Clif Bar. I didn't feel like eating, but I knew I should take in some calories. I was glad I had thrown in a few extra bars when we were packing. I usually liked to eat more on the trail than Doug did.

Doug, I thought. *He's out there somewhere.* My heart sank and my stomach turned when I thought about how long he might be gone. I might have cried, if I only had the energy. *Please let him find someone,* I prayed. When those thoughts made me fearful, I told myself not to think about that and to focus on getting comfortable and resting after all that exertion.

But "getting comfortable" was a relative term. I bent forward slowly and used my hands to lift my right leg and set it up on— surprise—a rock. I shoved the pack behind me for my head, and gently eased myself down. No longer busy with tasks, I began the wait.

There was nothing to distract me as I lay there. No birds flying by looking for food, since there was nothing around to eat but rocks. No bushes to harbor small animals. No trees to break up the view or sway in the breeze. The canyon floor dropped away in front of me, but the rocks blocked me from seeing just how far I still had to go. Above, the sheer rock walls were glowing in the last of the day's sunlight. But the shadows were starting to creep down the rocky slopes, changing the golden-kissed rocks into somber and more ominous shades of grey and rust.

With no other distractions, I tried to appreciate the beauty of the valley, but the colors of the setting sun on the mountains began to seem far more menacing than beautiful.

As I lay there in the stillness, questions began grinding away in my mind: How long will I have to wait here alone? Will Doug find anyone? Will he get back before dark? Will they send a helicopter to rescue me? I hope not, since those are very expensive...and besides, where would it land? How cold will it get? Will I die here?

I felt utterly helpless, alone, banged-up and bloody. Ironically, my body was in its best physical shape ever, after my months of training. But that was all moot as I lay there, exhausted and in pain. I was frustrated at not being able to get myself to safety.

Then, I had a thought that wrenched my stomach. Oh, God! I'm lying here helpless. Won't mountain lions be attracted to the smell of my blood? My mind raced. I can't stand up to make myself appear bigger by holding my coat out. I can't run away. How can I defend myself against a mountain lion? Then I thought, the ice axe! Relief flooded through me and my body relaxed as I imagined my triumph, fending off the predator by using that two-foot aluminum tool. It just goes to show what good friends shock and denial can be.

Still, some part of me was trying to delight in this magnificent scenery. I looked up at the ridge on my right. How could such a beautiful slice of wilderness feel so menacing? Will this be where I die? Will my rock friends hold me here in death? How strange that my love for rocks had brought me here. How had it come to this? My mind couldn't reconcile these seemingly contradictory facts. Random ideas continued to taunt me from the edges of my consciousness, even as I tried to force myself to stay calm.

Close your eyes and relax, I told myself, as I tuned in to the expansive silence of the canyon. The altitude, exhaustion and shock had slowed my mind, yet with my eyes closed, I was still plagued by visions and thoughts of the many ways I could die. *Will I freeze to death tonight? Could I bleed to death? Will I pass out if I let myself go to sleep?*

Shivers ran down my body and made my leg hurt. Was it from the shock? The cold? My fear of dying? I watched as the last of the sunlight slowly left the canyon. The cold gray of the sky began to penetrate into my bones as I continued the wait: either for Doug's return or for the freezing embrace of night.

Learning the Ropes

KRISTA AND I WERE catching up over dinner at one of our favorite restaurants. "What's up with you and Doug?"

"Oh, didn't I tell you? I had to end it with him again last week."

"But I thought things were going pretty well for you two," she said.

"For a while they were. After we got back together last year, we went on that fabulous backpacking trip to Yosemite and he seemed to have changed."

"So what went wrong?"

"Do you remember when I broke things off the first time, how he kept after me to try and understand why I called it off?"

She nodded silently.

"And I've told you how proud he is of being stubborn. Well, I explained that I didn't feel good about how he continually talked over me. And how frustrated I was when he wouldn't respect my need to get home at a decent hour on a 'school night.'" As a contractor, he could sleep in, but I had to get up in the morning. "He just made it harder and harder for me to get home to sleep.

"So, he takes a few months to think these things through and comes back to me with an 'I've changed' speech."

"Oh, yeah. I remember that after you broke up."

"Yes, after that first time, I was willing to give him a second chance. I mean, dating at my age..." I let the implications of my statement hang and shrugged my shoulders.

"Oh, come on, Cheryl. Don't believe those 'more likely to be killed by a terrorist' statistics. You don't even look like you're in your forties!"

"I know, people always say that. But there's this part of me that's tired of dating and wanted to make it work. After all, he's a really decent guy. Intelligent, good job, no kids." I counted off the pluses on my fingers. "And you know how I need to be with an intelligent guy."

"But you said he wasn't spiritual."

"No, he's not. But I'm trying to be more open about what kind of man will make me happy. After all, we do have such fun together!"

"So, why did you end it this time?"

"See, I tried to talk to him about our, um, how we are when we're, you know," and emphasized, "together." I tried to give her a knowing look so I wouldn't have to go into the details of our sex life.

"I mean, no guy wants to hear that he doesn't make you happy in bed, but Doug is super defensive. It took me a long time for him to agree that he wouldn't jump out of bed immediately afterwards. It wasn't enough for me to say that I wanted to feel more intimacy or connection with him. I had to break it down to the exact feeling and then define the precise motivation for my need. Figuring how to explain that was hard enough. Then after going round and round when he wouldn't understand, we'd hit another one of his 'My brain is different' places, and he'd totally shut down. We finally agreed that he would not jump right up to dispose of the condom, and he would stay in bed and hold me. But it ended up being just a mechanical change in his behavior. His behavior looked different on the outside, but it didn't shift anything between us on the inside or draw us closer." I shook my head slowly at the painful memory.

"That wasn't the only issue. See, I got tired of explaining over and over what I considered to be our common social contracts to him. You know, after we'd come home after dinner at a friend's house and he wouldn't understand something done by our hostess. Then he'd ask so many questions and I could never explain to him the 'why' of it to his satisfaction. It was all the more frustrating to have him not understand what I considered the normal dynamics of a relationship. I just got tired of beating my head against that wall, and of him never getting it. I'd had enough. I wanted out. So that's why we're not together any more."

***

Luckily, my plans for getting back into the mountains were coming together nicely, even if Doug was out of the picture. I had the new trekking poles by Christmas and by springtime, I was well into my weight-training program to strengthen my legs, abs and arms. I was glad, though, that it was only cows that saw me fumbling with my trekking poles as I climbed up and down Mt. Burdell after work.

Without Doug in my life, I was keen on looking for a new backpacking partner. So I went back to the local climbing club. I knew I would need to go with experienced campers and climbers since I still didn't have all the equipment, skill or audacity to do it on my own.

"Harrison is holding a basic ropes course in a couple of weeks," my new hiking buddy, Faith, told me. "I'm thinking of going with my son. What about you?"

I had met Harrison at the RIM club meetings and recalled his announcement about the upcoming weekend class. I knew I wouldn't do this course by myself. "How often does he do these?" I asked Faith, doing an internal calculation for my best timing for the class.

"Not often," she paused giving me time to think. "It would be great if you could take the class. Then you'd be able to join us on the club trip to Yosemite in June."

Faith sure knew how to work my weak spot.

"And if you do it with me," she continued, "it would be more fun. Then you can join Dylan and me when we go to the climbing gym. It would be great to have another woman there. What do you say? We can do it together!" she enthused.

"But I don't have a tent."

"Oh, that won't be a problem. We'll find someone you can share with."

I wasn't sure how all of this would work out, but the climbers I had met were all very friendly and I figured they would be willing to take in a novice like me. It didn't hurt that there were mostly men in the group, so a woman was welcome, no matter how inexperienced she was.

A few weeks later, Doug showed up unexpectedly near the end of one of my contra dances. I hadn't seen him for several months; he sat on the sidelines and watched until the dance was over. He didn't join in and looked a bit uncomfortable just sitting there waiting. I got packed up to head home and that's when he approached me.

"Can I walk you to your car?" My body stiffened at his request and I looked at him warily. The air between us crackled with tension.

I nodded my assent and we walked together out of the parking lot and down the street towards my car.

We broke the silence by broaching safe subjects, like how his father was doing and what my sister's family was up to. His hands were in his pockets and we both looked down at the pavement as we walked. When we finally got to my car, I turned to face him and looked up expectantly. I knew that he didn't come all this way just to walk me to my car. He was shifting from side to side, and seemed about as nervous as I was with the situation.

"I just wanted to tell you how much I've missed you, Cheryl," he finally confessed. "I really want us to be friends."

I was getting cold standing there and wondered where this was going.

"Yeah," I answered slowly. "I've missed you too," I said, trying to ease the awkwardness of our exchange. Then I added, "I've been looking for other folks to go backpacking with. So far, no luck."

We reminisced about the good time we'd had in Yosemite last fall. It was a safe and comfortable topic for both of us. I was remembering the good times I had enjoyed with my friend and after a while, we both relaxed a bit. Since we were on the subject, I mentioned the upcoming ropes course with Harrison.

"It'll be at Pinnacles National Monument," I said.

"That sounds like a great trip."

"I know Faith and her son are going, too. Do you remember her from the RIM Club meetings?" He gave me a rather blank look, so I just continued on, "Well, we've been doing some hikes together."

"That sounds like fun. Maybe I should go on that trip," he said.

Surprised at this turn in the conversation, I started to back-pedal. "Well, I'm not sure I'm going yet."

"Oh."

"Well, thanks for saying 'hi,'" I said, turning to unlock my car. "And," looking back at him, "give me a little more time to consider the whole 'being friends' thing. Okay?"

"Sure. Just think about it. Okay if I call you some time?"

I nodded and we hugged briefly, then I turned to get into my car. I was consumed with poring through and interpreting the entire conversation. Doug sure went out of his way just to come and see me. I was flattered and more than a little twitter-pated at having seen him again. I replayed the conversation again and again, trying to decide if it was a good idea to "be friends" with him. My heart was tender and cautious, my body was responding to him all too well, and my head was throwing roadblocks up faster than you can say, "Let's just be friends."

Faith was persistent, too, and I really wanted to join the group for the climb in Yosemite, so I agreed to sign up for the ropes course. To shop for the additional climbing gear I would need, I set my sights on Berkeley where, Faith said, was the best selection of wilderness stores to check out.

I had been researching sleeping bags all winter, and now added climbing gear to my shopping list. I got all tricked out with squishy rubber-toed climbing shoes, a red and pink-flowered climbing harness and what I considered the ultimate score, my own zero-degree sleeping bag. I had been pricing sleeping bags for months, ever since I froze that second night in Yosemite.

Most are rated down to 20 or 30 degrees Fahrenheit, but just to keep you from freezing to death. Me? I'm a girl. I want to be *warm*. After looking at sleeping bags online and wondering if they would be long enough for me, I finally resorted to crawling into a bag on the floor of the local North Face outlet, just to make sure I would fit. It wasn't the most attractive shade of green, but then I figured I wouldn't need to worry about somebody wanting to steal it.

Doug made good on his promise to call, and we had spoken a few times since seeing each other at the dance. And who better to appreciate my new acquisitions?

"Wow, you're ready to go," he said. "How much was the bag?"

"Only $99."

"Geez, Cheryl, maybe I'll mistake it for my bag," he teased.

"No way! It's this really bright chartreuse-green color. You would definitely NOT mistake it for your bag."

"Well, then, I should at least have you shop for me," he said, clearly impressed with my eye for a good bargain.

Now that we were on more friendly terms, Doug approached me about doing the ropes course together. I was a more than a little nervous about how it would be to spend that kind of time together as "just friends," and had to think about that for a while.

But I was willing to try — if he would agree to one thing.

"We can do this together under one condition, Doug. That we do not discuss 'what went wrong in the relationship.'" Since that was a regular topic for him to bring up, I figured if we avoided it, we could have a good time.

"I can do that, Cheryl," he said. "I just miss you as a friend."

I was motivated to make this new type of relationship work, because he was the one with all the right camping equipment. At the ropes course that weekend, we ended up doing very well working together as we set up the tent and prepared our food together.

The amazing thing about rock climbing is that it tests you and pushes you beyond what you'd ever thought was possible. Many times on my first 200-foot climb I had thought, *I can't go on. I'm stuck.* But something inside doesn't let you bail. Whether it's that you're on the side of a mountain and it's not so easy to walk away, or that you'd be embarrassed to get lowered down on the rope and be teased endlessly by the guys at the bottom. So, you don't give up and you keep looking for a solution.

And maybe the next moment, you figure out that there is some tiny ledge where your fingers can grip or some little nubbins of a rock where you can wedge your toe. And before you know it, you're out of that "impossible" place and moving forward again. After repeating that scenario over and over again, you come to know that even if it seems impossible, you've developed the confidence to keep looking for a solution, because it's there — somewhere. You just haven't seen it yet. My lessons in technical climbing taught me to never give up. Over and over, you keep looking for the solution, and never give up.

"You did really well this weekend," Doug said with satisfaction on the drive home.

"I'm still amazed that I climbed that 200-foot slab."

"And scrambled up behind it afterwards. That was at least a Class Three scramble we did."

"What's the difference between a scramble and a climb?" I asked.

"We used our hands and feet, but no ropes," he clarified. "Just different ways to talk about the difficulty of the terrain."

Whatever, I thought. For me, it was all about climbing around on the big rocks and having fun.

As we drove home together, we finally waded into deeper waters and talked about how this would affect our status as "just friends."

"It was fun," Doug stated in a tentative tone.

"Yes, I thought we did very well *as friends*," I added, to confirm my position.

"Yeah, I thought it went well, too," he added carefully.

"So we can agree that we're still friends and won't try to make it anything more?" I clarified.

"Yes, that's fine with me. You're a lot of fun to climb with."

Good, I thought. I was afraid he might read something more into the fun we had shared.

But Doug was already moving in another direction.

"How would you like to go on another climbing trip?"

I was surprised at his suggestion. "Where would we go?" I asked.

Doug had already been camping and climbing all around northern California, so when he recommended Desolation Wilderness, farther east, closer to Lake Tahoe, I took his recommendation. "Once you get in," he said, "there are nothing but rocks all around." Doug had clearly learned how to sell me on a trip, so I was in for our next climbing adventure, just two weeks away, on Memorial Day weekend.

Early Signs?

"IT'S THE FIRST WEEKEND that Desolation is open this season," Doug advised, "so we'll be hiking through snow at the higher elevations." I had enjoyed my previous snowshoeing experiences, so this didn't sound like that big of a deal.

On our way driving there, we stopped by the Ranger's Station to get our wilderness permit. I was excited as I flipped through the photo album on the counter of the different campsites. "How much snow is still on the ground?" Doug asked the ranger.

"These pictures were taken last week, so I couldn't say for sure." Turning her attention back to the map, she added, "Now these sites are already taken," pointing to the edge of Aloha Lake on the map. "But I can put you down for this area further north. Is that okay for you?" she asked, looking at me. My eyes widened in surprise. *You're asking me?* I thought. *I have no idea; I'm just following along here.* Doug was the one who knew where we were going. I shrugged my shoulders and gave Doug a questioning look. "We'll take it," he said.

"Let me get a picture of you with that pack on," Doug suggested before we started on the trail. "Now turn sideways so we can see how much you're carrying." I turned so he could see how the pack was towering high above my head. I was proud to be carrying the extra weight of the bear canister, since we already had more equipment with our snowshoes and climbing rope.

As we hiked in and slowly climbed, gaining elevation, I saw that there were lots of different wildflowers along the path. I wanted to stop and get a closer look, but the pack made it difficult to bend down without stopping. I could only hope I would get a second chance to identify them on our way back.

We hiked in over two miles before we even entered the Desolation Wilderness section of the Eldorado National Forest, passing by some very dramatic cliffs rising up along the path. "We could come back and climb these," he said. "That's probably not more than a 5.5 or 5.6. You could do that," he offered. I now understood these numbers as the numeric rating for the difficulty of various climbing routes. Doug knew that I could indeed climb at that level, and I was flattered. It was a nice thought, and they were wonderful bluffs, overlooking the lake. But the pack was heavy and I couldn't bear the thought of needing any additional energy, even if they were great climbing routes.

Normally, Doug and I would talk a bit as we hiked. But after a while, I fell silent, conserving my energy to carry the load on my back.

"You're quiet," Doug observed. "Anything wrong?"

"No."

"Pack too heavy?"

"No," I denied emphatically. "I can handle it." I was very aware that Doug was carrying extra equipment for this trip, and I wanted to carry my share too. I wanted to show him that I was strong—and capable for this more demanding trip. I felt lucky to be with him, out on the trail, with these magnificent towering bluffs alongside the sparkling blue lake. I wasn't going to jeopardize my chances for a peaceful hike by complaining or becoming a problem.

After I had denied his repeated offers of help, Doug finally stopped and put his pack down. I was glad for the rest and sat down with him, shrugging off my pack. Without saying anything, he unlaced the top of my pack, transferred the bear canister to his pack, and moved the ropes to mine. I was glad that he was lightening my load, but I would never have asked him to do that. I'm also fairly certain that I would not have lasted much longer on the trail, having to carry all that weight by myself.

Literally unburdened, and feeling mostly relief, along with just a tiny bit of guilt, I was now able to keep up with Doug as we climbed ever higher and passed the sign welcoming us to the Desolation Wilderness area.

"We're at about 8,500 feet," Doug said, after checking his altimeter watch. We were encountering more and more snowfields as we climbed higher. "Looks like it's time to put on the snowshoes."

The sun was just touching the tops of the ridge when we lost the trail under the snow. Doug pulled out his new Global Positioning System unit and extended it in front of him, waiting to pick up a signal. I followed him as we moved through the trees. I was brimming with all the excitement of being on a true adventure as we moved into unmarked territory.

"Hold on," he said, putting his hand up as he continued forward. He was started waving the GPS back and forth as he crossed the clearing. The way Doug wandered around the clearing, his arm straight out with the device made me wonder if we were lost. He did a fine impression of Captain Kirk trying to detect alien life forms with his Tricorder. I had to stifle a laugh as he continued to go back and forth, still trying to pick up a signal.

Then he stopped in the clearing and was fussing over the unit. I was just standing there, getting cold and feeling fear creep in. I wondered if we were lost. "Can I help?" I said, finally daring to approach him as he fretted over different buttons on his new unit.

"Well, it...umm... uh-oh."

"What?"

"I just... this unit...I thought...." he said in exasperation before his hand that was holding the unit dropped down to his side. He looked up and around, then said, "Let's just go this way," pointing off to our right.

I followed along, but didn't dare ask, "Do you know where we are?" or "Did you break the GPS?" or even worse, "Did you get us lost?" So I followed along in the awkward silence. Doug was now searching the printed topological map instead of using his beloved new GPS unit.

After hiking for a while longer, I asked, "Are we going to get to our campsite tonight?"

"I don't know," he said looking again at the topological map. "It's getting late. We haven't even come to Aloha Lake yet."

We trudged on through the snow and then climbed up a steep ridge. By now I was not only tired, but genuinely scared. I knew that Doug had been here before, but as it got darker, it was harder for me to trust his judgment. It wasn't like we could just set up camp anywhere around here. It was too hilly, and everything was covered with snow. He didn't say anything to make me think he knew where we were going or what we would do. So I bit my tongue and continued to follow along quietly.

We were descending towards a frozen lake, but it seemed too small to be Aloha.

"I'm getting tired," I finally confessed. "Can we find some place around here to camp?"

I continued to follow him as the fear crept up from my belly and took over my mind. *Was this trip a mistake? What has he gotten me into?* I stood there a few stunned moments, assessing our predicament. There was nothing but snow all around, but I was hopeful that we could find someplace, anyplace, close by that was flat and dry where we could pitch our tent.

"Sure," he replied looking around. "We can camp here."

He had to be kidding. If I had thought Doug was leading us astray, now I was certain of it. When I looked around us, all I saw was snow. And the only places that weren't covered with snow were filled with puddles of cold water from the spring runoff. *No way could we camp here*, I thought. *There wasn't any place to set our packs where they wouldn't be soaked. My indignation was rising. First he gets us lost, and now there's no place to pitch a tent without getting soaking wet. It's getting darker and colder, and I'm hungry. What are we going to do? But what choice did I have? We were out here alone in the snowy wilderness, with no camping options in sight.* I was on the verge of panic, but I kept all of these thoughts to myself as Doug continued marching on. I didn't know what he had in mind, but I knew I had to keep up.

Welcome to your adventure, Cheryl! Be careful what you ask for.

We trudged through the snow closer to the lake and finally he stopped at a small clearing where there were some dry boulders.

"Are we going to put our tent here? It's not very flat," I commented carefully, so as not to question his choice.

"No, we'll put our tent there," he said pointing to a snowy knoll a few yards away.

"We're going to put our tent on top of snow?" My mind reeled at the impossibility. I was in no mood for a joke. "No way. I mean, how are we going to…?"

"The tent stakes go in at an angle into the snow," Doug said, interrupting my confusion, "and I have the space blanket for a vapor barrier."

He must have been amused at the shocked look on my face, because he smiled, "You'll see. Come on," he nearly laughed. "I'll show you."

We stomped around in the snow to pack it down flat and then put up the tent. We angled the stakes into the snow, just like he said. "Let's point the door towards the lake," he directed, "so we catch the morning sun coming up." I saw that the tent could be set up, but I still had my doubts about sleeping on top of snow. But Doug was so confident and matter-of-fact about it that I didn't dare say anything more.

We boiled our noodles for a quick dinner and settled in for the night. Inside the tent there was only a sleeping bag, a Thermarest pad, and a space blanket between me and the snow. I put on a second layer of fleece once I was inside my sleeping bag. Then I used a trick I had learned from the sleeping bag salesman: hot water in my water bottle at the foot of my sleeping bag to keep my feet warm. It worked like a charm. I was very comfortable, if not entirely fashionable, in my new puke green zero-degree sleeping bag.

Doug, on the other hand, was not so comfortable. His bag was only rated to 25° or so, and he was cold. "Next time, I'm bringing TWO sleeping bags," he grumbled.

"Or maybe you'll want just one zero-degree bag," I said, smiling in the dark. I tried so hard not to sound smug.

"Sure you wouldn't like to share, Cheryl?" he said enticingly as he reached out for my bag.

"No way," I said, slapping his hand away, still trying to sound incensed. "You wouldn't fit in here with me, anyway." I said, like a petulant three-year-old, "You'll just have to get your own zero-degree bag."

"Yeah, I guess I will," he admitted.

I felt totally vindicated in my pursuit of a warmer bag. Sure, it meant a few more pounds to carry, but it was worth it to not freeze at night and actually get some sleep.

In the morning, the view out our tent's door was truly breathtaking. The sun came across the lake and turned the entire area into a fairyland of sparkling white brilliance as the sun reflected off the snow and ice. The trees glistened as the light shot rainbows through the droplets that hung from the branches. I basked in this incredible beauty as Doug, always the gentleman, brought me some hot tea to warm me up before I got dressed in the tent.

After breakfast, we strapped on our snowshoes and made good time heading out on our day hike. Doug marked our campsite location in his GPS so that we could to find our way back from our chosen destination, Pyramid Peak.

The joyous thing about snowshoeing is that you can go anywhere you want, and I had fun squeezing myself between the trees. Then the landscape opened up and the sun illuminated an expansive winter wonderland. We passed by several small lakes that were just starting to melt, and I was delighted by how beautifully the deep blue water glowed as it pooled above the ice. *Pinch me*, I thought. I really can't believe I am here in this spectacularly untouched wilderness. This is the kind of scenery you'd only get to see on some *Discovery Channel* special on polar bears or Siberia. The sun was shining, the sky was clear, and the snow blanketed the ground, giving it a soft, clean look. I only wished my camera could take more of it in. The tiny pieces of heaven I could fit into my viewfinder would never do it justice.

We crossed over snow and sometimes scrambled over exposed rocks. I was concerned that the rocks would damage the snowshoes, but Doug was trucking along and didn't seem to give it a second thought. He had a longer and more powerful stride, so I had to stay focused on just keeping up with him.

Our progress was halted when we came to a creek raging with fresh snowmelt. We heard it long before we saw it, and Doug had to shout at me so I could hear him over the sound of the rushing torrent.

"We'll have to take off our snowshoes to cross this," he shouted, pointing to indicate the fallen log that seemed to hang some 12 feet above the water. My eyes widened as I looked down and saw that there were rapids where the water churned over the rocks directly below the ersatz bridge. Doug was busy strapping our snowshoes onto the pack as I stood there trying to figure a way out of having to cross that log. It was long and sitting very high above those rapids. I looked around, but there didn't seem to be any other way to continue on. Doug didn't ask me if I could do it; he just assumed that I would.

It didn't seem to matter how much this situation activated my fear of heights; I would just have to move through it. I could feel my stomach tensing up at the thought. Normally, if you're crossing a creek, it's shallow — so maybe you'll slip, or get your boots wet, and it's no big deal. But if I was to slip off *this* log, I would fall a fair distance, get banged up on the rocks, then get pulled downstream by the icy current. And how stable was the log? Had it rotted? Would it collapse? Here was a seemingly simple task, but this time, it came with tremendous risk attached.

I stood frozen as I watched Doug walk across the log. He moved very carefully, holding his arms out for balance. He got to the other side, turned around and called back, "Go ahead. It's stable. Just make sure your boots are dry." I looked down and turned up my boots to see that the bottoms were still wet from the snow. A fresh shot of panic coursed through me. How could I dry them off? Everything around me was wet or covered in snow. I looked around quickly, found a dry rock, and rubbed the boots as best I could in order to regain some traction for the crossing.

As I stood there at the brink, I peered over the edge and saw the water gushing away down below. My heart sank. I looked at the log. Then I looked up to see Doug on the other side. There's no way I could get out of it now.

A chill ran through me as I took a deep breath and put my left boot on the log. I stared down at my right boot, and willed it to rise up, too. I stood still for a moment, begging my heart to stop racing as I silently affirmed how stable my boots were on its curved surface. I moved achingly slowly, and must have appeared like a marble statue. Then I turned sideways to maximize my contact with the log. I moved one foot, then the other. I took small steps to keep my body from swaying. I walked slowly, shuffling along, so I could pay close attention to my balance and not fall off. I held my arms straight out to the sides to steady me as I slowly inched myself across the log.

A novice on a tightrope — and no net.

When I finally got to the other side, I looked back in relief. I did it! I wanted to celebrate my successful crossing, but Doug was already moving on. I fell in line behind him and chided myself for making such a big deal about it. *It was simple enough,* I mused, *just walk across a log*. But try it miles from civilization, over a rushing river, and you've got something very different on your hands. I hoped it would be easier for me the second time, because I knew I would have to cross over that raging creek again on our way back.

When we came to a snowy slope on the last leg towards the peak, I got my first lesson in ice climbing.

"When you're climbing a steep incline like this, kick your toe into the snow to make your step. Lean your body forward and use your trekking poles to keep from falling backwards," Doug advised.

I was delighted at how simple it was to climb the snow, even with snowshoes on. Simple, but not easy. My heart pounded at the exertion of climbing, as if scaling a wall. As I got higher, I had a spectacular view over the trees and could see more lakes glowing with their brilliant blue ice. I even stopped mid-slope to take some pictures.

Doug greeted me at the top of the ridge. "You did great coming up, but that was really steep and you'll want to be more careful about your balance so you don't fall backwards." I'm glad he didn't tell me how treacherous he thought the climb was; otherwise, I might have been more nervous on my way up.

We took our lunch out on the rocky plateau at the top of the ridge. It turns out that Pyramid Peak was yet another steep valley away. "We're not in a position to descend the steep cliffs and go the rest of the way," Doug advised, reluctantly.

"This feels far enough for me," I said, lying back on the rocks to bask in the sun. It felt good to rest my body and enjoy some chocolate before packing up again.

On our way back down the slope, Doug wanted to show me other snow-climbing techniques. I was surprised to see that he had brought his ice axes. I didn't quite know what to do when he handed one to me. After all, there was no ice here to climb on. As I held the axe out at arm's length, it looked all business. One side had a narrow blade, like a smaller version of a pick-axe. On the other side of the head, instead of a flat head for pounding nails, it curved slightly into a thin, sharp point. That reminded me of a big animal's claw, because of the sharp jagged teeth on its underside. The skinny handle, about two feet long, had a sharp metal spike coming off the end. I held it away from me, afraid of its sharp metal points.

Doug saw my grimace and said, "Don't worry, I'll show you how to use it. Come on," he beckoned with his hand, "follow me. Kick in your toes like this." This motion created a step under my boot in the snow. He then proceeded to walk me sideways along the ridge and showed me how to plunge the axe into the snow in front of me as my anchor. *This isn't so hard*, I thought, following along behind him, dutifully stabbing at the snow in front of me.

Doug continued, "Be careful when you're near rocks, because they heat up the snow underneath and it melts. Except you can't see that from above, like here," he said, pointing toward a rocky ridge. Peering closer, I could see that, from above, the snow looked like it came very close to the rock. Yet underneath, the snow had melted. "Just give the rocks a wide berth when you're going by them," he advised.

"There are a couple of ways to go down a slope like this," he continued, once we had come to the top. "Plunge-stepping is just walking down and creating your step under your heel with the compacted snow." He demonstrated the technique with a few steps, and it seemed easy enough.

"Now, if you fall down and start to slide, you want to turn over onto your stomach and dig your ice axe in," he demonstrated as he turned and pointed the axe head toward the snow. "It will jerk you up when the claw grabs, so you have to hold on tight. And be careful that you don't roll onto the axe head with your stomach, or you can rip yourself up. Wanna try it?" he asked.

I didn't like the idea of sliding face down in the snow, let alone risking the axe tearing into my belly. "No thanks, I'll pass." I was feeling quite accomplished, now that I had learned how to use an ice axe. It simply wasn't worth getting all wet and cold just to practice a technique I'd never use again.

"Then I'll teach you how to glissade," he said. "It's easier and more fun. You hold your axe at your side and it acts as your emergency brake." He demonstrated by holding the axe close to his hip, with the sharp tip at the end of the handle pointing down. "Now take this," he said pointing to the axe in my hand, "and slide down."

"But how?" I asked, still puzzled at his suggestion.

"Just sit down with your legs out in front like you're on a sled," he explained.

"But my pants will get all wet," I protested.

"They'll dry fast," he said confidently.

I looked down the steep slope. It was a long way to the bottom.

"What about those rocks?" I asked, pointing to the bottom.

"You won't hit them. There's plenty of open space there to the left," he pointed, "and it flattens out. You'll slow down before you even reach them."

Having run out of objections, I took a deep breath and slowly sat down in the snow. I looked over and positioned my ice axe next to my right hip.

"Now hold your axe like I showed you," Doug instructed, as I moved my other hand on top of the handle. "Now go."

I scooted forward a bit and soon I was sliding down. It was steep, and I started to go even faster. At first, it was kind of fun, just like sledding, back when I was a kid. But as my speed increased, that excitement turned into fear as I bounced up and down, careening out of control down the slope. With only my pants between me and the snow, I couldn't steer like I would have done on a sled. When I pushed the ice axe deeper into the snow, it didn't seem to do much to slow me down. I felt certain that I was going to hit an icy bump, flip over and slam my face into the snow. My legs were getting battered and my butt hit every icy lump as I flew down the slope. When I finally came to a stop at the bottom, I was gasping for breath and flooded with relief that I hadn't wiped out on my way down.

Doug soon pulled in next to me at the bottom of the slope, a huge grin on his face. "Wanna go again?"

"No thanks. Really," I said dryly. "Once was enough." I was only now starting to breathe normally. *I hope I never have to do that again*, I thought, as I brushed the snow off my body. Then prayed that I wouldn't catch a chill on the way back, wearing my soggy pants.

The return hike presented us with different challenges because the snow was melting so quickly in the afternoon sun. Snowy places we had crossed earlier in the day had melted a bit and we had to be cautious as we picked our way back. We tried to cross over more of the rocky outcrops without the snowshoes, but still had to traverse a few snowfields. I was still doing my best to keep up with Doug's longer strides in the deep snow.

But the next step I took suddenly felt like the world was giving way underneath me. My head swam and my stomach flipped as the snow collapsed under my foot and I went down. The snow swallowed my leg, and my butt slammed hard into the snow. Suddenly I was surrounded by and trapped in the snow. I wasn't sure what had happened. My heart was stuck somewhere in my throat and I tried to clear my head, but a panicky feeling had started rising up within me. First the sudden drop, and now I had one leg sticking straight out in front of me and the other trapped =beneath the snow. I couldn't move my lower body at all. I tried to push myself up with my hands, but even with my fingers spread, my hands just disappeared into the snow.

"You've posted through," Doug said, upon seeing my struggle. "Don't worry. Just work your leg out slowly."

I glared up at him and thought, Whaddya think I've been trying to do here?

"Here, let me give you a hand." He moved towards me cautiously and extended his hand from a safe distance, slowly pulling me out of the hole I had created.

"That's what I warned you about, when you're walking close to the rocks."

"But I wasn't that close," I said defensively, pointing out how far I had been from the rock. I had been doing exactly what he said.

"The snow is a tricky thing," he continued, "especially when it's melting this fast. Are you sure you're okay?"

"Yeah, I didn't hurt anything," I said. "It was just really scary to go down so fast," I continued, shaking my head in disbelief.

"Why don't you follow in my footsteps from now on?" Doug instructed. "That way, you'll know it's safe."

I had to lift my foot up and above the snow, then stretch my leg way out in front of me to reach his next footprint. I was still a little shaken from my fall and was finding it difficult to follow behind him. "Maybe it's time to put our snowshoes back on," I finally suggested, and we strapped them on for the rest of the way back.

Doug's GPS was instrumental in finding our campsite, and I was glad, since our tracks in the snow had melted away and we had to find our way back through a thicket of trees. I was relieved to be back at our camp since the sun was already low, and I wanted to put on some warm, dry clothes. We were both bundled up in layers of fleece as we huddled on a small island of dry rock in a sea of snow to eat our ramen noodles. We then retreated to the tent for the promise of warmth and much-needed rest just as the sun set over the ridge.

The next morning we broke camp and reloaded our packs to snowshoe our way back to civilization and dry ground. After the softness of the snow under foot, the uneven surface of the rocky trail took its toll on my feet. "These boots let me feel every rock in the trail with this pack on," I explained to Doug. My lightweight hiking boots had served me well up to this point, but this terrain was different.

"You'll want a half-shank boot for this kind of trail," Doug explained. "Of course I like a three-quarter shank for climbing. That way you can put your toe in and it supports your foot better." I took the opportunity to pick his brain further about this next piece of equipment I wanted to get. I liked this higher, rockier terrain, and it looked like I was going to need a new pair of boots to be able to enjoy it.

Partnership
and Personal Power

THEY DON'T CALL IT "Desolation" for nothing.

When we were hiking in and hit the snow line, there was simply no one else around. That kind of isolation really clarifies your level of responsibility to yourself and to your backpacking partner, because everything you do makes a big difference for both of you. There's an unspoken trust in that reliance that builds minute by minute. You're coordinating every little act you do, from helping to pump the water, to fixing or bear-proofing the food, to changing your clothes. You're even accountable to each other when you're going to relieve yourself behind a tree.

Before being out there in the wilderness, I could never have understood how powerful that intimate dynamic of interdependence really is.

And it's not about the words, although verbal communication is certainly helpful. It's about the doing. Agreeing about the day's plan; looking out for each other on the trail; assessing what the other person can handle, or where he needs some assistance. It's about how you act, respond and react to every situation that arises. This is what creates the trust, and ultimately the joy in the adventure. It's about knowing that you can expect cooperation and support while you're dealing with basic human needs and so few creature comforts in the wilderness. It's the blessings in the cup of hot cocoa offered on a cold morning, or the patience required while you try to dig a six-inch hole in the frozen ground for your morning ablutions.

This interdependence is its own kind of dance, where you're both tuned in and present to the current situation, whatever it is. Situations change and are sometimes dangerous, but you must maintain that high level of awareness as you look out for each other. And in that, a real love and respect flows between you and your partner. In the moment, you're just doing the next indicated thing, whether it's using snow to scrub out your oatmeal bowl, or crossing over a log suspended high above a raging creek.

Other backpackers must understand this unspoken rule of the outdoors, but may not speak of it, for fear of ruining their rugged image of self-reliance. I've never heard anyone speak to its power and to the profound intimacy it generates. For me, it was truly compelling. I pushed through new boundaries and learned incredible new things about myself as a result.

A dizzying array of experiences had been crammed into the mere 48 hours that we had spent in Desolation Wilderness. My mind was overwhelmed when the images and feelings came flooding back, once we were off the trail and the pressure to survive had been lifted. Doug and I had definitely bonded more deeply through our adventure. But more importantly, my sense of self was irrevocably altered.

Where there might have been an "I couldn't ever do that" inside of me before, now there was an "I sure can do that." After having continually surpassed my own expectations, I had truly changed. I couldn't rely on my old beliefs and limits, so I was open and willing to try things that I had erroneously believed were beyond my capability.

Returning to the car, I was high on life, with a newfound understanding of what I could do. My possibilities seemed to be as open and powerful as the staggering beauty I had seen for miles around me. I had not only survived in the snow — I had thrived. It was a mind-bending thought that I had possessed the strength to bring myself to such a magical place. There were now unlimited possibilities before me. My inner paradigm had shifted somewhere between the rocks and trees back there in that snowy paradise, and I was ready for more adventure.

Paradise wasn't just about that snowy wonderland. It was about what I now had within me when I dropped my limiting beliefs, and embraced my new self as a strong and capable woman.

That's the paradise I was bringing home with me. I might show my friends the pictures of the landscape, but they would have to look more closely to see that brand new space for possibilities opening up within me.

It was only when we were safely back in the car and driving home that I began to reflect on all that had happened in the wilderness. There had been so many challenges for me throughout the weekend, one right after another. It took some time for me to unlock that treasure trove of experiences and appreciate all that I had done. The feeling came over me slowly. There were so many things for me to process, from having not only survived — but thrived in the snow.

After musing over all of these experiences in silence, I finally looked over at Doug in the driver's seat and whispered, "I slept on top of snow," my voice full of dreamy disbelief.

"Yes, you did," Doug agreed and smiled at my amazement.

"Never in a million years would I have thought that I'd sleep on top of snow."

I had had no idea what I would be asked to do over the weekend, either. I felt like I had been tested by the fates and won. I had pushed myself outside my normal comfort zone and had been rewarded with a profound sense of accomplishment.

"I climbed that snowy ridge," I continued, "and glissaded." I shook my head at what I had done. I saw Doug's smug expression and added, "And that was a steep slope," to emphasize my courage.

"You're a natural," Doug commented. "You learned so fast and you're not afraid to try something new."

I had to turn my face to the window to hide my impish grin, remembering when we were lost in the woods. Doug with his GPS had looked so much like Captain Kirk with his Tricorder, waving it around in the clearing. I had to keep from laughing then, and certainly didn't want to have to explain my laughter to him now.

But then I thought of the amazing scenery. "It was so incredible to see all those icy blue lakes," I gushed. "The rocks, the ice, the snow. It was all so amazing. I never imagined I would go so deep in the wilderness to experience that kind of beauty."

Doug smiled. "If you like the snow and ice," he said turning to look at me, "you'd love Colorado."

I had already heard stories and seen pictures from Doug's trips to Estes Park. He and his brother John had learned to climb both the rocks and the ice in the Rocky Mountains and go back there every year. The whole family comes, and even his teenage nephew climbs.

"There's nothing like being on a glacier," he mused, slowly shaking his head at the memory. "It's quiet. There's no one else around. The Sierras are nice, but they can't compare to Colorado."

I was surprised. What was he thinking? Here I had just done the impossible, and now Doug was upping the ante.

"Wow. A glacier," I was stunned at the possibility. "But I...."

"Don't worry. I'll take good care of you. You've already shown that you're good on the snow. You picked it up really fast."

I was surprised at what he said about my newfound skills. All weekend long I had just been trying to keep up with the next challenge. But he thought I had actually done a good job on the snow. I beamed. Then he added, "We could have a really good time in Colorado."

I was overwhelmed for a time, trying to sort out all the implications of such a trip.

"I couldn't go to Colorado," I finally said. "I've only got one week's vacation left, and I've already given my deposit for that contra dance camp in July."

He thought a minute, then asked, "How much was that deposit?"

"$120. I paid back in March. You have to register early because the camps are so popular and fill up fast." I suddenly felt torn between my love of dance and my love of rock-filled adventures. I sighed, then added weakly, "I've really been looking forward to it."

"But what if the deposit weren't an issue?" he suggested. "Would you be interested in Colorado then?"

Cheryl Berry

My heart leapt at the thought. "Of course I would." But then I added quickly, "But I can't."

"Well," he paused, thinking. "What if I paid you for your dance camp deposit?"

"What? But I can't let you...."

"It's only $120," he said matter-of-factly. "Just tell me. Would you still want to go?"

Oh, he had me. I was totally seduced by the idea. If one weekend on the snow had blown me away, what would a whole week of hiking and climbing feel like? "But it would be expensive," I countered.

"Not really. We'd split the cost. We could camp out, and that's cheap."

He saw my grimace at the idea of camping for a whole week.

"But we could stay in a hotel if you wanted, too."

"How much are we talking here?"

"Well, we could split the car rental and camping." He suggested some numbers and I started writing them down in my wildflower notebook. Then I halved them and announced the total.

"And for a whole week. How much was your dance camp?" he added to make his point.

"Yeah, okay. It's not too much."

"I tell you, Cheryl. You'd love it."

I looked out the window as we continued down the highway. Mountain climbing in Colorado. Climbing on a glacier. Me? I was stunned at the possibilities. But I had just done what I thought was impossible. My heart was soaring, and now Doug was putting a glacier climb within my reach. Glaciers seemed so foreign and mysterious to me. *What would it be like to actually be on one?* I thought. *What with glaciers melting so fast, maybe I should go before they all disappear. Doug's seen me perform in the wilderness. He's climbed a glacier and thinks I could do it, too.*

"I've even taken my nephew and his teenage friend on the glaciers," he added. "You'd do fine."

I had followed Doug into the wilderness over the weekend and had the time of my life. He'd seen what I'm made of. If he's willing to show me his corner of Colorado, how could I turn that down?

"I'd have to get those alpine boots," I said.

"Yeah, you'd probably want those. And I'll bet Jerry would be happy to loan you his crampons for the trip."

My mind started humming away, happily working out all of the logistics. Suddenly, Colorado felt like it could be our next fabulous adventure.

After driving a while longer, we pulled off in Placerville to find some coffee for Doug. As he got re-caffeinated, I continued down the street and stepped inside a wilderness store. My feet were still very tender from our long hike, and plans for Colorado gave me a good reason to get a new pair of hiking boots. Doug had suggested sturdier alpine boots on the trail. I stood in the store, perusing their selection.

"Looking for anything in particular?" the middle-aged salesman asked. It was late on a Sunday afternoon; I figured he probably owned the shop.

Now, what had Doug said I would want? Leather and a three-quarter shank. Or was it the half-shank?

"Um, an alpine boot with a three-quarter length shank," I repeated, trying to sound like I knew what I was talking about.

"Well, these Sundowners here are good. I climbed Kilimanjaro in these."

What had Doug said? Kilimanjaro was just a long walk. Not a technical climb?

"Uh-huh. Well, uh, I'm just going to need something to climb in Colorado," I wanted to sound matter-of-fact about it, as I tried out this idea on him.

"Oh, where are you going?"

"Estes Park," Doug answered, coming into the shop with his coffee. "I wondered where you ran off to," he said pointedly.

"I just thought I'd look at their boots," I said sheepishly.

"Would you like to try them on?" the man offered.

"Not right now," I said, pointing to my feet. "They're pretty sore from wearing the wrong boots in Desolation."

"Is it open already?" he asked, somewhat surprised. "How was the snow?"

"Well," I said, feeling incredibly proud, "we snow-shoed in and snow-camped beside Lake Marguerite. Then we made our way toward Pyramid Peak. The snow was melting fast, so it was kind of dicey on the way back."

He motioned to my feet and said, "You weren't wearing those, were you?"

I looked down at my Tevas. I chuckled to myself that he thought I would hike in these simple nylon-and-Velcro sandals. "No, I was wearing some lightweight hikers. That's why I need some alpine boots. My feet are killing me."

Doug launched in with his questions about the boots and soon the two men were swapping climbing stories and comparing their experiences of the Sierras and beyond.

I wandered further back into the store and marveled at all the minutiae for backpacking and equipment repair. Look, a backpack patch and replacement belt kit. Wow. This was a shop for serious backpackers! When I came back up front, Doug was checking out some MSR snowshoes.

"This is a good price. I'm going to get a pair. Then I won't have to borrow them from Jerry any more."

"Should I get a pair?" I asked expectantly, suddenly feeling the need for more serious equipment.

"No, this is the last pair of these," he said. I frowned. "Don't worry," he said, "you can borrow the snowshoes from Jerry until you decide if you want your own."

Somehow, talking with the shop's owner had made the Colorado trip even more real. He didn't look skeptical at the idea of me going there, climbing or even being on a glacier. He had found the right equipment for other women who hiked and climbed, and he would for me, too. "We'll have to remember this store the next time we head this way," Doug said, fishing around in his pocket. "I'll put it into my GPS so we can find it again."

The next time, I thought. Yeah. I could see it. Me coming back because I needed some new inserts for my alpine boots or a patch for my backpack. I couldn't wait to tell Carol! We had joked about becoming BMWs after our long hikes all throughout Yosemite. But by climbing a glacier, it would be official. I could then proudly call myself a <u>B</u>urly <u>M</u>ountain <u>W</u>oman.

I was excited to tell my friends and co-workers about my plans to go to Colorado and climb a glacier. It was a very different thing, however, to tell my family.

"Glaciers?" my sister, Marcia, said in the disapproving tone she usually uses on her kids.

"Yeah. Doug has done it before with his family," I countered. "He has even taken his nephew. He says it's not that big a deal; he's done it lots of times."

"I don't know, Cher," she reflected gravely.

"He's been teaching me a lot on these two weekend trips we've taken. He says I'm a natural and that I can handle it."

"Will there be someone there who knows where you've gone off to?"

Doug had done this all before and I had trusted him to handle all of the logistics. What I did know was that the rangers are the ones who give out the wilderness permits. I wasn't sure how it would work in Colorado. So I hedged, "Yeah."

"I just don't want anything to happen to you out there," she said, her voice full of loving concern.

"It'll be fine. Doug is extra cautious when he takes me out and always promises to keep me safe." I paused. "I thought I'd take my Arnica," I added, distracting her by talking about homeopathy to lighten up our conversation. We would often talk about the different remedies I could try after I had pushed my body a little too hard on the trail. Marcia had studied the healing properties of homeopathy for years, treating her four kids, and was "Dr. Mom" to me whenever I had a question about a runny nose or sore throat. "You'll probably want to pick up some Rhus and Ruta for your knees," she said.

"Yeah, I'll make sure that I have those."

"You're spending a lot of time with Doug lately," Marcia observed. "Are you sure you want to get close to him again?"

"Things have been very sweet between us lately. We do very well together on these camping trips. I'm kind of looking at this trip to Colorado as a test of the relationship. You know, to see how well we get along traveling together for a whole week."

Goodness knows she had heard the blow-by-blow accounts of the ups and downs with Doug.

After the fun we had had with our weekend climbs, Doug and I got back "together" just a few days before the trip. It was still a tender decision for me, so I was careful not to tell Marcia that we had just resumed our status as lovers.

I spoke to my sister one final time before I left.

"He's taken good care of me and shown me what to do on all our climbing trips, Mar. He promised to keep me safe on the glaciers."

"Well, Cher," she said, her voice heavy with resignation, "if you're going to go, at least give me some phone numbers and information about where you'll be."

I could understand her concern. After all, her husband had gone on a simple outing with their teenage daughter when they were in Europe. Carl wanted to retrace his grandmother's daily trek to sell the eggs from her farm across town. It was just a short stroll across the border from Poland into the Czech Republic to grab a soda and come back. But they forgot to show their passports when they returned, so they were swarmed by border guards and held in custody for several hours. I remember the look on Marcia's face when she got that call from the Polish police station. "No problem, Mar," I said with a smile. "I'll send you all of our travel information."

Beginning of the End

AFTER ARRIVING IN ESTES PARK, Colorado, our plan was to climb the glaciers after taking a day to acclimate to the higher elevation. The town itself was at 7,500 feet, but we drove to 12,000 feet for a spectacular view around the park. Mountain ranges reached up and into the clouds. There was a snowfield at this elevation, so Doug gave me a refresher course on using the ice axe and put crampons on my feet, where I used them in the snow for the first time. We also got to feel how much harder it was to breathe at that elevation.

Later we did a short hike along the Continental Divide, where it rained in the late afternoon. I enjoyed scrambling over the rust-red rocks that jutted out of the hillside, and was already noticing wildflowers that weren't familiar to me. I picked up a Rocky Mountain Wildflower Guide to help me learn the names of these local beauties.

We had set our tent up at a woodsy campground inside of Rocky Mountain National Park. It got dark early because the sun sets behind the mountains sooner, and the trees blocked what little light there was. The campsites were spread out, so we had the nice experience of feeling like we were alone in the woods.

I had awakened the next morning before the alarm, knowing that this was the day I would actually climb a glacier. Filled with excitement like a kid at Christmas, I was sure it was a good sign when we spotted a bear on our drive to the Bear Lake trailhead. He was just sitting there on the side of the road, looking at us calmly as we came around a curve. "Doesn't he look like he's waiting for someone to bring him his morning Starbucks?" I asked Doug. It would have been great to get a picture, but the bear probably would have fled if we had backed up to take the shot.

As we started on the trail, the mist was slowly rising off of the lake when the sun made its first appearance of the day. The groomed gravel trail near the lake crunched underfoot, but soon gave way to a quieter dirt trail leading us deeper into the forest. The dampness of the morning dew captured the mossy smell of the woods, and filled our nostrils with its cool, earthy scent. The early morning light gave sharp outline to the ferns and flowers on the forest floor. We continued into the dense greenery and eventually came to an elevation where all we saw were lots of yellow sun-rayed petals of heart-leafed Arnica along the path. My heart was pounding a little harder due to the elevation and my excitement. We hiked along in silence, enjoying the quiet of the forest, which was pierced only by an occasional bird song.

The trek up to the glacier turned out to be a long hike that took us through a dreamy landscape. As we gained in elevation, we could now look over the trees; the early morning fog had settled between row after row of mountains, as far as the eye could see. The quiet stillness of the morning added to the feeling of profound majesty. It was like one of those *National Geographic* spreads glorifying the natural splendor of the Rockies. What a quiet thrill it was to be there, breathing in the cool morning air and owning that spectacular view for myself.

Ptarmigan Glacier is the big patch of white above my head at the top of the ridge

We encountered an occasional snowfield that stretched for a hundred yards and crossed the trail as we approached 9,000 feet. It was still cold enough, and the snow had piled up thick enough, to be there in July. The trees started to thin out as we approached 10,000 feet, and we became more exposed to the wind. I had on my nylon t-shirt, a fleece jacket and a wind-breaker. I put on the outer shell and pulled its hood up to protect my ears. The wind became colder, stronger and more constant, and like a thief, reached inside my lungs to steal the body heat right from the core of my being. I wrapped my arms around myself to keep from being robbed of the last of my body's warmth.

After we left the trail, the trees seemed to hunker down themselves, so we literally bushwhacked our way up through a nasty tangle of trees stunted by the fierce wind and thinner air. Crossing open fields of barren rock, we hiked to an elevation above the tree line. That's when we started to enter the great gaping maw of the glacier's canyon, where Mother Earth extended her arms to take us in.

We advanced over the sharp-edged rocks and around the tarn (a pool of glacier water) at its base. I wanted to stop and bask in the beauty of the glowing ice and water, but Doug continued on. As I looked up, the sheer cliffs were bathed in the morning light and various streaks of blue, green and rust-colored rocks melded through the expanse. A white line snaked through all of them and hinted at the untold history of this place. The massive towering canyon walls rose up dramatically, surrounding us. They reached skyward and inspired awe, as if we were in a cathedral. I slowed down and felt great reverence as we approached the snowy edge of the glacier. Standing at its base, I looked up. The glacier seemed to go on forever, a vast expanse of white, reaching up to touch the sky.

I found it hard to believe that I would be able to climb all that way. It was one thing to join Doug in our weekend mountain climbing trips back in California—but climb a glacier? I still couldn't quite believe that I was here, standing right next to one.

Looking down, I watched Doug unloading the pack. I stood there, nervously shifting back and forth as he sorted out all our climbing gear. I wasn't sure what I was supposed to do next, so I waited for him to finish his inventory. I had put my trust in Doug for our other outdoor adventures, and felt safe in the knowledge that he was an experienced climber, and blessed that he was willing to extend his expertise so I could learn to climb a glacier myself. As my anticipation grew, I shook out my hands to release some of the tension that was building up in my body.

"Put your gaiters on first," he said, when he finally handed them to me. I had to smile at this familiar scene where he hands me some new piece of equipment for the next leg of our journey. We had already defined our roles and built a level of mutual trust that had carried us into increasingly difficult terrain. Now I was preparing to take an even bigger leap, testing my new skills on the face of Ptarmigan Glacier.

I looked around for a big, dry rock, then sat down to put the gaiters on. I wrapped the nylon around to cover each of my calves and zipped them up the back, finally hooking the bottom onto the laces of my boots. Then I checked to make sure they covered around the tops of my boots to keep the snow out.

"Now you can put your crampons on," he said, pointing to my pair, lying on the ground. They reminded me of medieval torture devices, with their pointed metal teeth protruding all around the bottom. I had no idea how to strap them on. Doug helped me secure the crampons over my boots, pulling hard on the thick rubber straps to secure them.

As I stood up to test how it felt to stand in crampons, he handed me my ice axe. I had received my first lesson with the ice axe a few weeks ago in Desolation, so I was less intimidated by this big aluminum "T" with the sharp metal points at each end. This axe meant business, and I had to hold it carefully so I wouldn't cut myself.

Doug stood up, holding his axe out in front of him, with one hand on each side of the crosspiece, the long stem pointing down. He stabbed the shaft into the snow just beyond his toes. "Try to get the ice axe to go in deep," he said as a reminder. "It acts as your anchor to keep you from sliding down if you slip." Emphasizing the strength of its hold, he rocked the ice axe back and forth, but it barely moved in the deep snow. "Keep both of your hands on the top of the axe head," he said, patting it. "Put your ice axe in first, then take your steps like this," and he kicked the toe of each boot into the snow.

"Ready?" he asked, looking me up and down to see that all of my equipment was in order.

I nodded excitedly, hoping to convince us both that it was true.

"Let's do it," he said, taking his first steps onto the snow.

I looked up at the snowy white slope and then back down at my feet. I certainly looked the part. Wearing borrowed crampons and gaiters, and using Doug's extra ice axe, I kicked my first steps into the surface of Ptarmigan Glacier. The snow was good and deep, so I could make the ice axe go in almost to the top of the shaft.

"That's right," Doug encouraged, still keeping an eye on me to evaluate my technique, "get it to go in as deep as you can."

I beamed. I could scarcely believe it. I was actually climbing on a glacier!

Doug was already several steps in front of me when he called out one more piece of advice. "Remember to keep both of your hands on the ice axe if you stop for a rest," he said, patting the top of his axe. "You really don't want to fall backwards," he said, tossing his head back with a grin. I didn't give any thought to the fact that we weren't roped together for our ascent. I had seen pictures of the climbers on Everest all roped together, but I was filled with nervous excitement, and my attention was on doing everything exactly the way Doug had taught me to do it. There was no space for me to question his instructions or technique.

I was careful to watch my feet each time I kicked them into the snow, on either side of the axe shaft. *Durf durf,* my boots sounded as they went into the snow. It took a lot of concentration to make sure I didn't stab my toes as I plunged the ice axe down; this was a highly orchestrated movement that demanded all my focus. The axe rang out with a *chreeng* as it cut through the snow. Stab, step, step. Stab, step, step. *Chreeng, durf, durf, chreeng, durf, durf.* It was like doing the Stairmaster, kickboxing and NordicTrack all at the same time!

I hadn't gone but a dozen or so steps before my heart was pounding and I had to stop and catch my breath. But it wasn't muscle fatigue that stopped me. No, I had been training steadily for months to be in shape for this climb. But the air is much thinner at 11,500 feet because it contains less oxygen. I couldn't believe how quickly I had been forced to stop and catch my breath. My lungs were aching, my breath was ragged and I had only gone a few yards before I had to rest. I was stooped over my ice axe, trying to catch my breath. I shook my head as I questioned my sanity, and gave a short laugh. I gave up a week of dancing with my friends for *this*?

***

"Geez, Cheryl, why didn't you just stop and go back down?" Krista asked.

"I really didn't think that was an option."

"Not an option? You sound like you're gonna collapse right there on the snow! What do you mean 'not an option?' Wait, I'll bet this isn't the first time you've done this with a guy?"

"What? Climb a glacier?"

"No, go along and follow him into something that's not right for you. Like you're trying to prove something. What were you trying to prove to Doug?"

Her question hit me hard. It was true. I had been with other men who had led me into treacherous territory. There was Tom, back in the 1980s. He was a biker and a swimmer; we trained together in the pool during college.

I recalled to Krista, "I joined him in a triathlon where I did the swimming start, even though I had a fear of open water from when I almost drowned as a kid. Tom and I had trained for the event in the pool; he would slap my feet so I could get used to bodily contact in the water. But so many people crawled over me at the start of the race, and then the course turned sharply and the field narrowed. When I turned my head to come up for air, a competitor would shove my face underwater. If you got dunked time after time, you'd panic too! I pulled out of the race because I was so freaked out."

"And what were you trying to prove to Tom?"

"I don't know. That I'm good enough? Or that if I did this with him, he would like me more?"

"Don't be so hard on yourself, Cheryl. I mean, we all do it. We follow our men and get ourselves into sticky situations. I guess it's just good to notice the pattern before...."

Her words hung in the air, for, of course, I had paid a big price for following Doug. She gave me a look like she had already said too much. But she was right. I had done this before, and now I was doing it again.

***

Already striding ahead of me, Doug looked back and saw me bent over my ice axe. He shouted across the snow, "Count your steps. It will help you keep your focus." Starting up again, I could only make it up to 20 steps. Then 24. Finally I could take 30 steps before I had to stop and pull my heart back into my chest. I was bent over my ice axe, trying to catch my breath, when something hit me. Startled, I looked up to see Doug smiling as he scooped up another handful of snow. I ducked his second snowball, and tried to scoop up my own to retaliate. But he was above me, making him a more difficult target.

My feet were planted in the snow, and I couldn't step backwards for more leverage, or I'd go tumbling backward down the snowy slope. After making just one snowball, my bare fingers were now cold and wet. I had to flex them open and closed to get back some circulation. I wasn't up to a snowball fight under these conditions, so I shook my head at a laughing Doug and quickly gave up.

I trusted Doug when he said he would take care of me on this trip. After all, he had been very patient as he taught me various mountaineering skills on our other three trips. I could tell he was keeping a close eye on me as we hiked up to the glacier. "You're doing really well hiking at altitude," he said. "I wasn't sure how you'd hold up."

I was delighted that he had noticed my strength, and I beamed at his compliment. I knew I had been diligent in my training, carrying a backpack full of water jugs up those hills twice a week after work. "Each body responds differently at altitude," he reminded me. I was glad that I was still measuring up. At that time, what I knew about the body's response to higher elevations was primarily academic. The thinnest air I had experienced was at about 10,000 feet, back in Yosemite.

Since we weren't roped together, and with Doug so far ahead of me, I was able to set my own pace as I continued stabbing and kicking at the snow. When I'd stop to catch my breath, it gave me a chance to look around. Most of the time I had to keep my focus on where I was plunging my ice axe, so I relished these breaks and drank in every detail of the exceptional landscape that was all around me — white, white and more white.

Beyond the glacier's edge, the rugged canyon walls rose to dramatic heights on either side. Each wall had been deeply carved by the elements and was streaked through with shades of gray, rust and blue. Above was the cerulean blue of a cloudless sky. I was pushing my body and working harder than I had ever done in my life. At times, my chest clutched in pain as my muscles demanded more oxygen. But it didn't matter. My heart was overflowing with gratitude for the opportunity to explore this rocky paradise. Not many people ever get to see these sights, let alone climb a glacier. I still couldn't quite believe that I was actually here!

I looked ahead and saw that Doug was already waiting for me at a rocky outcrop. "You're going to like what you see here!" he called out, teasing me. He knew I loved rocks, but those rocks didn't look particularly special.

When I crested the ridge, I was amazed to behold a glorious field of columbine sporting purple and white petals popping out of the rocks. "Look at how many there are. They're so beautiful," I marveled, "I've never seen wild columbine before." Doug grinned back at me, knowing how much I loved my wildflowers. It was so surprising to see these delicate beauties out here in the middle of such a stark and barren terrain. There was nothing around but rocks, snow and ice, yet these guys were standing tall and proud, happily waving in the breeze.

Close-up of columbine

I can't wait to tell Carol, I thought, knowing that she would share in my delight. Carol had taught me so much about wildflowers during the week I spent with her last summer in Yosemite. Her love for wildflowers was infectious and had inspired me to research the names of the flowers that I found along the trails back home in Sonoma County. It certainly added more fun to my hikes whenever I came across these little gems. I had even called her last night to brag about all the new flowers I was seeing in Colorado. It's hard to compete with Carol's wildflower sightings, since she hikes through Marin every weekend and spends ten weeks every summer at her home in Yosemite. It seems that I needed to leave California to find a wildflower that she hadn't already seen.

My new Colorado wildflower book noted that this wild columbine only grows at very high elevations; so of course, I had to have a picture. I was also grateful for the opportunity to sit down on these dry rocks. With such wide stretches of snow between rocks, it had been a long time since I had rested my legs from the grueling climb.

I bade farewell to the flowers, and we continued on without ropes, which allowed each of us to set our own pace in the thinning air. As we headed up the glacier, the snow curved around some boulders to the right. The pitch was so steep that I found it easier to make progress with a short zigzag approach rather than going straight up. The sun was now overhead and reflecting off the snow. I was working up quite a sweat after pounding away with the axe and kicking into the snow. I took off my fleece jacket and tied it around my waist, took a deep breath, and continued on, counting out each hard-won step.

I finally caught up with Doug, only after he had stopped again to wait for me. He was sitting on some large, dry rocks above the snow line.

"Want a snack?" he asked.

I nodded eagerly. He held out a bag to me and I reached in. Maybe it was the high mountain air, or maybe it was the ambiance, but a handful of Cheez-its have never tasted so good.

As we sat there eating, Doug leaned over and placed his hat on my head. "No," I protested, "you need it to cover your head more than I do," I said, taking the hat off and handing it back to him. He was trying to help me, since I had lost my hat on the hike up.

"It's okay," he said, "I have an idea." He put his headband on, then layered a few strips of toilet paper over the top and tucked them into the headband. At least it would protect his scalp from the sun. "How do I look?" he asked, modeling his new chapeau. "It looks good. You wouldn't even know there was TP on your head."

"No pictures, please...." he demurred when I pulled out my camera. "I would never live this down."

Giving me his hat was such a sweet gesture. I was glad to see that he was making good on his promise to take care of me in the wilderness. It was such an alien landscape; I was relieved that Doug seemed very at ease out here.

After our snack, we scrambled over the rocks to the next part of the glacier. The metal teeth of our crampons screeched underfoot as they struck bare rock. I picked up an elk vertebra from a small pile of bleached bones and considered taking it as a souvenir. Then I thought of the extra weight I'd have to carry and reluctantly dropped it before I took a deep breath and stepped back onto the snow.

Doug was always able to pull ahead of me quickly, so I was essentially climbing by myself, even on this steeper part of the climb. I didn't mind, because I could go at my own pace and stop when I needed to catch my breath. I could also take my time and appreciate the quiet stillness on the glacier, now that we were deeper into the canyon and protected from the winds. Without Doug nearby to distract me, I could bask in the more subtle experiences of the glacier. For example, I came to enjoy the sound that the ice axe made as it sliced its way through the first few inches of snow with a *chreeng*, followed by a satisfying *clunk* as it hit the ice some 18 inches below. The final sound in that subtle rhythm told me I was ready to take my next steps.

Since the glacier's pitch got much steeper as we climbed, all I saw directly in front of my face was a wall of snow. There, instead of extending my arms in front of me to plant my axe, I had to raise my arms high above my head to stab it into the snow very close to my face. After I had taken my steps and pulled the axe out, I could look down inside the long channel that the axe had cut into the snow. The reflected light revealed an incredibly beautiful blue light glowing within each tiny snow tunnel. There were dramatic walls of stone rising majestically all around me, yet I was even more delighted to see that radiant blue light each time I took a step.

The pitch was so steep, I felt like I was climbing up a wall. I looked up at how far I still had to go, then down at how far I'd come. *It's a long way down*, I reflected. I would have expected that my fear of heights would kick in and make me feel anxious about standing so high up, looking down at the rocks so far below. But those reflections felt more like an intellectual review of the situation.

I was curious about this absence of fear. Perhaps I had developed more confidence in my climbing, or I believed that the snow was soft and deep enough to stop me from falling very far. I didn't even consider the possibility that the thinner air had affected my reasoning skills; I simply turned back towards the glacier and went back to counting out my steps, stabbing my ice axe ever higher in front of me as I continued to climb. I wasn't wearing a watch, so I wasn't sure how long we had actually been climbing. What I did know was that ascending the glacier was excruciatingly slow.

I became intrigued by something else on top of the snow: all kinds of bugs were littering the white surface. There were frozen flies, desiccated grasshoppers and even tiny spiders. What were they doing here at 12,000 feet, in the middle of the glacier? It was so odd to see any sort of life form in the middle of this frozen white expanse. Then there were the shiny green beetles, huddled together on the few pebbles that had fallen on top of the snow. The beetles seemed to belong there, unlike their freeze-dried brethren. But what were they doing in the middle of a glacier? Then again, what was I doing there?

Hey, Cheryl, what IS a nice girl like you doing on a glacier like this?

The Tundra

AFTER FINALLY REACHING THE TOP of the glacier, my sense of accomplishment was supreme. It had only been two months since my first technical climb, and today I had successfully climbed the steep face of Ptarmigan Glacier. My heart was pounding, my legs were wobbly and the wind was howling in my ears. Standing now on the tundra, I saw that it was wide and flat, as if someone had taken a knife and sliced a smooth flat top off the mountain. The view was expansive and offered stunning 360° views for miles around the park. I could see over the top of eight or more mountain ranges, stacked up one right after another, fading off into the clouds. I was triumphant, and felt like I was standing on top of the world.

Under foot, I marveled at the yellow and purple splashes of wildflowers in bloom: yellow paintbrushes and king's crowns were everywhere. I was astonished to see some snow buttercups blooming right next to the edge of the glacial snow. Those flowers had certainly earned their name. The tundra was barren and very flat except for the wildflowers, a few scattered boulders and some dense patches of stunted green turf. I turned back to see how far I had climbed. Looking straight down, I realized that I had just climbed up a vertical wall. From this perspective, I had a very different understanding about just how steep the slope was. *Wow, I climbed that,* I thought, with an even greater appreciation of what I had achieved.

"How you doin'?" Doug asked as he came over to me to help pull off my crampons.

"Great," I said testing my legs for their ability to walk on flat land again. "I can't believe I climbed all that way."

"Yeah, you did a great job. Are you ready for some lunch?" he asked.

"I guess we'd better eat something," I said, not sure what I could handle. The altitude was making my stomach feel uneasy.

We looked around to find something large to hide behind to block the steady push of the wind. At last, we hunkered down behind a solitary boulder, but dining at 12,000 feet, we had to hold onto our food or it would have been ripped right out of our hands by the tormenting wind whipping around us.

"I can't eat any more," I said, after forcing myself to eat a few bites of my peanut butter sandwich. "My stomach feels kind of queasy."

"It's just the altitude. You can try to eat some more later," he said, rewrapping my sandwich. "So, do you want to go back down Ptarmigan or go on further?"

***

"Why is he asking YOU what to do next?" Krista demanded.

"I thought he was being considerate to check in with me."

"Didn't you have a plan for the day? I mean, this was a big undertaking."

"We had talked about our plan the day before."

I remember all too well that fateful conversation at the coffee shop.

Doug was explaining the different glaciers we could navigate on our return. "Look, this is where we're going to climb tomorrow!" he pointed out excitedly. There was a map of Flattop Mountain under the glass at our table, and he pointed out our options for tomorrow. It was only then that I came to understand how long the full hike would be.

The realization was hard for me. I was excited to get to climb, but I had a sinking feeling in my stomach when he showed me how far we would be going and explained how long it might take. Just this side of panic, I wondered what I had gotten myself into. Doug was so excited, I was afraid to tell him that I was afraid. After all, climbing the glaciers was the whole point of our trip, so I couldn't back out now. I felt like I'd been pushed into a corner; a sense of dread started to fill me.

"I don't know if I'll be able to do such a long hike," I said, looking at him intently. "And I've never been on a glacier before."

Doug assured me that he had done this many times before with his brother. He continued to cajole me.

"I've even taken my nephew and his friend." Then he pointed out any number of glaciers on the map. "Look, we can take any one of these back down to shorten the day's hike." He kept pointing to three different glaciers. "So we don't have to go the whole route if you don't want to."

I felt better knowing that we had options to shorten the trip. But there was still a gnawing sensation in the pit of my stomach for the rest of the day.

***

"No wonder, Cheryl," Krista chimed in. "Your intuition was right on!"

"Yeah, I had that feeling but I overrode it. You know, we trust our men when they say they'll take care of us. Sometimes it works out, sometimes it doesn't. But we can't just collapse under the weight of those betrayals."

"So then, what do you do with that feeling?"

"For starters, now I trust my intuition more than my man. And then you forgive. You take your lesson with you and move ahead. Do we really have much choice? We love our men, but they are bigger and stronger than we are. If we didn't keep going back, the species wouldn't survive so well, now would it?"

Krista was a bit surprised at my impromptu sermon, but conceded, "I guess you're right."

***

It was hard to admit that I somehow knew better than to agree to the hike, but I really felt that I didn't have a choice to back out at that point in time. Lots of little decisions had led me to this decision. And there were many more decisions still to go.

Standing at the top of the glacier, I was torn. I had worked so hard to climb all that way up. Surely there was something more interesting to do than just go straight back down. I had hoped to get inside a crevasse, but we hadn't seen any as we were coming up Ptarmigan. I was experiencing a whole new world at this elevation, and I wanted to see more.

Doug was still waiting for me to make the decision about continuing on or going back down Ptarmigan. My thoughts ranged from *we just got here* to *I worked so hard to get up this high* and *let's stay up here a little longer*. I sorted through these options rather quickly, and was a bit surprised that Doug, the lead climber, was even asking me to make this choice. I was still amazed that

I had climbed all the way up, and my curiosity and delight in my accomplishment got the best of me. So I said, "Let's go on a bit more," hoping we wouldn't have to hike that much farther before we could start our descent.

Hiking across the tundra was no walk in the park. Although the trail had a smooth, flat surface, the wind was constant and threatened to knock me over. I had to wrap one arm around my waist to keep the cold air from blowing up my jacket. I used my other hand to keep my hood closed tight around my ears, and bent my head down. Although the view was stunning, most of what I saw was the thin dirt trail right in front of my feet. Alongside the trail, the grass and plants, just recently out from under their snowy cover, were tough and low to the ground, finally out from the snow, now battered by the wind, just like me. They seemed better suited for it than I was. After the hike and the glacier climb, the wind seemed to suck the energy right out of me.

"I've taken this trail before with my brother when we've come in the past," Doug reminisced. "When John's leading, it's always the long way. Makes you feel like you're on the Bataan Death March," he recalled. *Well, here's a newsflash, Doug. You're not doing so bad yourself.*

We'd pass by one glacier, then another. Each time, I'd get my hopes up that we would be able to start making our descent, but Doug would say, "Can't go down that one, either. See how the cornice comes up," pointing at the big wave of ice curving over the top. "That could break off and kill you. Not a safe one to climb on." Deflated at hearing that we had to keep going farther, I bent my head into the punishing wind and trudged on.

Between the howling of the wind and the hood of my jacket flapping wildly against my ears, Doug and I had to shout to hear one another. My muscles were responding to the lack of oxygen, so every step was an effort. By mid-afternoon, I was truly exhausted.

I spotted a large pile of boulders that I thought might offer some protection from the wind and told Doug I wanted to stop for a bit. I hunkered down between the rocks with a few other hikers who were also seeking refuge. It wasn't the most comfortable position, but getting off my feet and away from the wind was all that mattered to me. I forced myself to eat a few more bites of my peanut butter sandwich, but that just made me feel even queasier. I took my boots off and rubbed my tired, aching feet. I really hoped that Doug wouldn't push us on again too soon. I was wondering how much farther we'd be going and was starting to have serious concerns about my body's ability to continue on.

There was only one other time when I had not been willing to follow Doug's lead in the wilderness. We were on the back of Cathedral Peak in Yosemite, on our last climb before coming to Colorado. He had decided it would be easier and more fun to take the mountaineering route, because it wouldn't require us to put on the harness and haul out the ropes. I liked that idea, too, since I wouldn't spend all of my time pressing my nose to the rock face as we could only ascend inches at a time doing a technical climb.

It was the first time we had climbed in Yosemite and Doug went ahead of me as he scouted the backside of the peak, trying to find the route that one of the other climbers had suggested. I spent more time admiring the spectacular view and the slope as the back of the peak dropped straight down several hundred feet on its way to the valley floor. After a few minutes, Doug beckoned me to follow him out onto a tiny ridge.

I looked down to see the small crack in the rock face where I was supposed to put my feet. I was wearing my new alpine boots, which felt way too big for such a narrow ledge.

"Shouldn't I put on my rock-climbing shoes to grip this rock?" I asked.

"You don't need to. The rubber on those boots is "grippier" than you know. You'll do fine; just watch where I put my feet."

Easier said than done. Doug, at 6' 4", had a longer reach and stride than I did at 5'7".

My heart was in my throat as I stepped out onto that ledge. I turned to face the rock and pressed my hips against it as I inched my boots along the narrow surface. It helped to keep my eyes on the rock in front of me rather than on all that empty space behind me. Since I was hugging the peak with my entire body, periodically I'd stop and rest my cheek against the cool rock, willing my heart rate and breathing to slow down.

"You're doing great," Doug called back to me.

I came to a place where the ledge was wider, and turned around carefully, still leaning my back into the rock. *Look, Ma, no hands*, I thought, as I saw how far down it was. "Nobody is going to believe this," I murmured to myself. "I've got to take a picture." I got out my camera and pointed it down, framing my toes along with the steep descent. This is what they call "exposure." That's the fancy climbing term for how stupid you are to be that high up without being secured on a rope.

"Did you see how I maneuvered around this area?" Doug said, pointing to a bulging section of rock he had just come around. I looked ahead and couldn't see where I would put my feet. The panic must have registered in my eyes, because Doug continued reassuringly, "You can't see it, but you can feel it with your feet. There's a ledge that you can't see from there. Just reach out with your toe."

I couldn't believe that he expected me to pull my body away from the rock and reach out and across that area. It just didn't look possible.

He pointed above the bulge. "There are some good handholds here, too," he added, still trying to convince me. "Really, Cheryl, you'll do fine."

I heard the words. I looked at my feet. I saw the rock. But my gut just said, *No way*.

I tried to push through my fear and figure out how my legs could reach the places he had indicated. But I just couldn't force myself to do it. These were the last words I wanted to utter, but I felt like I had no other choice: "I'm sorry, Doug," I said soberly, "I just can't do this. You've got longer legs than I do. And it's a long way down," I added, tipping my head as a gentle reminder that we weren't roped up. We stood there looking at each other, eyes locked, for what seemed like an eternity. I didn't like disappointing him by being too afraid to follow. I don't think I had ever said no to him before while climbing, so he had to know that I was serious.

I didn't know what he might do or say. Oddly enough, I felt much more vulnerable to what his reaction might be than I did to such a high level of exposure. My stomach got tighter as I waited anxiously for him to respond. But I knew that the move he wanted me to make was just too risky for me.

Finally, he broke the stalemate. "Okay, maybe you're right. This is a bit dicey through here," he said, reflecting on his chosen route. Then he paused to think for a bit. "They said the mountaineer's route was lower on the backside. Maybe we didn't look far enough down."

I felt such a wave of relief come over me as we slowly backed off that ledge. I was so glad that he didn't hassle me or try to push me into it.

Doug and I had grown to trust each other more on these outings. Our first trip to Pinnacles National Monument is where I learned the technical rock climbing with a rope and harness. Then, we had that mind-blowing weekend camping and climbing in the snowy outback of Desolation Wilderness. The trip to Cathedral Peak in Yosemite was our last trip in preparation for our week of climbing in Colorado. I had covered a lot of ground in just two months, and Doug had been wonderful about showing me the skills necessary to be safe and have fun while mountaineering. He had learned my strengths and weaknesses and had worked with me to build my confidence and experience. Earlier in the day, Doug had been impressed with my capacity to climb at altitude. But as the day wore on, I started to have serious doubts about how much more I could take.

We stepped back out into the wind and continued our slog across the tundra. Doug had led us beyond the trail, so now we were walking on the stunted grasses and flowers. I was hopping from rock to rock, trying not to harm the delicate vegetation. Eventually I gave that up because it was all I could do to put one foot in front of the other.

Doug was now looking for landmarks that he could recognize, but the terrain offered little in the way of visual clues. There was only a slight variation in the heights of the surfaces on the mountain as we trekked over it. And there were no discernible objects on the landscape, a brownish-green carpet in every direction. I couldn't imagine what sort of landmark he was expecting to find within the monochromatic expanse of the tundra. Come to think of it, we hadn't seen any other hikers for a while, either. How much further would we have to go? I had been willing to follow Doug up to this point, but I didn't know how much longer I would even be able to hold myself upright.

"How much farther is it, Doug?" I finally asked after we had hiked quite a bit more. I already felt like toast, and we hadn't even started our descent.

"I think it's just beyond that ridge," he said, pointing to a shallow valley that rose again on the other side.

I dropped my head in disbelief. *I don't know if I can climb up that ridge*, I thought to myself. The altitude was taking its toll—first my lungs, then my stomach. Now my entire body felt like it had been wrung out like a dishrag. I was exhausted and had begun to fantasize about just stopping and letting my body collapse; that was my best response to the endless plodding over the undulating sea of tundra grass. My judgment was compromised due to the lack of oxygen, so the idea of just surrendering my body to gravity truly seemed like a good idea.

Since that was not an option, I soldiered on, taking small steps and trying to conserve my energy as I attempted to keep up with Doug and climb to the top of that ridge.

When we finally found the "DANGER" sign atop Andrews Glacier, I was a mere shadow of myself.

Believe the Signs

THE BIG RED "DANGER" SIGN drew me in. "ANDREWS GLAC-IER. HIDDEN OR OPEN CREVASSES." it read. "DESCEND WITH EXTREME CAUTION." I laughed. "I didn't see signs on any of the other glaciers that we passed," I pointedly said.

THE most ironic picture in the world

Doug explained, "Those other glaciers had even more perilous descents and dangerous cornices than Andrews." Still highly

109

amused at the paradox, I asked him to take a picture of me with the sign.

Even though this glacier seemed to invite the opportunity of a crevasse, I was too tired to even remember my dream of climbing into one. As we approached the glacier's edge, I saw that it descended into a long and steep canyon. We were still far above the tree line, so the only things in the canyon were more rocks and snowfields.

"You've got to be extra careful late in the day," Doug advised. "It's at a time like this, when you're tired, that you can make a mistake in judgment and get hurt. I've been down this glacier many times with my brother over the past 12 years. I tell you this is the best part of the route, because we can slide down the snow for a fast and easy descent."

Fast and easy sounded good to me, so I sat down in the snow, my ice axe at my side, and prepared to glissade. But the snow was very deep and wet, and I had to work hard just to keep from sinking in and coming to a stop. I finally scooted my way to the bottom of the slope after having to restart myself three different times. I didn't really need my axe as a brake because I sank into the snow, which kept me from going very far or very fast. After a long day of hiking, the glissade really boosted my spirits and made me laugh, even though my butt was now cold, wet and a little tender from the bumpy ride. Doug ended up walking down the slope because he weighed more than I did, and every time he prepared to glissade, he only sank down into the soft snow and couldn't budge.

Doug filled our water bottles by pumping from a large pool at the base of the glacier. I sat down to rest my legs next to the cool, clear water, then took some pictures of the glacier and the water that glistened and danced in the golden light of the late afternoon sun.

The easy, safe slow descent down part of Andrews Glacier

"This second part of the glacier is steeper and there's all those rocks at the bottom," he said, pointing to a field thick with boulders about 100 yards down. "That's not good for a glissade descent. For this part of the glacier, let's plunge-step down,"

Doug suggested. *Good, that's easy*, I thought, *just walk down it and create my own steps in the snow*. Doug started walking down the slope with ease. Following his lead, I jammed the heel of my boot into the snow to create that first step for myself. But there wasn't much snow, so I didn't feel like I had a solid footing. I wondered if I could scoop more snow under my boot if I turned it sideways. Didn't Doug call this the French technique? I turned my boot to the side and took a step, but discovered that this snow was icier and more shallow than at the top part of the glacier. When I tried to adjust my step, I lost my footing and fell down on my butt. "Ouch," I said, then tried to stand back up.

But I had already started to slide down the steep and icy slope. *No problem*, I thought. I had my ice axe looped around my wrist, ready to act as my brake. *You just need to dig the tip into the snow*, I told myself. With the head of the axe in my left hand, I placed the axe a few inches from my right hip as my right hand pushed down on the shaft to force the tip further into the snow. Even though I was pushing hard, it just scraped along the solid ice a few inches below the snow's surface. I realized that there was no resistance from the snow, as I watched the axe merely scratch a long line on top of the solid ice sheet. I leaned over to put more of my weight onto the axe, trying to make it dig in. *I'm doing this right! This is what Doug showed me to do!* I insisted. *Why isn't this working?* I thought. *This axe is supposed to stop me!*

I didn't have the luxury of consulting the owner's manual or waiting on hold for tech support. I do confess that I wanted to shake the axe to make it work properly. Let's face it; if I ever needed an ice axe to work properly, it was NOW! And, although I was picking up speed, my mind was still fixated on this idea that the ice axe should start working for me. But since it could neither stop nor slow me, a dark feeling of dread started to grow inside my gut.

My body, which was starting to register the menacing nature of my freefall, soon cut through my singular focus of making the axe work. I was now confronted by the disturbing idea that I had no control over my acceleration down the slope. I was picking up speed and sliding out of control, filled with the horrific realization that something terrible was about to happen.

I looked up. Doug was right in my path.

"Doug!" I yelled.

He turned his head to see me coming towards him and held up his arms up as if to catch me dropping out of the sky. *Oh, good*, I thought, *Doug will stop me*. I felt such relief, confident that surely Doug would know what to do. Doug knew about climbing. He had promised to keep me safe. Powerless to stop myself, I placed all of my hope in him.

I released the ice axe from my right hand and shifted my weight towards Doug on my left. In a matter of seconds I had reached him. We collided in a tangle of flailing limbs. I used both hands to try to grab hold of his arm or leg. I lurched and raised my arms, desperate to attach myself to him. He was my last hope to save myself from those rocks.

His jacket and legs brushed over my face as we grappled. I searched frantically, trying to grasp something solid. His arms were above me, out of reach, and I was sliding so fast I couldn't get a firm grip of his leg. In the frenzied swish of nylon and Gore-Tex, I caught the hem of his jacket. That meager handful slipped through my fingers as I sped past his legs. One moment Doug was in my face. The next instant, all traces of him were gone.

Now there was nothing between me and the menacing rocks below.

I was consumed by an explosion of desperation and terror as the shock of this new reality ripped through my body. Denial rose up and demanded a stop to this unholy nightmare. If Doug couldn't stop me, I knew I was as good as dead. My chest clenched and my belly froze, but that didn't change the reality that I was speeding wildly out of control.

My ice axe was dragging beside me, still looped around my wrist, so I grabbed for it and fiercely tried to wedge it back into the ice. But the axe still did nothing to slow me and my mind raced in a panic. What else can I do? Doug couldn't help, and the ice axe still didn't work. I was running out of options, and those rocks were growing bigger and closer by the second. *There has to be something more I can do!* I demanded. Then a new idea flashed into my head. *My heels*, I thought. *Dig your heels in, Cheryl.* I dared to hope and tilted my boots to dig my heels into the snow.

But instead of stopping or slowing me, my boots shot up two huge rooster tails of snow that arced eight feet into the air.

Although my body and thoughts were moving at top speed, time seemed to slow down as I watched my consciousness start to expand. Precious seconds were ticking away as my awareness grew and became filled with a myriad of people, scenes and feelings.

Is this how I will die? If I was grieving my own death, I was firmly stuck in the denial stage. How did I get here? The utter absurdity of the situation felt like a brutal jab to my gut. This can't be happening! But my own refusal could not stop me from coursing down the ice into the cruel fate of the rocks lying in wait.

Overwhelmed by the unruly crowd of questions and my defiant dissent, I held firmly to the belief that a girl like me would not die on a glacier like this. My mind just could not accept my impending death on the rocks.

I flashed on an image of my office back at work. No scenes of my entire life flashing before my eyes, just a vision of my office.

The dull grey cubicles covered in cloth; the putty-colored desktop. My chair, empty and beckoning me. Normally a mundane or neutral sort of space, it now offered the incredible allure of the comfort, peace and stillness that my body craved. A curious choice as a balm to my terror, my cubicle had been transformed into a beacon of safety and comfort.

Then everyone I loved flashed before my eyes. I saw them all in an instant. A lifetime's collection of family and friends I would never see again. All of the people I loved but would never have a chance to say goodbye to. A spike of grief shot through my heart as I wondered how they would learn that I died on this glacier. It was definitely not the way I thought I'd go. I'd never see my dad or sister again, never be able to say goodbye or I love you to them or to my friends. More sadness surged through me, and added to the cruelty of the situation as I reflected on being robbed of my final goodbyes.

These tiny little vignettes popped up and then got tossed around inside my maelstrom of terror.

And by now, I had exhausted all possible means to save myself. The wall of boulders grew larger and more dynamic before me, as I could now distinguish their individual shapes. Brown and grey with jagged edges, the boulders stood a foot or two high, forming a formidable barrier before me. I could not avoid this surreal dream, and a new level of clarity emerged that narrowed my thoughts to one cold, hard reality: I was going too fast to survive when I hit those rocks. There was nothing more I could do or think. I shot a quick prayer to my angels for help, shut my eyes, tucked my chin down and prepared to die.

The clash of rocks and boots and axe exploded in my head. The force of impact was powerful and the shockwaves coursed through my body. I had built up such momentum, that after I hit the rocks, I flew beyond the ice sheet and was projected mercilessly onto the field of boulders. I bounced and scraped and slid over their jagged surfaces. They pounded at my legs and back until gravity and friction had their final say. I came to a stop on top of the boulders, many yards beyond the snow and ice.

And suddenly everything was dark and black and quiet.

Return of Hope

HAVING PULLED MYSELF through the thick pile of boulders for almost two hours, all I could do now was continue to wait for Doug's return. Feeling vulnerable as I lay on the ground, alone in the canyon, I had moved beyond my concerns about being able to fend off a mountain lion. Now I simply tried to keep my thoughts a half-step ahead of the terror. After crawling down the canyon and getting through the rocks, I was finally able to give my exhausted body some rest. Fears continued to buzz through my mind, but in the aftermath of the climb, my crash and utter physical depletion, I had no energy left to play out the different scenarios or their awful conclusions.

It was from that daze that I saw Doug's head pop up over the rocks. "What are you doing back so soon?" I said, not believing that he had returned before dark. "I didn't even have time for a nap!" I teased. Suddenly my smoldering fears were quenched by a huge splash of hope. My heart was beating so fast, as he and another man climbed up to where I was lying. I couldn't believe my eyes. Doug had actually found someone to come and help.

"Hi, I'm Tim," he said, introducing himself. "Doug here said you needed a little help." A trim 40ish man sporting a Detroit Tigers baseball cap, he flashed what had to be the most beautiful smile I would ever see. If his mere presence didn't make me feel better, that smile convinced me that everything was going to be okay. As grateful as I was for his presence, I was still a bit wary and wanted to get a measure of the man Doug had brought.

So I chatted him up while Doug was focused on loading everything back into the pack. "So you like the Tigers?" I started. "I'm from Michigan. I grew up in Royal Oak."

"I'm from Fenton," he said, identifying the similarity of our backgrounds, another Detroit suburb. It was important for me to connect with him somehow, and this felt like a very good start. "My wife and kids are back at our tent. We backpacked up here for the night," he explained, somehow sensing my need to understand his presence a bit better. "Then we heard Doug calling out for help," he stated matter-of-factly, shrugging his shoulders as if he responded to distress calls in the wilderness every day.

"I'm so thrilled to see you two," I said, "I was afraid I'd be here all night by myself. Thanks so much for coming." Helping Doug assess the situation, Tim seemed genuinely delighted to help get me down the mountain. Now that there was a second person to help, we considered different strategies for them to carry me.

"Put your arms around our shoulders," Tim suggested, "and see if we can all walk together." We quickly discovered that the terrain was still too rocky for us to have stable footing.

"Here, let's make a seat for her," Doug offered, clasping his wrists into a square with Tim's. But they couldn't walk sideways over the steep, uneven surface. We couldn't go far as such an ungainly unit, so I ended up crab-crawling and scooting my butt down yet another boulder field.

Doug put me up on his back again when the boulders cleared for a path and the ground was flat enough. We made better time, because Tim carried the pack while Doug carried me. This way he wouldn't have to cover the distance twice, first with the pack, and then with me. We continued on like this until we came upon a sloping snowfield. They suggested that I glissade down it. "I'm not doing that any more," I insisted. "My last attempt didn't end so nicely, and my butt is still cold and wet." I didn't even want to scoot over the snow because of the cold. They stood there for a while, not knowing what to do next.

"How about if you sit on my raincoat?" Tim offered. I was willing to do that, so they pulled me down the snowfield, like a kid on a sled, until we reached dry land again.

Soon we fell into a rhythm, as we made our way slowly through the rugged terrain. Tim carried the pack and picked the best route around the rocks while Doug carried me on his back. To get me up, he'd bend over and I'd reach around his neck. He'd grab under my knees, which generated that deep, searing pain in my thigh, and an intense throbbing in my right foot each time I climbed up and jostled my right leg. I had to hold on to Doug's neck for dear life (quite literally) as he started to slowly pick his way through the narrow, rocky passages.

We crossed over another dome of a snowfield, this time with me on Doug's back. Arriving at the crest, Doug's leg pierced through and we both dropped straight down, slamming into the snow. I felt another shock of pain shoot up my leg and was stunned by this, my second fall of the day. It took me several moments to figure out what had just happened. We were pinned down in the snow, with me straddling Doug's hips and his hands buried in the snow around my thighs. I wanted to pull my right foot free from where it was jammed at a painful angle. I started to move in order to free it, but Doug warned, "Don't move! I don't want to fall through if it collapses." His words stopped me cold. *Oh God*, I thought, *we're on a snow bridge, and Doug is already halfway through!* "Don't let us drop through!" I prayed.

Tim stood at a wary distance while Doug worked cautiously to free my legs from his grip. Afraid that any movement I made might make it collapse, I laid back, spread my weight out as if I were in quicksand and scooted away very slowly. Once I was safely off to the side, I watched intently as Doug leaned back, spread his arms and slowly extracted his hidden leg. Tim stood at the edge of the snow and leaned over, extending his hand to help pull Doug away from the dangerously fragile crest.

Falling into that snow bridge was a potent reminder that I was still vulnerable, even with Tim's help. Doug's back no longer felt safe for me, as I was sensitized to the fear of being dropped again. And now a chill was creeping up my back and down my legs from sitting in the snow again. But I really had no choice except to climb up on his back and hope I wouldn't be dropped yet again.

The three of us continued slowly in short shifts, going only as far as Doug could carry me before he had to rest. The terrain flattened out a bit and he was able to carry me for a slightly longer stretch. "Hey, try not to strangle me," he implored as my arms pressed against his throat. "Sorry," was all I could offer him.

I didn't have the strength to hold myself properly on his back, and it took tremendous effort and concentration not to let go and fall backwards. I focused all my strength on locking my wrists as I hung them around his neck. Doug is tall, and I was swaying back and forth with each step. Glancing down periodically at the sharp rocks, I was terrified. My hold was tenuous as he stepped over and around the rocks on the steep trail. I absolutely dreaded the thought of being dropped again, this time onto more rocks, and finally had to close my eyes against the threatening image of their cold, hard surfaces. I could no longer watch his boots on the uneven ground as we swayed endlessly through the boulders.

Closing my eyes, however, only left me with fears that had been splashing around inside my head all the way down the mountain. Are we going to topple over? I can't hold on any longer. I know my hands are going to slip. Is my foot going to hit another rock? I know he's going to drop me. Oh, my thigh hurts!

My inner vision showed a darkness creeping up my back and reaching up for me. The feeling was as if hands were trying to grab at me and loosen my grip, but it had the look of black flames of fire, seducing me into the darkness. I was trying to keep my awareness above these dark, beckoning tongues, but was compelled by their seductive allure. I looked at this odd apparition starting to consume me, and it filled me with abject terror.

I didn't understand this at the time, but I was right on the edge of losing consciousness, and had I let that darkness consume me, I would have passed out.

I felt the message the flames we sending me: 'You can let go of the pain,' they enticed me. 'You're exhausted. Go ahead, surrender.' They taunted. 'Just let go...'

As my figurative and literal grip on reality was slipping away, I knew that if I were to surrender my hold now, I would fall and surely die.

But even as I was afraid of the black flames, I was compelled by curiosity to look at them.

Doug had no way to know that in that moment, there was a tremendous battle taking place on his back. I was torn between the physical forces of friction and gravity that pulled at my body, and the choice of consciousness in the light or the easy release into the dark. Whichever I chose would ultimately determine if I continued on in life or in death.

My body must have slid down a bit, and Doug chose that moment to reach back on my thighs and hike me further up his back. That jolt to my body and the pain that racked my foot and coursed through my thigh shook me out of this nihilistic reverie.

I opened my eyes, looked around and saw that we were crossing a creek, and I was afraid we would fall or I would be dropped again.

As I closed my eyes, I recommitted to holding on, and focused on the locking of my wrists around Doug's neck.

Focusing on the pain in my wrists was the only thing keeping me from falling back into the darkened abyss.

I knew I needed to look away and distract myself. What could I do?

I flashed on singing to chase away fears, as I had done in the past, so I started in.

You are my sunshine, my only sunshine,
You make me happy, when skies are grey.

It was a simple song, and came with an added dose of comfort because I remembered singing it with my sister when we were kids.

You'll never know, dear, how much I love you,
Please don't take my sunshine away!

I opened my eyes again and saw the steep rocky path we were going down. I shut my eyes against the treacherous scene and continued singing.

I must have sounded awful croaking away, out of tune. After my second or third time through the song, Doug asked, "Are you singing about me?" His voice startled me, and my thoughts scattered. I struggled through the fog of exhaustion to find any sort of response. Did he want the song to be about him? Would he drop me if I said no?

No, it wasn't about you, Doug, I thought. But I couldn't verbalize an answer for him. It was too much of an effort to stay grounded and connected to my body. Every fiber of my being was screaming at me to let go, collapse, and allow the pain and exhaustion to carry me away into oblivion. *No, I wasn't singing to you, Doug, I was singing to life itself.* I hoped that this happy tune could edge out the demon fears that threatened to take me down, poised as they were and all-too-ready to consume me.

I dared to open my eyes once more and looked down to see the log he was balancing us on as we crossed over a creek. Oh, no! Please don't let him slip! I don't want to land in the water! I didn't know how much more I could take. It was harder and harder to keep a grip loose enough around his neck so as not to choke him. And I dreaded climbing on and off his back. Doug was also quickly getting exhausted. We had to stop every few minutes to give us both a chance to rest.

Tim was keeping the banter light as he told us about his family and picked the best route for us. A thin trail began to emerge as the terrain started to flatten out, which made it easier for Doug to walk and for me to hang on.

"I need to stop," I gurgled at Doug. He set me down on a thick log and I wanted to lie down and stay there. That's when Tim's family emerged from the edge of the woods. Tim had told us that his daughter Anna had been studying French at Michigan State University, so I surprised them all with a weak but audible, "Bonjour, comment ça va?" Anna, his wife Donna and their pre-teen daughter Allison were all staring at me wide-eyed, as if they were encountering some new alien life form. *They can't freak out at how bad I am and let me die*, I thought. "I can't tell you how grateful I am that you're here to help me," I said to them. I wanted to distract them since they continued staring at me, so I said, "Doug suggested we could stay on the mountain." Then I added with dramatic flair, "but I would have noooo part of that."

I mocked myself in an attempt to make light of the situation. I wasn't going to give Tim's family any reason to not want to help me. I should have focused more on resting before we continued on, but I felt a deep drive to make sure these people liked me. I believed my life depended on their good will, strength and resources. And, feeling so vulnerable, I didn't want to give them any reason to abandon me. "Well, this isn't quite what I had in mind for my first day on the glaciers," I said, indicating my bloody pants, "but, hey, at least I didn't have to walk those last few miles." I tried to downplay my injuries, not wanting to appear to be too much of a burden.

Some inner voice pushed at me: "Humor your caregivers, Cheryl, your life depends on it."

Donna, the mother, cut through my feeble attempts at humor and brought us back to the task at hand. "The tent is just a little ways back," she indicated, pointing behind her. "We came out looking for you because it was getting late," she said, looking at her husband with loving concern. "We've got lots of water and other things back there."

"Oh, thank you," I said as my body filled with relief. They were prepared and willing to help me. I mentioned that I was on my period and wearing contact lenses, and she reassured me that they were equipped to deal with all of that.

"We backpacked up to this remote site for the one night," Donna said, "because the rangers said that there would be no one else around except for a few climbers," and then she added brightly, "and here you are." They were surprisingly receptive to the idea of having the "injured climber" at their camp and adding this unexpected twist to their family vacation.

"Hey, we'd better move on," Tim suggested, looking at the sky. "It's getting darker by the minute."

Meeting the Family

DOUG CARRIED ME on his back through a final stretch of trees until we came to the small clearing with the Peters' tent at Andrew's Creek campsite. Doug eased me down to the ground and Anna, their eldest daughter, reached out to help me stay steady while I perched on my left leg.

Their first concern was to look at my right leg and identify the source of the bleeding. I teetered a bit as my left foot sought to maintain balance, and Anna moved in closer and put her arms around me for support. I turned my head and rested my cheek on her shoulder. Anna's body was soft and warm, in sharp contrast to the endless sea of cold hard rocks or the constant sensation of bouncing up and down on Doug's back.

I moved in closer and my whole body relaxed as I melted into her embrace. Her offer of support was like a lifeline to me in my sea of despair and her presence was a balm to my battered body and soul. My brave façade crumbled and unleashed a flood of emotion that had been kept at bay. Hot tears rolled down my face as I gently sobbed into her neck. Anna didn't push me away and I appreciated that she could accept my grief and tears so easily.

I was relieved to have this family's help, but I wasn't really sure what to expect. Their various conversations were hard for me to follow and there was still so much I didn't know about my condition. I had no choice but to trust them and whatever support they were willing to offer me. I was still terrified of what horror they might find under my bloodied pants. As I continued to stand there holding on to Anna, Doug crouched down and unzipped the bottom half of my right pant leg. He gently eased the material down and over my right boot, exposing the bottom half of my leg. I nearly tipped over, swatting at the mosquitoes that were aggressively going for my newly exposed skin. "Allison," her mother said, "keep the mosquitoes away from her," and she moved in, waving her hands as if she were fanning my leg to cool it off.

Doug leaned in to take a closer look. When he lifted the shortened pant leg, all eyes were on my leg. All conversations stopped and the silence was deafening. I could feel their shock; it was that palpable. Each additional second that ticked by terrified me all the more. What were they seeing? How bad was it?

"Well," Doug finally said in a very measured tone, "it has stopped bleeding." By choosing his words so carefully, I knew it had to be bad.

"Yes," Tim confirmed, leaning in closer, "it has stopped." I tried to look down to see for myself, but it was towards the back of my thigh, so I could only see the top of a cut.

"It's a nice, clean cut," Doug offered. "If I had a needle and thread I could stitch it back together." "No ragged edges," Donna added encouragingly.

With a bit more effort, I turned and saw the deeply cut valley of exposed and bloody tissue where my upper thigh had been. It had been sliced clean through and my leg was laying wide open. My first thought was of disbelief. After all, how could there be so much space where my thigh is supposed to be? Then I focused on what surrounded the space and I nearly gagged at the sight. I recoiled into Anna's arms, squeezing my eyes shut, trying to block out the surreal image. The laceration ran perpendicular to the bone and seemed to cut half way through my thigh. It was a ghastly mess of my own flesh — gaping, bloody and raw.

"It's long and deep," Tim said gravely. "We've got to cover the wound up. Keep the dirt out." "Here's my camp towel," Donna said, offering him a small, gray cloth. Then she thought to look at me. "It's clean," she said, "really." I nodded my consent to her.

"Do you have any tape?" Doug asked, holding the cloth over my exposed flesh.

"Here," Tim offered, "I've got some duct tape on my water bottle," peeling it off.

"I got you a new bottle," Donna reproached. "And you brought that old one."

"Yeah, and it's a good thing, I did, isn't it?" Tim tossed back at her with an easy smile.

They taped the camp towel to my thigh, while my mind raced with other thoughts. Beset with new worries about the huge gash, I began to wonder if I would now die from blood loss or infection. What about gangrene? I felt as though I had unwittingly bumped into death's door again, and started to wonder if I would ever get off this mountain alive.

After sealing up the cavern in my thigh, Tim took charge. "Let's get you into the tent, Cheryl. Go in and lie down. You won't be leaving the tent tonight."

What? I thought, *Not leave the tent?* His edict was like a slap in the face. I felt like a petulant child being sent to the corner for a time-out. But this flash of indignation was quickly drowned out by the crush of my new reality. What else could I do? Where else would I go? A fresh wave of exhaustion came over me and I acquiesced. After all, what choice did I have?

I surrendered to Tim's direction and put my arms around Doug's and Anna's shoulders. As hard as it was to hear at the time, ordering me to rest was the most loving thing that Tim could have done. With this one statement, he took charge of my situation and prepared his family to tend to my needs within the confines of the tent. Doug and Anna maneuvered me towards the family-sized tent. I only had to duck my head down a bit to enter its doorway. It seemed strange to be stepping into the tent with my boots still on. They lowered me to the ground, and Anna helped me into a sleeping bag along the right side of the tent.

Doug went back outside, where he talked further with Tim and Donna about what they should do next. I could hear bits of their discussion. Yes, it was getting late, they agreed, but someone needed to continue down and get help for me tonight.

Doug eventually came back into the tent with their decision. "I hate to leave you again, Cheryl," he said, reluctantly. "But I'm the best one to continue on down." My heart sank. I felt so vulnerable with these new people. I'd just found out that my leg was torn wide open and now Doug was telling me that he was going to leave me again. Everything was happening so fast, it was hard to adjust to the implications of all these revelations.

Doug was the only constant in my fragile and tenuous connection to this world. He reached for my hand in a silent offer of comfort and hope. I wanted to say, "But we just got here! Don't go. I don't know these people. I'm scared. I don't want to die. Please don't leave me again!" But this wasn't the time for an emotional display. There's no way I could speak those words in front of the Peters family.

"I'll be leaving now. You'll be okay," he said, squeezing my hand. "Don't worry," he said, as if to acknowledge the fear-stricken look I was giving him. "I've got my headlamp." He ducked out of the tent and started down the trail.

His departure had a powerful effect on me, as if I had just taken a punch to the gut. I flopped my head back down onto the pillow and squeezed my eyes tight against the tears that threatened to flow again. Having no more strength left to struggle, I surrendered. I gave in and felt my awareness starting to collapse inward. I felt the pull from inside, slowly tearing me away, as if my fingers had finally released their grip on this absurd reality. I continued to feel myself falling inward, away from the pain, away from Doug, away from life. I was falling away from everything I thought I knew about myself and my world. I felt like I was falling through darkness, floating through a spacious black tunnel.

All alone. Again.

Inside the Tent

I WAS PULLED BACK to the present and when I heard the *zring* of the tent door unzipping, I opened my eyes and glanced to my right to see that Donna was ducking back into the tent after seeing Doug off. I was still cold, cocooned inside one of the family's sleeping bags. Donna looked down at me, her hands on her hips, and said, "We've got to get you warmed up; you're still shivering." She looked around quickly. "Try another sleeping bag," she told Anna.

"Should we take your pants off?" she asked.

"Yeah, I guess so," I responded weakly. "They're cold and wet." Because of my blood, I didn't add.

Anna was already seated at my side as she bent forward to fold back the top of the sleeping bag. Her back then straightened and she composed herself, as if about to perform surgery. "Don't worry," she said, "I've worked in elder care, so I'm used to this." She unzipped the sleeping bag further and started to ease my bloody pants down my leg, careful not to touch my duct-taped thigh or bump my throbbing right foot.

Donna took the bloodied pants, held them up, and crinkled her nose. "These are disgusting. I should throw them out."

"No," I protested, feeling very awkward to be asking anything of her, "I can wash them. They're still good," I said, seized by a curious need for thrift. "Please don't throw them out."

"Well, if you really want them," she conceded, shaking her head, "I can put them in some plastic. I just don't want to attract any wild animals with the smell of blood." I thought of how I was preparing to face down a mountain lion back in the canyon and shuddered at the memory.

"Your underwear is all bloody, too," Anna said. "Can you lift your butt up so I can slide them down?"

I guess this isn't the time to profess any sense of modesty, I thought, as she leaned in to hook her fingers around the waistband. *We're all women here*, I mused. They've looked deep into my thigh. These people were trying to keep me from catching a chill and dying. What could I say? "I hardly know you"? Or, "Won't you at least buy me dinner and a movie first?" I gave a questioning look to Anna, but she seemed unaffected. I finally gave her a resigned "okay," and raised myself up on my elbows. I slowly rocked my hips so as not to aggravate my thigh and she eased my underwear down, carefully stretching the pants around the duct tape.

"Uh-oh," Anna said as she held them at my ankle. "I can't slide them over your boot."

"Why don't we just cut them off?" Donna suggested. She produced a pair of scissors and *snip snip*—off they came. She then went outside again to dispose of my bloodied underwear.

I was now naked from the waist down. That is, unless you count my socks and right boot. We decided to leave the boot on to support my swollen ankle. I was still wearing my t-shirt, fleece and windbreaker as Anna zipped me back in. They gave me one bag for each leg because of the need to let them move independently to ease any painful pressure for my leg, hips or foot.

"Tim's heating some water for you to drink," Donna advised. "And here's some Motrin." She paused after handing me the two pills. "What else can we do for you?"

Their kindness nearly overwhelmed me. I couldn't believe all the things they were doing for me, the stranger who had practically crashed through their tent roof in the middle of the wilderness.

"Well," I said, sheepishly, "my left foot is really cold."

"Allison," Donna said, addressing her youngest daughter, "Go over and see if you can warm her foot up." Allison looked pleased that she was finally able to pitch in, and practically jumped towards my legs. "Be careful about her foot!" Donna warned. Allison slowed down and cautiously moved around my feet, back in the corner of the tent. She looked at me shyly as she removed my sock and put my left foot between her legs. I smiled back my thanks to her.

"Here's Tim's hat," Donna said, offering me a fleece beanie. "That should help."

"You guys are being so great to me," I said, still not quite able to believe their incredible generosity.

"Well, you're making it easy by telling us what you need," she returned. I was settled in for the time being and my most immediate needs had been met. That's when Anna seized the opportunity. "So...what's with you and Doug?" she asked, her eyes alive with curiosity.

The sudden shift in the conversation caught me off-guard. It took a moment for me to switch gears and bring my mind around to try to address this new topic. My mind was running at least a half a beat behind in being able to process any thoughts. "Doug, well...." I searched for where to begin. "This is our first vacation together in Colorado. My first day on a glacier." The details of our relationship history would not be so easy to explain.

"No, no," Anna clarified, "I mean, like, the two of you... are you... you know..." she leaned closer with an expectant look in her eyes, "together?"

"Yeah, I guess we are," I finally replied. "We've been off and on these past two years," I said distractedly. My mind was moving slowly as my awareness struggled to access those particular memories. I was all the more upset when I thought of how Doug had led me into this mess. But I didn't want to seem like I was blaming him or mention any of our problems from the past to sully their view of him. Doug must have seemed like a hero in their eyes, carrying me down the glacier on his back. It took some effort, but I decided I could find good things to say about Doug and me. "We just got back together again before this trip," I continued. "Climbing has been really good for us."

"Where did you meet him?" Anna pressed on, clearly more interested in the details of our relationship than my climbing stories.

There was not much else to do now besides talk, and this was a welcome change from having them fuss over me and my wounds.

"Doug," I started, "well, now, let's see...." it took me a few moments to remember exactly. "That's right, a party. I met him at a Halloween party about two years ago. He was made up like a cowboy. Tall and lean with his hat, chaps and spurs." A small grin crossed my face at the memory. "And the clicking sound he made when he crossed the floor coming towards me... well, what can I say, ladies," I paused for dramatic effect.

"Spurs are *very* sexy." They all laughed at my story and that alone made me feel better.

But the tender nature of my reunion with Doug was still very present for me. I had struggled to try to make it work with him in the past. After both the times I'd broken it off, he'd come back to me later with an "I've changed" speech. Ever the engineer, he had considered the specific behaviors I had identified, and told me he had made the necessary changes to meet my needs. Doug is smart and kind and I really did love him. So I'd find myself back with him for a time, until there was something else he couldn't understand or wouldn't budge on. Doug seemed almost proud when he admitted that he could be so stubborn.

Anna was holding the cup of hot water her father had heated up for me. It was an effort, but I slowly propped myself up on my elbows and sat up to take it. I sipped at the drink slowly and enjoyed how it warmed my cold hands. Then I asked Anna, "So, what about you? Is there someone special?"

"Well...his name is Gabriel," she said, with a telling smile. "I met him up at State. We've only been dating for a few months," she said somewhat shyly, "but he's a really nice guy."

We compared notes on our men and talked alone after her mother and sister had left the tent. I suppose I appeared to be somewhat of an exotic creature to her after she heard about my life and how I had traipsed all over these glaciers with my lover.

After we had been talking for a while, I had the uncomfortable realization that my bladder was full. Frustrated that I couldn't deal with this on my own, I had to bring Anna in on my problem. "Oh," she said, puzzled about what to do. "Let me go see," and she got up and left the tent. I had no idea how they were going to help me with this particular problem. If Tim had decided that I would not be leaving the tent, it wasn't going to be easy. I hated the thought of one more embarrassing thing they would have to deal with for my sake.

A few minutes later, Anna came back in. "Okay," she said, pressing some items to her chest as she entered the tent.

"Let's slide this plastic bag underneath you and then I can help you sit on this pot."

"That's your cooking pot," I said with alarm. "I can't use that. It's the only pot you have."

"Don't worry about that," she said, sitting back on her heels. I rocked back and forth slowly as she slid the plastic underneath me, then she pushed the pot at my hip and commanded, "Up."

I was mortified that I was about to foul their only cooking pot. What would they do after I had peed in it? Backpackers travel light. Did they have other pots to cook with? This felt like I was taking too much away from them. But Anna was poking at me again, so I reluctantly raised myself up on my elbows. I rolled a bit to my left and shifted all my weight onto my forearms and left foot. Then I slowly started to arch my back to lift my hips above the pot. Suddenly, a sharp pain shot up my right leg, and I cried out.

"Are you okay?" she asked quickly. I shook her off and closed my eyes to breathe through the deep burning of the aftershock. *Will this never end?* I thought, exasperated again by intense pain from such a simple movement.

"Can you help me up?" I said through gritted teeth, offering her my arm. She gave me her shoulder and slowly lifted me on-to the pot. I agonized over each little movement to lift my hips up just high enough. "A little lower," I hissed as she positioned the pot strategically underneath me. I lowered my weight back onto the pot and felt yet another pain. The pot's rim cut sharply into my flesh, but it didn't hurt quite as bad as my leg. *God*, I thought, *I hope I don't pee on the plastic or their sleeping bag.*

Now she sat there, watching me. I closed my eyes to create a sense of privacy and tried to relax. But my body was arched back awkwardly, and the fullness of my weight pressed my flesh painfully into the edges of the pot. I wanted to let my pee out slowly, so I wouldn't splash or miss my tiny bedpan. God. How embarrassing! After what felt like an eternity, I heard the familiar tinkle of water on metal. Good, I thought. I made it inside the pot.

Getting me off the pot was harder. As I lifted my hips, the pot full of pee came up with me because it was now stuck on my backside. Anna didn't seem to have enough hands to hold me up and peel the pot off my butt, but somehow we managed to extricate it without christening their sleeping bag with my pee.

After she had emptied it out, she and Donna came back in. "Are you doing okay?" Anna and I exchanged knowing grins.

"Anna is taking great care of me," I answered, my eyes still on Anna. We had bonded over our talk and the improvisational bedpan routine.

"She's been telling me about Doug," Anna said brightly.

"Oh, I was wondering about the two of you. How did you end up climbing here in Colorado?" Donna asked.

I knew they were bound to ask sooner or later. Where could I start to explain the rich dynamics of the past few months? I mentioned the three trips we had taken, and how Doug had suggested we come here to Colorado to climb on the glaciers. I winced internally as I flashed on how his latest idea had turned out. But I pulled myself back to continue the story. "Climbing has definitely brought us closer together," I concluded, trying to sound upbeat.

Through the spring, Doug and I had done surprisingly well getting back together and staying in friend mode, even through all of the intimate challenges of our snow camping in the Desolation and Yosemite backpacking trips. Then after dinner one night, just a week before our trip to Colorado, Doug took a bold step away from just friendship and spoke to me about his feelings.

"These past few weeks have been wonderful," he said, measuring each word. "I love climbing with you, and I don't want to do anything to mess that up."

Uh-oh, I thought, where is he going with this?

"I never stopped loving you, Cheryl," he confessed. "I feel so good when I'm with you." Then he looked down at his plate and fingered the cup of salsa. "I can't change the way I feel," he said, full of resignation. "I just had to tell you."

I sat there stone-faced. Doug had just changed the rules. Our agreement to be friends had just been tossed out the window. I didn't know what to say. Truth was, I was full of hope too, and I was having lots of fun. But we had been through this too many times before.

"Thanks for telling me, Doug." I finally said, but nothing more.

"I'm not asking for anything, Cheryl," he said, sitting back and holding both his hands up as if to stop me from saying anything else. "I just wanted to be able to tell you."

Over the next few days, I reflected on how much I admired his courage for sharing all that he had. I sensed a shift in my feelings too. After all, things had been very sweet between us lately. Maybe this was what we had needed all along, I mused — to just relax and be friends. I felt his words of love moving through me over the next few days and was fascinated to see how they worked on me and opened my heart to him again.

We had a sweet and tender reunion as lovers, and with just a few days left before our Colorado trip, I prayed that our revised relationship status wouldn't complicate things. I was filled with an underlying hope that this time, we could make it stick. After all, you learn a lot about someone when you travel with him, and I felt confident that after an entire week with him, I would finally know if Doug and I were meant for each other. But after nearly getting killed on this climb, the relationship had unwittingly entered an entirely different realm.

Tim had been outside of the tent for most of the evening, but then he came inside, as it was now getting late.

"Here's that contact lens case and solution I promised you, Cheryl," he said, handing them to me. Then he turned to his wife. "What do you think, Donna? How are we going to work this?" he asked, sweeping a hand over the remaining pads and sleeping bags on the tent's floor.

"Well, Allison's sleeping bag is too small, and we can't zip it to ours, so she gets to sleep in her own bag tonight. I guess we can put these three sleeping pads together and lay the sleeping bag on top."

One bag for three people? "But I don't need both sleeping bags," I started to protest. I wasn't comfortable with hogging two of their sleeping bags. Tim cut me off.

"Don't worry, Cheryl. I wasn't planning on sleeping, anyway. I'm going to stay up with you tonight." What he didn't say is, "So you don't lose consciousness." He was on the night watch. He would make sure I didn't go comatose or die on them.

I was both grateful and embarrassed to be the recipient of such thoughtful and generous support. I took out my contacts as they each put on more layers of clothing. Tim continued to chat me up. "My brother won't believe this when we see them back at the camper tomorrow." Donna nodded in agreement, with a mischievous grin. They were vacationing with his brother's family and had backpacked up here for a night of solitude in the wilderness.

"I guess I've ruined your quiet night in the woods."

"Oh, no problem," he smiled at me, "We're sure gonna have a great story to tell them!"

Before they settled in for the night, I had worked up the courage to ask something more of Anna. "I hate to tell you this," I said apologetically, "but all that hot water has hit bottom." Then I lowered my voice, "I need to go to the bathroom again." I so hated to make her do bedpan duty for me a second time, but she seemed unfazed and brought their cooking pot back in. There was no precautionary plastic bag this time. Was this a vote of confidence? I didn't think that such trust in my aim was warranted, so I was extra careful not to miss my mark. I hoped the rest of that water would just stay put. I didn't want to wake up the whole family just so I could go pee again in the middle of the night.

She covered me up afterwards, and it dawned on me that the reason I was still cold inside the sleeping bags was because I had nothing on below the waist except my socks and my right boot. I wasn't generating enough body heat to warm the bags, and with one bag on each leg, there were gaps between them where the cold night air regularly rushed in.

Once everyone was settled, they turned their flashlights off. Then Tim, Donna and Anna snuggled beneath their one sleeping bag. Tim and I continued to talk in the dark. I was interested to hear about life back in Michigan since I had grown up there. He asked about how I had come to live in California and what my life was like in Sonoma County.

It was wonderful to talk and think about anything else besides my injuries and fears. The Peters were so incredibly gracious, taking me into their tent and tending to all of my needs. Yes, I needed physical and logistical support for even the most basic activity. But their biggest gifts were how they made me feel comfortable and distracted me from my fearful ruminations about the future. Theirs was the truest gift of hospitality, to make this uninvited guest feel like one of the family.

But after a while, I didn't feel like I had enough energy to keep talking. "I'm really tired, Tim. Why don't you go to sleep?"

"Are you sure? I can stay up with you," he said.

"Don't worry about me. I'll be fine," I said, for my benefit as much as for his.

Now that there was no conversation to distract me, the silence made the darkness feel even more ominous. I was beyond exhausted and wanted to sleep. But once we stopped talking, my thoughts conspired with the pain to keep me awake. Both of my legs were cold, and my right foot and leg ached with a deep and constant pain. Left to my own thoughts in the dark, I was besieged by a flurry of feelings and images that swirled through my head. What was really going on in my foot? Was it broken, or just sprained? How fast can you develop gangrene? Could I lose my leg? How would I get help?

Then there were the recurring images of my slide down the glacier's ice sheet, my terror on the way down, then the impact with the rocks. Why didn't we go around? Why didn't he rope me up? My mind continued to wrestle with all those implications for my life. I didn't want to die of some weird infection out here in the wilderness. The onslaught of these fears would not let me relax, let alone sleep. Instead I returned to wondering if I would now die here instead of back with the rocks.

Rescue Rangers

HAVING FACED THE REAL THREAT of dying only hours earlier, it was curious to me that I was lacking any thoughts about wanting to die. What had once been a regular response to feeling overwhelmed, thoughts about suicide or somehow promoting my own death were gone. In their place, I felt the inexorable pull towards life, despite the crazy unknowns that continued to threaten my existence. It was as if the memory of those suicidal ideations and escape plans had totally been swept away. There was now something else exerting a firm grip on the whole of my being, that deep primal instinct that had welled up from within and gave me strength back up on the rocks. It felt as if it were still standing guard over my thoughts even as I lay there in the tent.

It didn't matter that my imagination was generating a constant visual montage of bleak outcomes for my future. The curious fact was that I was looking ahead at my life, not for a way out of it. This newly awakened part of my being was in it for the long haul and wanted me to stay in the game. I was cold, afraid and in pain, with no idea how I'd get down the mountain or receive medical attention. Yet there I was, wondering about how my future would unfold rather than my old pattern of planning different ways to escape it. I didn't understand how profound the shift would be at the time, but first on the rocks, and now in the tent, I was finally choosing life.

As I continued to lie there in the dark of the tent, listening, I heard nothing from the Peters family sleeping right next to me. At least I was hoping that they were asleep, not lying awake all night, like me.

I was stiff and my body ached all over, but I didn't dare move anything, because that only brought more pain and the extra bonus of cold air rushing into the sleeping bags. My right foot was cold enough to keep me on the edge of chilling. The two Motrins probably helped some, but I could not get comfortable enough to relax or sleep, no matter how exhausted I felt.

After several hours of this purgatory, I saw a movement out of the corner of my eye as small circles of light started to dance on the side of the tent. "Rangers!" a male voice shouted from a distance. I couldn't believe my ears. Help had finally arrived. "Rangers!" they shouted again as they got closer, but it felt more like the cavalry had arrived. All of my fearful "what ifs" collapsed to the ground and a gust of new possibilities started to swirl around me as I realized I probably wouldn't die after all. A wave of hope rushed in and filled my body as they approached. Silent tears of relief left cold traces down my face, and I was all the more grateful that no one could see that I was crying.

Donna sat up and turned her flashlight on. "It's 1:30," she announced groggily after checking her watch. "We've got company," she said, wriggling out from under the sleeping bag.

"I've got to put my contacts in. Where are my contacts?" Tim said.

"My nose is bleeding," Allison announced, on the verge of tears.

"Again?" Donna asked.

There were swishing noises as nylon bags were discarded, followed by a furious fumbling in the dark. By the time the ranger poked his head into the tent, the Peters had run a full-blown Chinese Fire Drill.

"Hi, rangers here. Is Cheryl in here?" one of them asked, poking his head into the tent.

"Is Doug okay?" I asked anxiously.

"Yeah, he's fine," the ranger said, "he told us where to find you."

"There's five of us in the tent," Tim advised.

"Could you please step out of the tent so we can evaluate her?" And with that simple request, the ranger politely evicted the Peters from their own tent.

My gratitude for their appearance became a fresh round of embarrassment, as my kind hosts were being kicked out in the middle of the night.

Two rangers entered the dark of the tent with a flashlight that cut a dusty beam through the air before it landed on me. I squinted at the sudden brightness.

One of them sat down next to me, holding some forms. He leaned over with his face close to mine. His head floating in the darkness was softly illuminated only by the reflection of light off the forms. "I'm Dave and this is Steve. We'd like to get a little information."

He started with the standard name and address. Their perfunctory inquiry made me feel like they were detectives filling out a police report and I was somehow a guilty suspect. "So where did this happen?"

"Andrews Glacier. I lost my footing, slid down and hit the rocks." My first attempt at defending myself for the shape I was in.

"You weren't roped up?"

"No," I answered softly. Suddenly I felt as if I was on trial. "My boyfriend said we should just walk down it."

They returned their focus to an assessment of my body. "Where does it hurt?"

At this point, I thought, *what **doesn't** hurt?* But I kept that comment to myself and replied, "My right foot and leg mostly."

Dave continued on checking my pulse, my pupils, and asked me to breathe deeply. He then checked my hips, and rolled me to my left side to feel my spine. I knew I wasn't paralyzed, but maybe he could tell something I couldn't. "Any tingling or paralysis?"

"No," I replied.

He jotted all these things down on his form while Steve brought in supplies.

"Okay, now let's see about that foot." He unlaced my boot and opened it up. My foot had swelled tremendously and filled the entire boot. Each little movement sent sharp, burning pains through my foot and leg, and I gritted my teeth as he removed my boot and layers of wool socks.

He looked at my foot closely while his partner held the flashlight.

"What do you think?" I asked. "Is it a sprain? How bad is it?" I asked, desperate to understand my fate.

"Well," he hedged, "it's hard to say."

"But, if you were a betting man," I pushed, "what kind of odds would you give me on my foot?"

He smiled and shook his head at my insistence. "I'd say a 51 percent chance that it's not broken." I felt a little better, but I could tell that he was just trying to ease my concern without raising my hopes too high.

"This is an inflatable splint to hold your foot steady," he said, unfolding something clear. "I'll put your sock back on so you don't stick to the plastic." He slipped it over my foot, then leaned over and blew the splint up like a balloon. Once my foot was floating inside it, they moved up my body.

"How does your leg feel?"

"My knee is aching a lot."

"It's swollen, but not too bad. Let's take a look at that thigh. Can you lie on your other side so we can see it better?"

I had been holding the sleeping bag over my midsection, since I was naked from the waist down. I figured they're going to get a full moon view. But I'd already been racking up the humiliation points. What was one more? They helped me turn onto my left side so they could access the camp towel covering the gash on my upper right thigh.

They peeled off the duct tape. Once again, an eerie silence filled the tent as they inspected the gruesome carnage inside my thigh.

One ranger put his hands around my thigh and squeezed to close the gash, but it kept popping open. "Let's try to hold it closed with a butterfly bandage."

They could hold the wound closed with their hands, but the cut was so deep that the tape just couldn't hold my flesh together. After several attempts, they taped it as best they could before covering it with a clean gauze pad. "Don't move your leg to-night," one of them advised in frustration. "That bandage isn't holding it together very well."

Then they rolled me gently onto my back again. We then discussed the problem of getting me down the mountain in the morning.

"Can you ride a horse?" Dave asked. I was confused by their question. What difference did it make if I could ride a horse or not?

"If you can't ride the horse, then we will have to carry you down on a gurney."

A gurney! Carried? Me? I flashed on a M*A*S*H-styled triage, with me on a piece of canvas stretched between two broom handles. I won't let them carry me down. No gurney for me, I decided. "I can ride the horse," I stated urgently, with perhaps a little too much confidence. Apparently I wasn't too convincing, from the look they gave each other.

"No, really. I can do it. I've been on a horse before."

"Okay, in the morning, we'll have a horse come up to carry you down." I felt certain that I could sit on top of a horse, even if they were skeptical.

"Well, that's all for now," Dave advised. Remember not to move your leg and try to get some sleep." They offered that as helpful advice, but still it felt like a cruel joke to me. They then went outside to explain the plan to Tim and Donna.

They had brought up a bivy tent for me, some kind of all-in-one tent and sleeping bag combination. Tim was intrigued, and I heard him offering to try out this new piece of equipment, so he slept outside of the family tent for the remainder of the night, leaving Donna and Anna to share the one remaining sleeping bag. Once everyone was settled again, I heard one of the rangers on his walkie-talkie, calling in the report at 3 a.m., with an update on my condition and confirming the horse for the morning.

Even after the rangers had patched me up and everyone had quieted down, I still couldn't sleep. My hips and lower back muscles ached from the impact with the rocks. I wanted to find a more comfortable position, but couldn't move my right leg without destroying their fragile tape job. The rangers were here and I'd been evaluated, but I was still concerned about my foot. What was really wrong with it? What would become of my thigh? Why did my knee hurt so much? I was more hopeful about my chances of survival, but I still had no idea what was wrong with me. For the next few hours, my thoughts floated and bounced randomly between these fearful musings as I tried to anticipate the future of my life and my leg.

***

I woke up groggy and somewhat surprised that I had actually dozed off for a little while. I heard someone say it was 8 a.m. as two more rangers arrived at camp. There was activity outside the tent, and I could only listen in as they introduced themselves, prepared food, answered questions and told their ranger stories to the Peters family.

Stranded inside, I heard everyone talking and laughing just a few feet away. I was upset at being left alone while I was feeling so scared and vulnerable. I was completely exhausted, in pain, yet felt strangely put out. The excruciating irony was that most of the people had come up because of me, yet I was all alone, stuck on the tent floor. My thoughts spun around even more as I considered all of them fussing over my injuries, adding fuel to my feelings of humiliation, but I didn't have the energy to understand or express why. Even through this altered state of mind, I was convinced that my life depended entirely on the willingness of these people to get me down the mountain. I overcame my relatively petty frustrations, and the "don't upset your caregivers" mantra took firm hold that morning and continued to shape my reality.

"How are we doing in here?" Ranger Steve said brightly, as he ducked into the tent. "Your splint deflated," he said with surprise, and bent over to blow it up again.

No wonder my foot hurt last night. It was just lying on the hard ground.

"It doesn't seem to hold any air. Hmmm. I'll get another splint for you. Here," he said, holding up some packets, "I've got some MREs. You know, 'meals ready to eat'?"

"What've you got?" I croaked, my first words of the day.

"Beef stroganoff, raspberry cobbler," he said reading off of the different foil packets.

"Beef stroganoff," I grimaced, "for breakfast?" I didn't want to appear ungrateful, but not even the raspberry cobbler sounded good if it came from a dehydrated pack. "I'll pass. My stomach isn't too keen on food."

"Well, how about a trail bar," he said, tossing half a dozen bars at me. "You should really try to eat something."

"I can't sit up," I protested weakly. I couldn't budge. My entire body felt like a solid lead weight.

"I'll be back with some water and give you a hand," he said, exiting the tent.

"Looks like you chose wisely," Steve said, coming back in. "That cobbler looked pretty messy if not downright inedible."

I smiled at his attempt to cheer me up.

"Let me put this splint on, then I'll help you sit up so you can drink some water."

I was so weak that Steve had to push on my back to help me sit up, then had to sit with his back against mine, to prop me up while I ate my trail bars and drank some water.

"So," I said, searching for some kind of normalcy in this strange little arrangement. "How long have you been a ranger?" I listened as he told me of his ranger experiences and his girlfriend in Texas.

"We only get one big accident each year," he said with a hint of pride, with the implication that I was somehow the highlight of this ranger's season.

Because of this, they had no trouble finding volunteers who wanted to come and help.

I was surprised at the effort it took to follow along in this simple conversation. My thinking was unclear at best, and I struggled to hold up my end. But this luxury of a regular conversation that did not involve my foot, the pain or my bladder was short-lived.

"If you're done eating, we need to get you ready for the trip down," Steve advised. That's when it hit me. Donna had taken my bloody clothing, and I had nothing to wear below the waist! I'd be a gimpy Lady Godiva!

"But my clothes...." I said, with a mixture of desperation and bewilderment.

"Let me go check on them for you," he said, leaving me in the tent to wonder how I could ride a horse with no pants on.

Donna came into the tent and started rooting through her pack.

"What size are you, Cheryl?" she asked. Donna was coming to my rescue once again. I marveled that she not only produced a spare pair of undies, but also an extra pair of hiking pants. My goodness! What did these people NOT have tucked away in their packs?

"But, Donna, really. I can't."

"These should fit you. The pants are too small for me," she said.

"Are you sure?" I felt terrible taking something else from them.

"I'm glad to let you have them," she said sincerely. "Put them on," she said, making little sweeping motions at me with her hands before she went back outside.

Except I couldn't even sit up to pull on my pants.

"How we doing?" Steve asked, coming back in.

I held up the pants and underwear. "I can't put them on, and I've gotta go pee," I said, exasperated at needing help to do every little thing.

"Okay, let me help you."

Great, now this guy is going to pull bedpan duty with me and then put on my underwear. I shook my head as yet another layer of normalcy was ripped away from me. I couldn't even bend to pull on my own underwear!

Steve and I managed to do the bedpan routine without a hitch, as the humiliation points just kept adding up. Steve then gingerly threaded my splinted foot first through the underwear, and then through the pant legs. He pulled them both up over the thick bandage, gently as if he were dressing a sleeping child. He was doing his best not to burst the butterfly bandages they had applied to keep my thigh from gaping open again. He saw how quickly I tired from these simple efforts. "Try and rest some more before we leave." Having been fed and dressed, I settled back down into the sleeping bag and closed my eyes.

"Bears!" someone shouted.

"A mother and two cubs," a male voice clarified. "But they're a good 100 feet from the campsite," another added dismissively, as if to calm everyone.

"You're going to leave us here with the bears?" Donna cried out. This was clearly the last straw for her. "Do something!" she entreated.

I heard someone on the radio reporting the bear sighting.

"Leave us your bear spray," Donna demanded of a ranger.

"What are the bears doing?" a deep voice crackled over the radio.

"Bear things," Dave replied, indicating that the bears were not looking to raid the campsite. "Digging for something inside a log."

"Please, leave me your bear spray!" Donna asked again.

"Then we won't have any," a ranger retorted.

"But what about us?" she asked desperately. "You can't leave us here with those bears so close!"

While they were outside worrying, I wanted to get out and see the bears! I was frustrated because I couldn't even get up to take a look. Can't pee, can't dress, can't look at the bears! ARGH! My body felt like it was held down by a lead weight, and I could not even will myself to sit up.

My emotional tirade was cut short by the rangers as they brought a big metal gurney into the tent. It wasn't flat, but came up around the sides, ostensibly to keep a body from rolling out.

It took all four of these young men to help lift me into it. Gee, Doug, did you realize that you were leaving me in the hands of a bunch of cute guys?

As I settled in, I thought, Great, I'm trying to get away from my fear of dying and now they've put me into this casket of a gurney! I didn't have much time to reflect on this eerie fact as they quickly carted me outside, stuffed padding underneath my leg and then Velcro-strapped me into my custom-fitted hearse.

Then it hit me, like a splash of cold water. There was no horse, and these four guys were going to carry me down! My head was slow to register this change that only added to my frustration. I did not ask for this! I was supposed to ride the horse! Where's the horse? I don't want people to carry me! As confusion raged inside of me, it was obvious that the rangers had come up with the full understanding that they were going to carry me.

These ever-changing circumstances overwhelmed me as I struggled to cope, and came as yet another stab to my pride and independence. What kind of person has the audacity to ask to be carried? Who would impose upon people she doesn't even know like some modern-day Cleopatra carried along by her men?

Yet the rangers were taking care of their final preparations to do that very thing. They seemed nonchalant about it, just tending to the business at hand, which happened to be all about me — my helpless state, my incapacitation, my need for their muscle to transport me to medical attention. It was a startlingly intimate agreement. These young men suddenly appearing with the unspoken understanding that they will be bearing my weight down the mountain. No opportunity for "Hello, I'm Cheryl. Would you please carry me down the mountain?" I've never seen a Dear Abby or Miss Manners column explaining how to best handle this delicate situation. I felt eternally indebted to the Peters for taking me in and keeping me alive through the night, and now I was mortified to have to accept this outrageous courtesy and allow these young men I didn't even know to carry me. What must they think of me? I felt that my status as a woman, competent hiker, capable human were all being called into question, and I desperately needed to validate my worth to them. If I could only muster the energy to explain myself to them. Wasn't I in the best shape of my life? Hadn't I just climbed Ptarmigan Glacier? Didn't they know that I was capable and strong enough to have crossed the tundra at 12,000 feet?

These thoughts and fears coursed through me as I lay there on the ground, feeling more helpless than ever, looking up at all of them while they walked around me and packed up their belongings.

"I chased the bears away, Mrs. Peters," Ranger Dave said, returning to the camp. "You won't have to worry about them after we're gone."

I looked over and saw the Peters family standing together watching the rangers pack me up.

"Let us know how this turns out," Donna said, coming over and giving me their address and phone number. She placed the small folded piece of paper in my hand, closed my fingers around it, and held my hand there briefly.

Even if I had had full presence of mind, I would never have been able to express my gratitude to them for having taken such good care of me. Did they understand what a profound gift they had given me? Did they realize that by treating me like family, they had eased my pain and suffering? Did they know they saved my life?

I looked into her eyes and placed my trembling hand over hers. "I will." Then I looked down and tried to search for the right words. "Thank you so much. I..."

"You're welcome, Cheryl." She cut me off and saved me the awkward embarrassment of fumbling for words that would have been woefully inadequate or all too cliché. "We were obviously guided to be here for you last night," Donna said quietly. "And we're so glad we could help." She released my hands and stepped back with her waiting family as the rangers moved in closer.

"Take good care," Tim waved as he put his arm around her waist.

"Say 'hi' to Doug for us," Anna chimed in.

Then the rangers were fussing over me again and I began to sense the depth of my exhaustion. Feeling totally powerless, I was deeply in need of their muscle power. They checked my straps and the cushioning on my leg to make sure I was comfortable. My mind struggled with all of the implications of my predicament and my impending status as cargo. Would they drop me? Could I trust them to get me to safety? It was probably just another day on the mountain for these rangers, but this unexpected adventure left me struggling for my sense of self-worth as a human being.

My mind veered off uncontrollably in yet another direction as I became aware of my disheveled appearance. How did I look? Would that affect how they treated me? It was a reflexive attempt to gauge how these young men were likely to deal with me. My life was quite literally in their hands and beyond being their cargo, I was a helpless female. It was a strange calculus, to be sure.

My vulnerability was painfully clear to me as I prepared to embark on the next stage of my journey in the hands of these strapping young men.

Starting Down

"ON FOUR," DAVE CALLED OUT to the other rangers holding on to the rims of my gurney. "One...two...three... UP!" I held onto the metal myself as I was tossed from side to side while the gurney leveled out. As they adjusted their respective grips, it felt rather like a Keystone Cops routine, with everyone jostling for a comfortable position. The four rangers synchronized their steps and settled into a comfortable rhythm as we proceeded down the path. I continued to hold onto the sides as I kept shifting back and forth inside all their Velcro straps and foam packing. The emotional toll of this enterprise was mounting; all I could feel in that moment was the crumpled remains of my pride. I guess any odd bits of pride were left back at the campsite, as each step they took carried me deeper into dependence and humiliation.

I was lying quietly in the gurney, looking straight up at the trees overhead, feeling very self-conscious and wishing I could disappear. It was as if they were balancing the bubble inside a carpenter's level. Dave managed the process from the back with a variety of verbal cues. "Right up," if my feet were starting to drop too low. At the call of "rock," they would halt to allow someone to negotiate around a boulder that was imposing itself into the narrow trail. We were such a cumbersome juggernaut! I thought, *Surely a horse could have picked its way through the trees more easily.*

I didn't have the strength to lift my head up to look around. Their arms and backpacks created a veritable wall around me, so I wouldn't have been able to observe anything on my right or left anyway. Resigned to my fate as cargo, I tried to distract myself by looking at the individual branches of the trees towering above. But the drama unfolding with each step kept me on edge. "Front down," someone called and my legs would be lowered. I braced myself, my hands tightly grasping the metal rim like a nervous passenger with a student driver. "Left up," and I was slightly shifted to the right, "back down," and my head would dip.

"You doing okay there, Cheryl?" Steve asked, checking in.

"Well," I shrugged, reflecting on my powerlessness, "under the circumstances..."

If I had turned my head to the side, I would have bumped my nose into someone's forearm; they were that close to me. The men traded verbal barbs between their calls of "rock" and "tree" and "down." Finally I started to loosen up and joined in on their banter.

"You know," I added, "this isn't exactly the way I expected to be coming down the mountain. Don't get me wrong, I *do* appreciate the service," I added dramatically. "So nice of you boys to make a house call!"

"No problem, ma'am," someone drawled, adding, "Happy to be of service." We all laughed. These bits of humor helped, but were not enough to eliminate the strain I felt. I knew that if there was one slip or if one of them lost his grip, I'd go down.

Doug had already dropped me unexpectedly on that snow bridge, and I was registering every movement inside my leg like a pain-induced seismograph. Even though I was strapped into the gurney, I had to brace my arms and legs against the inevitable dips and jolts. I was somewhat mollified knowing that the rangers were only carrying me a short distance to the horse.

All the water that I had been forced to drink before we had left had been shaken down, and I had the distinct and uncomfortable realization that I needed to go to the bathroom again. The last thing I wanted to do was to tell these young men that I had to pee. However, I couldn't slink away and go discreetly behind a tree. I would have to ask for their help, and I had no idea how we would manage that, with my leg out of commission.

When we arrived at the meeting place, they set me down in the small clearing and introduced me to Ranger Paula and her horse, Chief. I finally said, "I, uh, hate to tell you guys this, but, um, I have to, well..." closing my eyes against their reaction "...go to the bathroom," I mumbled into my chest.

Paula sensed my distress and took charge. "Help her out of the gurney and place her over there," she said pointing to the edge of the small clearing. Four sets of strong arms lifted me up, working carefully to avoid my bandaged thigh and the splint on my foot.

Next they carried me a few yards over, where they set me up to stand on my left leg. I became a complex puzzle as they carefully positioned themselves around me to support me without touching parts that were too painful or too private. Three rangers held up my torso, one under each arm and another supporting my lower back. The fourth reached in gingerly to stabilize me from tilting sideways as they balanced me upright on my left leg. Once they were in place, Paula did the honors and moved in to carefully unzip my pants. "I'm going to ease them down your legs," she said, lowering first my pants, then my underwear, carefully stretching them over the thick gauze bandage. "Let me know if I hurt you," she added. I didn't know which was worse, the pain of moving my leg, or the overwhelming embarrassment of having to pee in the middle of this crowd of men. Not even when I was two years old did I have so many people attending to my toilet habits. *I can't believe I'm doing this!* I told myself silently.

"Ease her back," Paula instructed, as the four men moved in unison to slowly tilt me and my naked butt backwards.

Sure, so now I'm just supposed to relax and pee. I kept thinking, Am I going to pee on this guy's foot? How can I do this with them watching me? This is somebody else's bad movie! Then with a deep breath, Oh, please, bladder, I said to myself closing my eyes, don't think of these people. Feel how much you need to go. Just...relax.... I heard my pee splashing on the ground for what seemed like an eternity, flashed on the absurdity of this little scene and thought, Never in a million years... I was so grateful not to have a shy bladder, especially in front of such a large and attentive audience.

When I was done, I had a reflexive desire for some toilet paper, but let that go quickly and went with a "Let's just get the pants up without anyone getting hurt" approach.

Paula eased my pants back on and I avoided looking at the guys because of the awkward "after they've seen you pee" moment. Luckily, they were all distracted by figuring out how to get me up and onto the horse. Once again, my brain was a little slow and the *concept* of getting on a horse did not catch up with the *reality* of getting onto a horse. How would I get up there? My leg won't bend!

Everyone seemed to talk at once, offering different opinions on how to leverage me into the saddle. "What if we lift her up from the side..." or, "Wouldn't it be better if she went..." or, "How about if we try..."

They finally settled on two guys lifting me up and holding my body straight. Someone directed my left foot into the stirrup, and another ranger guided my right leg gently over the top of the saddle. I know he was trying to be gentle, but I gritted my teeth against the pain that shot through my foot. I held my breath and hoped they wouldn't drop me as they lifted me high over their heads and slid me over the saddle, aiming me like a surfboard onto a car roof. My thigh burned like I had been stabbed with a searing hot poker as they positioned me to straddle the horse. Even so, these pains were easier to bear than the endless jostling and angst of the men carrying me in that damned gurney.

Paula checked my position in the saddle, making sure my left foot was in the stirrup and both my hands were on the pommel. My right leg stuck out to the side in the splint, which set my torso off at an odd angle, veering left. "Hold on to the pommel here and keep the reins up," she instructed. It was hard to hold the reins and the pommel and not fall over sideways, with only one foot in a stirrup.

The rangers dismantled the gurney and loaded the two halves back into their packs before they fell in line behind Chief. With Paula and Dave leading me on the horse, we continued down the mountain with our little caravan.

Staying upright took a tremendous amount of abdominal strength and concentration as I swayed back and forth in the saddle. I was balanced very tenuously on the horse and listed heavily to the left, with my right leg sticking out. Chief's gait shook my entire body up and down with each step, but I was glad to be upright and on the horse's back instead of lying flat on that gurney. We were still in the thick of the forest, where boulders and trees crowded the edge of the narrow trail. So I was not only trying to maintain a balance with only one foot in the stirrup, but I had to constantly shift my body to prevent my right foot from banging into the trees. I could feel a deep burning pain, as my thigh was slowly torn open further by the horse's speed. When I had a chance to look down, I saw that the bandage on my thigh was already bright red and soaked through. "I'm sorry he's acting up like this," Paula said, pulling at Chief's halter in an effort to slow his pace. "He's anxious to get back to the stable now that we're headed down."

It may seem like a simple act, but just being able to sit up again made me feel more in control of my situation. Looking ahead and down the trail, instead of up through the trees, prompted me to think of where I was going and my future. This was a radical shift in my thinking, since my every thought since the crash had been focused on survival and on protecting my leg.

My brain was now slowly piecing together the implications of my injury for the rest of my week. It felt like quite a revelation when I realized that I wouldn't be able to hike anymore. I started to think about what else I could do. I continued bouncing up and down on the saddle while I envisioned Doug pushing my wheelchair into a restaurant in Estes Park. That simple vision of my future was surprisingly satisfying, and was probably the most pleasant thought I'd had since yesterday. *At least I could enjoy some good food*, I happily mused. It sounded like a reasonable enough plan for my week and was enough to tame my fretful and curious mind. This was important because it left me the precious mental focus to continue ducking branches and keeping the trees from playing a painful game of tag with my protruding right foot.

As our caravan continued on, I was relaxing more and more, away from the intensity of survival mode. I began to feel more of my body's exhaustion. In pain and in danger of breaking into tears, I felt ready to collapse in a heap at the side of the trail. I didn't even have the bandwidth or mental energy to consider where Doug was or how he was doing, beyond that earlier thought of us at the restaurant. It was all I could do to concentrate on protecting my body through the various obstacles as the horse plodded his way down the mountain.

I could hear the relaxed and friendly banter between Paula and Dave up ahead as they led the horse down the trail. I was glad they were enjoying themselves and not fussing over me. I basked in this one tiny slice of normalcy, clinging to the idea that everything would be fine. I yearned for a time when I wouldn't be such a burden to everyone.

Our procession plodded on down the trail when suddenly the trees gave way to a breathtaking view and led us into an open meadow. The morning mist was rising from a lake and the entire scene was illuminated by the morning sun, which was still low in the sky. Its first rays slowly crept over the eastern ridge. Everyone quickly got warmer, now that we were out of the trees' shade and entering the bright sunlight. The caravan stopped so everyone could take off a layer or two of fleece.

Maybe it was the heat. Maybe it was the exhaustion. Maybe it was because I had lost more blood. "I'm feeling light-headed," I told Paula, as my stomach was doing flip-flops. She frowned as she looked up at me, "Are you sure you won't throw up?"

"No," I countered weakly. My voice trailed off as I said, "I need to get down." Then, as if the strings that were holding me up had just been cut, my shoulders dropped and my upper body slumped forward. I started to slide off the left side of the horse. The last thing I remember was the rangers rushing forward to catch me before my eyes rolled back and everything turned white.

Slightly confused, I blinked a few times and found myself now lying on the ground at the side of the trail.

***

"How did you get there?" Krista demanded. "What happened after you fell off the horse?"

"I don't really know," I replied. "The rangers must have caught me and carried me over to the edge of the meadow. There was a bit of shade, so I guess they found a bush nearby so they could keep me out of the hot sun until I revived."

***

Steve was in my face, rattling off questions, a worried look in his eyes.

"What's your name? Do you know what day it is? Do you know where you are?"

My head was clearing as I heard his questions, and I felt irritated that he felt he had to ask. "Yes, yes, I'm Cheryl. We're in Colorado. I'm fine," I said, still coming to terms with my new location. I didn't have a strong sense of where my body parts were, or understand that I owed my seated and upright position to Dave, who was sitting behind me to prop me up.

Steve plucked at the skin on the back of my hand, "She's tenting a bit," he said watching my skin stay peaked instead of springing back down. "Make sure she drinks more water," he said as he wrote down more of my vital signs on the accident report. "Can you eat some of this trail bar?" he asked, unwrapping it for me. I made a face and turned my head away, the smell alone turned my stomach.

Other hikers stopped by to take a look, curious about the trailside attraction. A man crouched down right next to Steve, insinuating himself into our tight little trio. "I'm a doctor," he announced authoritatively. "What's wrong?"

A doctor! Could he tell me if my ankle was broken? I had a million other unanswered questions that had accumulated from last night—and I wanted some answers. But I hated the fuss they were making and the concern I saw in their eyes. Questions and thoughts swirled in my head, but the words got stuck

166

somewhere between my ears and I couldn't bring them out of my lips.

I was pleased to finally have access to a doctor, but my two rangers were less thrilled. Steve was intently focused on my vital signs, and though the doctor was well-intentioned, Steve moved in closer to me.

"Have people go around us," Steve shouted, craning his neck around so the other rangers could hear. "Thanks," he said dismissively to the doctor, "but we've got it handled here." After the doctor and the others had been cleared out, Steve and Dave gave each other a knowing look. "We can't put her back on the horse," Dave said gravely.

My vision was starting to clear, and I didn't like what I saw. The swirl of activity all around me was disturbing. It was about me, I knew that, but the whole scene seemed to be unfolding in someone else's life. I should have been very concerned at my predicament, especially after losing consciousness and falling off the horse. But all I could muster were a few scattered questions. *What will they do with me now? Would I die here instead of at the glacier? What if they can't move me from here?* Agonizing thoughts floated through my brain before quickly drifting away, leaving me in an altered stupor, unable to make sense of the situation.

When I couldn't even follow the rangers' conversations, I retreated back inside of myself. I closed my eyes and took refuge in the safety of Dave's arms. This was the only bodily comfort I had received since Anna held me during my leg inspection the night before. I felt how warm his arms were as they wrapped around me. I felt the tension of his ranger-like hold on me, but I was raw with need. I hoped he didn't mind that I was seeking the sweet comfort of this intimate connection. I was afraid that he would feel me reaching behind the professional hold of his ranger's façade. I was thirsty for something more personal from him. I basked in the comfort and protection of his embrace, tentative as it was, as if I could somehow drink in his energy and strength. After a few minutes of feeling the shelter of his arms, I started to relax.

Away from the worried faces and fretful conversations, I finally surrendered. A torrent of tears filled my eyes and rolled down my cheeks. I turned my face into Dave's shoulder to hide them. My tears seemed so extravagant and out of place — a waste of energy or at least a waste of my precious bodily fluids. I felt that they were too "girly," and signaled a weakness I didn't think I could indulge. I didn't want them to think that I wasn't strong enough to continue on. I feared that they might decide to leave me if I became too much trouble. After all, I'd already complicated things by passing out and falling off the horse.

When I finally dared open my eyes again, I saw that Tim, Donna, Anna and Allison had caught up to us and were checking out the commotion from the far side of the meadow. I wanted to wave a greeting and offer them a big smile as if to say, "Yes, it's me again. I'm really okay," despite this train wreck of a scene. But my body would not respond. I could only raise my hand slightly to acknowledge them before they moved out of sight.

Although they had only continued down the trail behind some trees, it seemed as though they had dropped off the earth. A sharp twist of grief squeezed at my heart, thinking they were now lost to me forever.

Back on the Gurney

I WAS STILL LYING in Dave's arms at the side of the trail when I heard Steve calling down to the rangers' station. He was sitting close by, but his voice seemed far away. He asked them to bring up the wheel.

"A wheel?" I asked groggily, my voice struggling to pierce through the fog.

"We put it under the gurney to hold the weight," he said, "It'll be easier to carry you the rest of the way down."

I should have been mortified at the thought of going back in the gurney, but I didn't have any energy left for that. The gauzy veil through which I experienced the world freed me from any worry about my situation; time and space no longer had relevance. The rangers scurried to reassemble the gurney and strap me back in, and we continued down the trail. The sun was now high overhead and its heat was bearing down. Steve covered my face with his ranger's hat, to protect me from the sun.

"You're awfully quiet," Steve commented after a short while. "You okay under there?"

When I could only muster a grunt in reply, he called for the caravan to stop. "Let me take your blood pressure again," he said. I couldn't focus or care about what they were doing with me anymore, as he held my wrist and plucked at my hand.

Steve must have been worried. "We're going to have to stop every fifteen minutes so I can check her pulse."

***

Krista was looking at me with a surprised look of disdain. "Gee, Cheryl, you never mentioned how bad things got on the trip down. "

"It's hard to explain. I was so spacy and out of pain," I commented.

"That's called losing consciousness! I mean, you had already passed out once! You were practically comatose!"

I shrugged my shoulders at her alarm. "To me, it just seemed like a silly game, stopping every 15 minutes to check on me," I said derisively.

"A 'game'? Cheryl, that's not a game. You had lost a lot of blood and you had passed out. They had to make sure they weren't going to lose you."

I didn't say this to Krista, but I was so weak and disaffected at that point, I wouldn't have cared.

***

The caravan of five rangers, the horse and what was left of me continued on like this for an hour or two before we connected up with the two rangers who had hiked up the mountain with the wheel. Somewhere along the way I came to understand that Doug would be coming up with them.

"Let's put her in the shade," Steve called, as they set me down gently beside some trees.

Dave helped me sit up again to drink more water.

That's when I saw Doug, crouched down on the other side of the trail. He was looking at me with the hollow, frightened eyes of a wounded animal. He was only a few feet away, yet I felt a great chasm stretching between us.

I wanted to put on a smile for him, a reassurance that things weren't so bad. Or at least give him some sign that I was doing okay. But I couldn't. As for Doug, he remained on the other side of the trail, said nothing to me and just continued to stare.

My first impulse was to take care of him, but I was floating in my own carefree world, and didn't have the ability to reach out to him. I longed to have him hold me, to offer me some words of comfort and make this absurdity of a nightmare go away. But he just sat there crouched on the side of the trail for what felt like an eternity, hugging his knees and staring.

***

But Krista would have none of this. "He didn't even come over to say something?"

"No." I replied, "he didn't."

"I know you've told me how socially awkward Doug can be, but, *come on*, Cheryl. He didn't even say, 'Hi, glad to see you'?"

It pained me to remember how much more devastatingly isolated I felt when he just sat there and stared at me. All I could do was shake my head "no" to her pointed inquiry.

"I can't believe he didn't have the decency to even come over and hold your hand!"

It may have been a weak defense, but I said, "Maybe he was cowed by all the rangers standing around."

"That shouldn't keep him from showing some basic human kindness, Cheryl."

***

I was actually grievously disappointed that Doug failed to offer me even a word of comfort. *Didn't he have anything to say to me? Did I look that bad? Was he wracked with guilt? Paralyzed with fear?* Beyond those fleeting thoughts, I had no follow-up emotional energy to consider his curious lack of response. And with no expression on his face, he gave no sign of his thoughts. Then, before he could change his mind and offer me some consolation, the rangers were coming over to place the oxygen tank beside me and put a plastic tube up my nose.

There were now six rangers, who proudly positioned themselves around the gurney and lifted it and me up to attach the wheel underneath. I heard Doug ask if he could help carry me, but six people was enough. So Doug was directed to take up a position out in front of our caravan to ask people to step aside. This was starting to have all the morbid elements of a classic Monty Python scene, where Doug should be calling, "Bring out your dead!"

Once we were back on the trail with me in the wheeled gurney, Dave got out his radio and called down for an ambulance. I was disturbed by all the fuss he was making. Altered as I was, floating in my own distorted reality, I was feeling fine. I didn't feel that I was in need of an ambulance just for a ride to the hospital, and proceeded to tell him so.

"But you should have one," he insisted.

"No, I don't think so," I groaned. I figured that Doug was perfectly capable of driving me there in the car. *Those ambulances are expensive*, I thought, *especially for such a short trip.*

Dave tried reasoning with me, but I would have none of it.

"Take the ambulance," he implored.

I didn't have any more energy to argue with him, and let my refusal stand.

Finally, accepting defeat, he called back. "Cancel the ambulance. Patient is going AMDPOV," he said, exasperated, "I repeat, AMDPOV."

"What is AMDPOV?" I asked.

"Against Medical Directive," he spat out, shaking his head in disgust, "Personally Owned Vehicle."

After pushing water on me every fifteen minutes each time he checked my pulse, my full bladder demanded that I ask Dave to stop so I could take yet another pee break. My original four rangers knew the drill, and had more confidence and speed with where they placed their hands to support me. This time, they didn't need to carry me anywhere, just tilt the gurney down and slide me off, like a cookie from a baking sheet. The four were all in position to help me balance on my left leg. This part of the trail was in a slight gully, where the mountain rose up on either side. There was no bush to take me behind, so the two extra rangers were sent to block traffic a safe distance away to allow some degree of privacy. My rangers once again leaned me back to let me relieve myself, this time right on the trail where I was standing.

At this point I could muster no energy for the luxury of embarrassment. Paula guided the operations and I no longer cared that there were so many people watching me relieve myself on the trail. All I felt was an odd discomfort in not being able to at least go behind a bush or a tree. Although my brain function still had warped perceptions, I did register that somehow it was discourteous for me to be peeing right in the middle of the trail.

Earlier in the day, I was aware of the conversation between the rangers and even had the energy and presence of mind to joke a bit. But it was now after 3 p.m. and we had been travelling on foot for over seven hours. At this point in our descent, I heard the comments from the rangers only as strangely distant background noise.

There were starting to be signs, though, that we were getting closer to civilization. This area was more crowded, and I glimpsed folks who were older, heavier and wearing street clothes. "This is Alberta Falls," Steve announced with the brightness of a newly minted tour guide. He was probably doing it for my benefit, to lift my spirits and keep me connected to the outside world. I felt that I was about to miss something important, so I had to reach deep inside for the strength and will even to turn my head and open my eyes. I briefly saw the falls, as well as many people with inquisitive looks. I shut my eyes to block out their curious stares.

Doug had been sent ahead to get the car. When we reached the agreed-upon bend in the road, the rangers lifted my gurney over the split rail fence and set me on the ground next to the rental car.

The rangers busied themselves with unstrapping me from the gurney. I was sorting through six pairs of legs trying to get Steve and Dave's attention. I desperately wanted to thank them for taking such good care of me last night and on our trip down the mountain.

But I struggled with even constructing a coherent phrase, let alone producing the words to tell them how much their late-night appearance and care had meant to me.

"We brought you down the mountain," Steve said with resignation. This is as far we can go," he added, motioning with his hand toward the end of the trail. "But we can't help you heal," he said, shrugging his shoulders. "You've got to do that on your own."

Had I known all that lay ahead of me, I'm sure I would have begged the rangers to take me back up the mountain, lay me out on the rocks and leave me there to die.

An Awkward Drive

THE RANGERS' LAST TASK was to lift me out of the gurney and into our rental car. Doug was parked on the left side of the road next to the trail. From the driver's side, the rangers loaded me into the backseat, which allowed me to keep my legs straight in front of me and lean back against the door.

Doug got in and we started off to the hospital. Soon he was going very fast as we careened down the winding mountain road. Unfortunately, by loading me in from the driver's side, my wounded right leg was placed next to the seat cushion. I expended precious energy jamming my elbows between the seats to brace myself from being tossed back and forth and to keep my bandaged thigh from rubbing against the seat cushion.

At that moment, I understood why that ambulance might have been a better idea. I tried to free up a hand to get into my toiletry bag and root out my tube of homeopathic Arnica for the pain. But with my elbows pressed outwards into the back of Doug's seat and the back of my seat, my hands were a fixed distance apart. It took tremendous focus on my part to get my hands together so I could unscrew the tiny tube, all the while bracing my body not to roll off the seat as he tore around the curves.

This was our first time alone since he had left me alone in the wilderness. Doug started to explain what he had been doing since I had last seen him at the Peters' campsite.

"I got down to the first ranger station and no one was there," he said, full of desperation, "so I had to go to another station before I could talk to someone. I told them what had happened and they asked if you were still bleeding. I told them that had stopped; that's why they didn't send a helicopter.

"The rangers were packed up and ready with their plan in just 30 minutes. They told me that I should go to my tent and someone would come by once they had an update on your status."

Although I was sitting right behind Doug in the back seat of the car, I felt as though I was receiving his words via a grainy transmission from some distant planet, somewhere deep in space.

"My knees were killing me," he continued. "They were as big as grapefruits. I took some Advil, but I still couldn't sleep. A ranger came to the tent late in the night, after they had seen you, and told me you were okay. I wanted to go up with them in the morning, but they wouldn't let me join them. Said I'd be in the way," he added disgustedly. "I had to wait in the parking lot for them to bring you down. God, that was hard. There was nothing I could do to help you."

I was getting a little nervous about how much faster he was taking these hairpin turns, and had to brace myself even harder from rolling off the back seat.

"When they called down for the wheel, they said I could go up with them." "I wanted to do something, anything," he emphasized with emotion, "to be of some help. And then I saw you," he said weakly, his voice trailing off. After a moment's pause, he added with more conviction, "The hospital isn't that far. I'll have you there soon."

The fullness of his story rattled around inside my brain: his concern, his wait, the not knowing. I was confused. I was grateful for his help, but after my night in the tent, passing out and being carried down, I was also feeling a profound sense of disconnect—from him and his experience. He hadn't even spoken to me on the trail and was only speaking *at* me now. Meanwhile, I had a growing fear for my safety as I was tossed around in the backseat. After he stopped talking, I could hear the wheels protesting loudly as he sped around the sharp turns.

In that moment, I didn't know how I felt about Doug. My relationship with the Peters and my "Rescue Rangers" had been pretty straightforward. They were all good people who had showed up to help me out of a bad situation. My relationship with Doug, however, was more complicated. I had watched his roles change radically in the last 24 hours. When he and Tim had come back for me, Doug became the hero, the one who carried me down on his back. Before that, he was the one who had sold me on the idea that I could climb and then descend that glacier. He was "safety man," with all of his "I'll keep you safe on the mountain" speeches. After I fell, he was "not much help man," bewildered and not able to formulate a plan or make a decision. I had hoped that this trip would draw the two of us closer, but so far the opposite was happening.

Since I had seen him last night, we had gone through so much and been so close, but now I felt very removed from him. I tried to reach for a point of common understanding between our two disparate experiences. "The Peters were really good to me," I croaked weakly, "but I really felt that things would be all right when the rangers arrived."

Doug continued, "I heard the radio calls with their updates while you were coming down the mountain," he added, shaking his head. "It was terrible."

At the time I couldn't fully appreciate what he might have heard — that I had passed out, fallen off the horse or that they needed to bring up oxygen for me. Doug was not big on showing emotion, but he was clearly distraught after worrying about me for so long. Now he was channeling that emotion into driving me to the hospital as fast as he could.

My accident and rescue had launched our relationship into an entirely new dynamic, and the transition felt clunky at best. How was I supposed to feel? Should I be grateful that he had carried me as far as he had or angry that he didn't protect me better?

Whatever my feelings were, I would have to tuck them away for now. I didn't have the clarity of thought or power of choice to accept or reject him at this point. He was all I had. But things were about to get worse.

At the Hospital

"WHY DIDN'T YOU come by ambulance?" the nurse scolded as they gently lifted me out of the car. I couldn't formulate a response fast enough, so I let Doug take the flak for my decision to arrive by car.

As I passed through the doors of the hospital, I entered a world that seemed very foreign to me. Gone were the natural shapes of the green and brown mountain. Everything here was all white and steel with straight lines and sharp angles. Wearing my dusty boots and blood-caked thigh, I felt like I was seeking to gain illicit passage into this sterile universe. My passport? A current health insurance card.

I was wheeled into an exam room, where a nurse gently peeled open the bandage on my thigh. She recoiled and made a face when she first saw my gaping wound, then hesitated a moment before bending in closer. I felt a bit like a traveling freak show as she beckoned to another nurse to come and take a look.

"When did this happen?" she asked.

"Last night," I mumbled.

"Why didn't you come in sooner?!" she reprimanded.

"We were on the mountain," Doug interceded. He was standing several feet away, on the other side of the exam table from the nurses. "It took us that long just to carry her down."

The nurse frowned and shook her head, clearly upset that my wounds had gone so long without being cleaned or closed up. "Let me see if they're ready for you in x-ray," she said and left the exam room.

Doug did his best to keep me in good spirits while we waited. "You know, Cheryl," he started, "I've been thinking. You got to camp out on the mountain without a permit, then you got a free horse ride," counting out each benefit on his fingers, "and you didn't even have to walk the last part of the trail." His voice was bordering on cheerful. "You got a pretty good deal, if you ask me." I guess from where he sat, he could make it sound like a pretty nice vacation package. I cracked a weak smile of appreciation of his attempt at humor. Doug might be a brilliant engineer, but he couldn't make this "new" math add up for me.

Returning with my x-rays in her hand, the nurse said flatly, "Your heel is shattered."

Her statement came as a shock. Not sprained. Not broken. Shattered. I struggled to grasp this strange new idea. It was a jarring development after having waited so long for a verdict. I envisioned many little pieces of bone, dissolving like sugar in a glass of iced tea. It created the impression that these bones were just melting away. Try as I might, I just could not wrap my head around this idea of "shattered" as a reality inside my foot.

"I'm not sure about the leg here," she continued, holding up another x-ray, this one of my knee joint. She sighed. "We can't deal with this here, anyway. We're going to have to send you down to the hospital in Longmont; they'll be able to tell whether it's broken or not." She seemed rather pleased to be able to pass my problem leg along to the next hospital.

As they prepared me to leave, Doug approached. "They won't let me ride in the ambulance," he said, "so I'll follow you down. See you there."

The gurney's wheels folded up as they slid me into the back of the ambulance, and then I was covered with a thin blanket. A man accompanied me, but I couldn't even muster the energy to smile at this unknown guardian. That disturbed me, that I didn't even have the strength to acknowledge his presence. I was hooked up on a monitor and he was watching closely as the red digits flickered up and down. To me they were lights flashing danger signs, indicating my fearful and tenuous hold on life.

If some part of my brain registered the seriousness of my situation, it only showed up as a clammy sensation, filling my body with dread. I could cry, but felt uncomfortable doing so in front of this stranger. I tried to stop the tears, but a few still leaked out. As they rolled back into my ears, I did my best to hide them. There was some abstruse fear that he would judge me as a weak or silly person if he saw tears. The ambulance ride was a 30-minute stalemate of fear, chills and emotional constipation as I awaited the final verdict on my life at the hospital in Longmont.

Upon my arrival, there was a flurry of activity. They whisked me into pre-op and a flock of nurses and administrators gathered around me. They asked me a myriad of questions, took my jewelry and had me sign a gazillion forms in preparation for surgery.

The nurse undressing me was trying to get around my thickly bandaged thigh and splint. "It would be easier if we could cut off your underwear." It was strange how this was quickly becoming a regular occurrence for me.

"Go ahead," I said flatly, "they're not mine." Her eyes shot up in disbelief, then narrowed slightly, puzzled. I confess that I enjoyed her shock at my provocative response. It was a small flicker of pleasure for me, though it was quickly drenched by the rising tide of fear about my impending surgery.

A nurse informed me that Doug was in the lobby. "He's quite insistent upon seeing you," she said. "I'm sorry, but due to HIPAA regulations, he cannot come into pre-op. It's a matter of privacy for the other patients," she explained, nodding her head around the room where other patients were probably resting behind each of the many curtains.

I really wanted to see him, hold his hand, look into his eyes and offer him some measure of reassurance that I would be okay. We both felt alone through this—he in the lobby and me surrounded by the hospital staff. The nurse saw my worry and offered me the use of her cell phone. I dialed his number, but struggled for what I would say: "I'm doing well"? "Things are great!"? "Wish you were here"? Ours was a stilted conversation, given the circumstances. "I'll be okay," I said softly, trying to be upbeat for his sake. "I'll be here for you," he offered back.

Dr. Monroe, the orthopedic surgeon, appeared by my side in cheery purple scrubs strewn with moons and stars. A bemused grin crossed his face as he perused my splint and gaping thigh and asked, "How did you do *this*?" he asked, pointing to my wounds.

"Uh, well, see, there was this glacier..."

His upbeat sense of humor put me at ease. He held up the x-ray of my leg, "Yep, it's broken, all right." He then explained both the benefits and risks of putting some screws into the top of my tibia, right under my kneecap. "Weight-bearing part of bone," he advised, "tough place to heal." He was looking for my decision on the screws very matter-of-factly, as if I were standing at the supermarket checkout counter, choosing between paper and plastic. It seemed like a big decision about whether to put metal in my body. But did I really have a choice?

He moved up to look more closely at my thigh, then pulled my thigh apart to open the wound wider. "Hmmm," he reflected, "clean and deep." He turned his head at an angle and looked closer. I felt like an expensive cut of meat he was considering buying at the market. "I'll have to make two more cuts to open it up some more to clean it out. Make like a 'Z.'" He drew in the air with his finger.

I brightened. "A Zorro scar? I'll be getting a Zorro scar!" It was the best news I'd heard all day.

After I wrote out a fresh round of signatures in preparation for surgery, he said, "You ready? Let's rock 'n' roll!"

Post-op would have been an unremarkable fog, except for one thing. Just as I was coming out of the anesthetic, a nurse leaned in to adjust something above me, which then fell and hit me on top of my head.

"Oh! I'm so sorry," she exclaimed as she lifted the heavy black box from where it came to rest on my shoulder. My leg throbbed, but now at least I was more balanced since I also had a pain in my head. Silly me, here I thought being in a hospital would be safer than being on the mountain!

I woke up the next morning after surgery, spaced out, stiff and in pain. It took me a while to remember where I was and why. My whole body ached, but my right leg's pain was through the roof. A nurse appeared after I had awakened and handed me a cord. She pointed to the little black button, and up to a bag suspended bedside.

"Morphine," she explained.

My new best friend. I would regularly pound that little sucker with gusto. I didn't care that it could only kick out more happy juice once every eight minutes. It made me feel better thinking that at least one of those clicks was going to give me some kind of relief. Anything to ease the intense burning in my sewn-up thigh, the ache in my newly bolted knee or the throbbing in my still-shattered foot.

My right leg was elevated and my foot poked out from under the sheet. I could see that they had placed a new and sturdier splint on my leg, one that came up over my knee. All I could see were my toes. However, they did not look like MY toes. Situated at the end of my leg, those foreign entities were purple and swollen, like Vienna sausages crowded into a jar. As I considered them, I wondered if I could move them. I gasped as that slight movement shot a bolt of pain through my entire foot. I decided that I wouldn't be trying that again. It turned out that it hurt for me to move any part of my body. I looked around the room for something that could distract me from my pain.

"Could you bring those notebooks over here?" I asked the nurse. Puzzled, she found my spiral notebook and my new Rockies wildflower book and handed them to me. I held them reverently. They felt like magical keys to a world I once knew. A world filled with beautiful mountains, majestic trees, and my wildflower friends. A wondrous world where I could walk. A world with no pain. I so wanted to dive into that reality and remember the joy of striding along the mountain paths, the beauty of the flowers and the trees. But as I opened the book and tried to compare the shapes and colors of the flowers with my notes, my mind could not focus, and I couldn't distinguish the various details required to identify them. What previously had been a joy for me had become a frustrating exercise in futility. After struggling with trying to read for a few minutes, I came to realize that an incredible mental fog had taken over my brain. Ah! This must be the morphine. It has finally kicked in.

Doug arrived later that first morning to check up on me. I know I didn't look good, because when he finally saw me, it increased the worry that was written all over his face. "Let me do something for you," he pleaded. I didn't have any specific requests, so he set about assessing my needs, taking an inventory of the various tubes flowing in and out of my body. He seemed happy to be tasked with chasing down the nurses for me when I needed something that he could not handle himself.

My next visitor of the day was the surgeon, Dr. Monroe, who gave me an update on last night's surgery. "It went well. I put two screws in your leg," he said, glancing down at the notes in his hand. "And I was able to put my hand inside of your thigh without making any further incisions," he happily demonstrated his technique by waving his hand back and forth, like a windshield wiper. The movement seemed bizarre to me.

Then it hit me. "What? I didn't get a Zorro scar?" But he had promised! The one bright spot of this whole experience was gone with the wave of his hand.

"There was some degloving of the tissue," he said, moving his hands apart to show me that the tissues had separated, "and we did have to flush it out for a long time, but I think we got all of the necrotic tissue out."

I bristled at the thought of these creepy things going on in inside of *my* body.

"That gash was three centimeters deep and eight centimeters long," he reported with a smile. He was clearly impressed, as if he had won some surgeon's contest for the biggest incision of the week. "You lost about two units of blood before we got you."

I looked at him wide-eyed in the face of all of these revelations. It was a lot of information to receive through a mental cloud of general anesthetic and morphine.

"I'll check in on you again tomorrow," he said, closing the chart, "Just try to get some rest."

Thoughts of his hand deep inside my thigh were mind-boggling. I struggled with the physical impossibility of it. I mean, is my thigh big enough for his hand? How far up and down my thigh did he have to go? His reference of necrotic tissue made me feel like a prop from some creepy B-grade horror flick. But all his fancy terms couldn't hide the fact that my thigh had been chewed up pretty badly. And I had lost a lot of blood.

Doug heard the report and offered his opinion on what had sliced me open. "It was the rocks that cut you," he offered quite confidently.

***

Now wait a minute, Cheryl," Krista interjected. "Were those rocks sharp enough to cut you like that?"

"I didn't think so, but I didn't have the energy or mental capacity to either doubt him or argue with him."

"I've seen your scar. It goes across your thigh, not along the length of it."

"I know. If the rocks had done it—a: the scar would run along this way," I motioned up and down along the line between my knee and hip, "and b: those rocks weren't sharp enough to give such a clean slice. I know it was the ice axe that cut into me."

"Well, that makes sense. Did you ever share that with Doug?"

"Oh, yes, but he couldn't bring himself to believe it. He would say, 'I saw you sliding, Cheryl,'" I said, imitating his deep voice, "and the ice axe was pointed away from your body.' You could say it was a bit of a sore point with him, so I didn't bring it up again."

***

A few hours after the doctor left, the walker lady came by. She unfolded the walker proudly and patted the top of it as if I should easily jump up and start wheeling it around the ward. Every move I made caused my body to ache, and now, after struggling to swing my legs over the side of the bed, I had to hold all of my weight on my hands and my left leg. Unsteady in my hold, keeping myself vertical inside of the walker, I also had to bend my right leg to hold it up and keep my foot from touching the ground.

Just like crawling down the mountain, I was having to coordinate my movements to avoid hurting my foot. It was slow progress using the walker as I rebuilt my strength and endurance. Doug was there to encourage me, and helped me practice balancing on my left leg, using the walker to go a tiny bit farther each day. First I made it only a few feet, over to the chair by the bed. Next, I went all the way to the bathroom — a stunning ten-foot distance. On the third day I could go a full thirty feet, to the end of the hall.

Doug shuffled alongside me, rolling the IV bag, since my hands were busy on the walker. There were chairs by the window at the end of the hall, so we sat there while I rested from my efforts.

"You know, it takes a lot more energy to use a walker than to just walk," I explained. "I have to lift up all of my weight onto my hands with each step forward." I looked at my palms. "I think I'll be getting blisters soon."

"Just think of the upper body strength you'll have," he said enviously.

"Yeah, that's some consolation."

"Well," Doug countered, "just think about what a great movie this will make," smiling as he pitched it to me. "Great scenery, lots of adventure." That got a smile out of me.

"Yeah, well, who's gonna play me?" I shot back.

"Hmmm. She'd have to be beautiful," he said looking at me. "Tall and beautiful. Kate Winslett or Uma Thurman."

I was touched. I felt like a total mess, yet he still thinks of me as beautiful!

These happy thoughts were interrupted by a nurse who came speeding out of a doorway near our seats. As she rushed past, she inadvertently kicked my splinted foot. I bent over reflexively, but too late to protect my foot from intense and throbbing pain.

First, I was hit over the head in post-op, then my catheter was botched up (yes, I spared you those details), and now a nurse kicked my tender foot.

"We've got to get you away from here before something else happens to you!" Doug said, as he helped me up to head back to the relative safety of my room.

Dr. Monroe appeared again later that afternoon and discussed the future prospects of my right foot. "You're going to need a really good surgeon to fix that heel," he said gravely. "I see you're from California. Are you near Stanford?"

"How about UC Davis?" Both my dad and sister lived in Davis.

"They should have someone good. You'll need to give this to your employer," he said filling out a form. "It explains that you'll be out of work for at least a month."

His statement caught me off-guard. "But I have to work," I asserted.

"Not with that foot, you won't," he said, continuing to fill out the form.

Then it hit me. With my right foot in a cast, I couldn't even drive to work. Oh, how small my world had become. Why hadn't I thought of this before? I couldn't even *get* to work.

"Your foot surgeon might revise this, but for now, you'll be off for at least a month." He signed and gave me the disability form before he left.

In his wake, the realities of the outside world came crashing in on me. The life I once knew had been stripped away. I had been coping fairly well with all the support from the Peters, the rangers and the nurses. But the doctor's pronouncement on my work life forced me to look beyond the limited confines of my hospital bed.

I have to work, I thought, *and who's going to take care of me?* There were too many details for me to consider, and I could only see one issue at a time. I could barely get around on a walker, let alone navigate the stairs in my home. I couldn't drive. I couldn't do anything myself. I couldn't go home; there would be no one there to take care of me and I could not even get to my bedroom upstairs. After all, I was still struggling just to get to the bathroom.

I couldn't even conceive of how to take care of my life outside of the hospital. I shook my head, still unable to sort it all out. My brain was so clouded, first getting sloshed inside my skull after hitting the rocks, and now by all the drugs. As hard as I tried, I could no longer hold multiple thoughts or options inside of my head.

Doug could see my distress and helped me think it through.

"Both your house and mine have stairs," he said, dismissing those two options. "Do you think you could stay with your family?"

Oh, God, I would have to stay with someone else. That reality hit me hard.

Doug continued, "He said that UC Davis should have good surgeons to fix your foot."

Although I could only start to glimpse the painful implications, my needs pointed to a frightening state of total dependence.

"Dad has a guest room," I said, absentmindedly. I stayed there on weekend visits and the holidays. The morphine still clouded my thinking, but one thing was clear. Once I left the hospital, I would have to rely entirely on other people and would need someone else to care for me while I recovered.

Once we had settled on Davis as my best option, I needed to make the call. However, I discovered that the *idea* of staying with my family and the *reality* of asking them for help were two separate matters. I was loath to tell my family about the accident, let alone ask for their help. I had told them over and over that Doug knew what he was doing and not to be concerned about our climbing adventures. My body after the crash was clear evidence that they had been right, and now I was going to have to eat a big dose of humble pie and ask for their help.

Doug spent the third and last night on a cot next to my hospital bed and helped me get packed up Friday morning. "You need to call them," he said, handing me his cell phone. I had been in the hospital four days and I was now dressed and ready to leave. We were on track to make the return flight on Saturday, in accordance with our original vacation plans.

I sighed, took the phone, then collapsed back into the chair. I was already exhausted just from getting dressed.

"I *so* don't want to do this," I said, punching in my sister's phone number.

My sister answered. "Mar? It's Cher."

"Hey, great to hear from you. How's your trip?"

"Uh, well, that's why I'm calling," I looked up at Doug for moral support. He nodded me on.

"See, I had an accident," then added quickly, "but I'm okay."

"What happened?"

"I lost my footing and fell down a glacier. I broke my leg and shattered my heel," I got it out as matter-of-factly as I could.

"A glacier? Shattered? What were you…where were… I mean where was Doug?" She demanded, her voice slowly rising. Then in a more demanding tone, "What was Doug doing?"

"Doug carried me off the mountain," I said brightly, in contrast to the heavy implications of her question. I looked up and smiled weakly at Doug. "He's been really great." Then I looked back down at the floor and tried to regain my focus. "Listen, the reason I'm calling is that I'm getting out of the hospital today," I continued on, trying to sound upbeat as I laid out all the facts. "They patched up my thigh, but I still have to deal with my foot once the swelling goes down. The doctor says I should have a really good surgeon to work on my foot. He said UC Davis should have someone good." I paused slightly before continuing, "and since you guys are in Davis," I proceeded carefully, "I thought maybe you could see if I can stay at Dad's place."

I held my breath and waited.

"Oh my gosh, Cher." She paused a moment to take in this shocking news. "Are you sure you're all right?"

"Well," I said. *Not really*, I thought, but plowed on. "I've still got to get on the plane tomorrow," my voice starting to crack with emotion, "and I'm still not great with the walker and..."

"Okay, okay, Cher. Listen, I'll talk to Dad and we'll work it out here." I heard Marcia's take-charge voice, and it was very reassuring.

"Thanks for talking to Dad for me," I said, feeling my shoulders relax. I wiped at the tears welling up in my eyes. "I didn't want to be the first one to tell him."

"You just get home safely, and call and let us know when we can expect you. Okay?" I guess when you're a mom who has raised four kids, you're good at responding to these sorts of emergencies.

"Thanks, Mar," I said. "Really." I was still uncomfortable with having to ask her for this kind of help.

"Just call me if anything changes. Okay?"

"I will. I love you," I said weakly.

"I love you, too, Cher." Then she emphasized, "Just get home safe."

I hung up, relieved to have finally delivered the bad news, then closed my eyes and sank back into the chair, counting my blessings. Marcia would talk to Dad and rally the troops.

Thank God for family.

Heading Home

MY FIRST NIGHT OUT of the hospital we spent at a Red Roof Inn close to the Denver airport. Doug asked for a room closest to the entrance so I wouldn't have so far to go with my walker. I psyched myself up for a record-setting distance: from the car to the room, drawing questioning stares from the staff as I slowly clunked my way by the front desk.

Before it got too late, I called my office and let them know what happened and that I wouldn't be in on Monday.

Stopping the hospital's drugs must have uncorked my kidneys, because I was up four times to go pee. Doug insisted on getting up to help me each time. I tried to be quiet with the walker, but the metal clanging around the bathroom was a dead giveaway. Consequently, neither of us got much sleep that night.

We flew out of Denver and deplaned at Oakland airport, which was much busier. Doug pushed my wheelchair through the crowds, but my leg felt terribly exposed, sticking straight out into the sea of bustling people. After retrieving our bags, Doug had to leave to go get his truck. He placed my wheelchair in front of our luggage and handed me my walker, which was folded up. I held it in front of me, pointing its aluminum tubing forward.

Left to my own devices in the middle of Baggage Claim, I was wary of the crowds, vulnerable to anyone who might try to wheel me away or walk off with our bags. So I hunched over the walker, scanning the crowd of travelers with a fierce scowl. I held my walker menacingly, as if it was a machine gun, warding off everyone. Looking around me, I channeled my best Clint Eastwood sneer as if to say, "Don't you DARE even THINK about coming CLOSE to me or my leg."

The sidewalk leading up to my father's house in Davis had never seemed so long. Dad and my step-mom, Judi, were standing on the porch looking at me with the expressions of parents who were waiting for their wayward daughter after curfew. I approached them slowly with my walker, weighed down by apprehension as much as by exhaustion. I already knew Marcia had spoken to them, but I had no idea how the conversation had gone. Doug helped me and the walker negotiate the final two steps up to the porch.

Once inside their home, I fell onto the sofa next to Doug. Judi sat in her rocker, and Dad was in his recliner, his hands knit over his stomach as if he were ready to lay down the law. His expression said, "This is my daughter. What have you done to her?"

I felt very much like a teenager who had not only broken curfew, but totaled the car, gotten pregnant and had been arrested. And here I sat, asking my Dad to help me clean up this awful mess.

Dad seemed like he was looking for a darned good explanation for the state his daughter was in. He addressed Doug sternly, like a judge before a recalcitrant criminal. "So how did this happen? Marcia didn't give us much in the way of details."

I leaned a bit closer to Doug, in a conscious move to try and protect him from my father's wrath, and jumped in to tell the story. It was the first time I had recounted the whole tale and I struggled to remember the details that would be important to my family. "Doug carried me on his back and then continued down the mountain to go get help." My father didn't seem to be moved by my recitation of Doug's heroics, and turned his attention to the matter at hand. "What do we do about your heel?" he asked.

"Now I look for a good foot surgeon. Hopefully, someone associated with the med school here." The implications of that surgery, and a long recovery, hung in the air.

"Well, you must be exhausted," Judi interjected quickly. "I've already cleared out the guest room for you. Would you like to lie down?"

My mouth said, "Yes," but my eyes said, "Thank you for saving me," as she got up and helped me clunk my way down the hall towards the guest room.

I could only imagine what kind of conversation my dad was now having with Doug. You see, through my adolescent years, my dad had made it known that he was a National Champion fencer, and he leveraged that with my suitors, implying that they had better treat me and my sister very well, or they would suffer the consequences. The thick steel blades of naval boarding cutlasses hanging on the wall of the family room easily backed up that impression. So now Doug was alone with my father. Doug had clearly failed in taking care of me. What would my dad do now? He was always fixing swords for tournaments, so there were probably some weapons near the living room. Would he literally rattle his sabers at Doug?

I was arranging pillows and settling in on the bed when Doug peeked his head around the corner. "Need any help?"

My eyes shot wide open with curiosity, and I motioned him into the room.

"What did my dad say?" I asked in a nervous and hushed tone.

"Oh, he's just worried about you. I told him more about what the doctor in Colorado had said. He thanked me for bringing you here."

Good, I thought to myself. I was afraid Dad would really give it to Doug once I had left the room.

I just felt a sort of numb exhaustion as Doug lay down beside me. I sank into the warmth of his body and relished the simple comfort of his presence amidst the newest challenge of facing my family.

"I've got to be getting back home," he said after only a few minutes. "I still have to prepare for that conference call on the Harvard contract tomorrow, but call me tonight and tell me how you're doing, okay?"

Doug had become my protector and caretaker, shepherding me through the hospital, the airports and now delivering me into my family's care. I wanted to acknowledge and thank him for helping me through everything. We had been through so much together, but all I could do was issue a weary, "Thank you."

I laid back and tried to grapple with what it would be like for me to spend my days recovering at my dad's house. How would you feel if you had to move back in with your parents at 43? Never mind that you're helpless and needy, all because you trusted and followed your boyfriend!

I didn't get to muse long before Judi appeared and started arranging things around the room for me.

"I rented a wheelchair for you, and I'll pick it up tomorrow. I also went to Long's and got you a raised toilet seat," she said unwrapping what looked like a big plastic doughnut, "and I'm putting these little tables next to the bed so you can put your things on them." After she had unfolded the tables, she held up some little plastic baskets. "You can put your smaller things in these to keep them from rolling off the table." I was amazed at how Judi seemed to anticipate my needs.

"Judi, this is so great. But how did you…?"

"My mom fell and broke her hip last year," she said with a big sigh. "That's how I know what you'll need. Now, here's some extra water and some tissues. Need anything else?" she asked with her hands on her hips, surveying her marvelous additions to the room.

Judi had jumped in and taken command. Everything was within reach from the bed. I couldn't seem to think a clear thought, and she went ahead and pulled all of this together for me without my even having to ask. I was overwhelmed. "Judi," I fumbled for words looking around at this miracle of industry and foresight. "I don't know what to say. This is so amazing. You're amazing. Thank you."

She looked down, a shy smile on her face, and waved me off. "Just holler if you need anything. For now, you just try and get some rest before dinner."

What a gift! Just when I was feeling so vulnerable and uncertain about my future, Judi came to my rescue. Dad had brought her into our lives after he had moved out from Michigan to be closer to the grandkids in California. He married Judi several years after Mom had died, and they had been married for 12 years by the time I arrived on their doorstep that day. "I'm your wicked stepmother," she would say with a delighted grin. At a time when I really did need a mother, with life crashing down on me, Judi was totally there for me—full of strength, grace and love.

The next morning, Dad was gone for the day and Judi went to work, so I found that the simple day-to-day logistics of life on my own had become tremendous hurdles. I slept a lot and tried not to drink too much. It was my attempt to avoid any unnecessary trips to the bathroom, which was only ten feet from the foot of the bed. But the simple act of standing up caused the blood to rush into my foot, making it feel like it was being crushed in a vise. And bending my hip to sit on the toilet pulled at the incision in my thigh. Normally, I drink a lot of water to help my body function better, but now I was happy to be dehydrated if it meant I didn't have to make those painful trips to the bathroom.

Judi surprised me that first day when she came home at lunch to check on me. She brought hummus, pretzels and fruit right to me as I lay there on the bed.

"You really don't need to do this, Judi."

"Oh, it's no bother. I don't work too far from here. I like to get out of the office on my lunch break, and I didn't want you to get lonely." She was a good mother hen, coming by to make sure I would eat something. Even though my dad was retired, he was gone all day. During the summer, he volunteered to teach fencing all day to disadvantaged kids as part of the National Youth Sports Program.

"Is there anything else you need before I leave?" she asked.

I had been thinking of something, but I was embarrassed to impose upon her for yet another favor. "Do you think you could help me wash my hair?" It was hard to not be able to take care of even this basic task by myself.

"Sure," she said. "I'm sure that will make you feel much better. We can do that tonight," she added brightly before going back to work. I had no idea how we would do it, but I thought, *if there's anybody in the world who would know how, it would be Judi.*

Sure enough, later that night she laid out a bunch of towels on the floor alongside a plastic tub of warm water.

"What are you girls up to?" Dad asked, surveying the setup in their bathroom.

"I'm going to wash Cheryl's hair," Judi replied matter-of-factly. "If you could just help her get down here on the floor, then you can leave us alone." My dad cradled me in his arms as he lowered my body down to the floor, while I focused on keeping my right leg out of the way.

"Thank you, dear," she said. "Now you can leave us alone," she added, dismissing him easily. He shuffled away, muttering, "I just do what I'm told," and closed the door behind him.

Judi and I chuckled at his classic curmudgeonly behavior.

"I just love that man," she said, grinning, as she dipped my head back into the basin.

The paneling in the guest room is dark, which makes for a good sleeping environment. However, being stranded on the bed day after interminable day, it seemed to encourage the shadows that had started to eclipse my soul. It hurt to move, I was exhausted all the time and food held no appeal. There was nothing I could do. A simple walk to the kitchen was out of the question. Go watch a movie in the living room? I didn't have the energy to pay attention for a full two hours. Read? I couldn't focus long enough to read anything. My life had devolved into one long, boring, painful blur.

I rested a lot those first weeks, but sleep was a harder prize to claim. There came a time each day, usually at night, when the memories of the accident would play over and over in my mind. I would see myself standing at the top of the glacier and try to figure out what I could have done differently. *If only I hadn't turned my foot.... How could I have used the ice axe better...? What else was I supposed to do?* I would argue back and forth with myself — *but that was a solid sheet of ice! You did everything Doug taught you. You were going too fast for the axe to work!* So it continued, night after night, as I would replay the whole thing, still trying to get it right.

I started a journal soon after arriving at my dad's, and wrote down what I could remember. It had a surprisingly calming effect on me and gave me some feeling of control over the memories when they came flooding back at night. It was a definite improvement over lying in the dark and contemplating my uncertain future after the rest of the world had gone to sleep. The fear of not being able to walk, let alone ever dance again, could have easily overwhelmed me. Those fears were so much bigger when they haunted me in the hours of darkness. So, each night, I'd get a page or two written. It may not have seemed like anything big, but looking clearly at the whole crash and descent actually gave me comfort. I was not going to let the fears and visions stalk me at night. Each evening there was a standoff, and as I continued writing, I developed the confidence to look the fears squarely in the face.

I found a surgeon associated with the UC Medical School in Davis, wanting to schedule the surgery soon after the three-week waiting period, as suggested by my Colorado surgeon.

Dr. Loomis examined the reports from the surgeon in Colorado, looked at the x-rays and explained the options for my heel. "We could just let the bone heal without any surgery, but your foot would spread," he motioned with his hands outward. "The whole idea of reconstructive surgery is to give the heel a good shape. Is that what you'd like?"

"Yes. I like the idea of being able to fit into a pair of shoes again."

"How long before she can walk?" my sister asked.

"You won't be able to put any weight on the foot until six to eight weeks after surgery. Then we can look at a walking cast."

Two more months! It felt like a prison sentence. The last ten days had been difficult, and I was desperate to find some kind of end to my painful incapacitation. I looked at his wall calendar and counted...August, September... Maybe I could still dance at the Fall Fling on November 3. I had heard my dance friends speak highly of this dance because it would be on a sprung floor and I wanted to experience that for myself. I continued to muse about being able to go to that dance while Dr. Loomis took the stitches out of my thigh and knee, scheduling my surgery for the following Tuesday.

Waiting another week for the surgery was almost as painful as the foot itself. From the moment I decided that I was willing to fight for my life, I had been moving ahead with progress, doing whatever it took to get my life back. But lying around day after day, stranded on the bed, was taking its toll. There wasn't much I could do, so when Doug suggested that I come to his house for a visit, I jumped at the chance.

Our First Conversation

DOUG CAME TO DAVIS to gather me, my walker and the wheel-chair for our weekend together at his place. His house is built into a hillside, so there were two sets of stairs for me to scoot up backwards. I was exhausted after the long drive and the stairs, so I headed straight for his futon, where I collapsed. Doug came over to lie down, snuggling up close to hold me. It had been three long weeks since the accident and this was the first time we had been able to enjoy any quiet time together to connect.

After resting together for a while, Doug started to speak. "I lost my footing when I made a grab for you," he said. "I had to use my ice axe to stop myself from sliding down the slope."

This was a surprise. Doug had never mentioned any of this in the hospital, on the plane or in our conversations on the phone. It seemed strange that I was only learning about his experience on the glacier so many weeks later.

"I couldn't stop myself," he continued, "so I had to turn my body over on top of my axe to stick the head into the snow." I recalled that this was the advanced self-arrest technique that he had described to me back in Desolation Wilderness, prior to our fateful climb.

"But," he continued, "instead of how it normally jerks you back up when the ice axe grabs," he motioned with a quick movement, "the ice was a solid sheet, so I continued to slide for another 10 or 15 feet before I was finally able to force it into the ice and stop myself."

His confession was a revelation. I had been beating myself up for not being able to stop myself on the ice, and now I learned that Doug also had had a hard time stopping, even considering his size, strength and experience. Applying the advanced technique, he had continued sliding down on his belly before finally stopping. Only then did I realize that I couldn't have done any better for myself. I was surprised to realize, in fact, that my inexperience had probably saved me from more serious damage. If I had been trained and used that self-arrest technique, the rocks would have really ripped me up. I wouldn't have been able to stop myself that way either, and I shuddered when I thought about what I would look like after slamming into those boulders on my belly.

But Doug wasn't through. "When I saw you just lying there," he continued, "I felt like my world was falling apart. After I reached you, I still thought you might die. I was scared that any decision I made could kill you!"

My first impulse was to comfort him, so I buried my head in his shoulder and pulled him close. But as I lay there holding him, I was trying to sort through all of this new information he was giving me.

I had been all alone with the memories and beating myself up for not doing the right thing on the ice sheet. Hearing Doug's struggle created a whole new dimension for me to consider. These memories represented a slow festering wound for both of us. It felt good to be able to hear him talk about it, but I wasn't ready to share my own feelings since I was still trying to figure out how I truly felt.

I raised my head and looked him in the eyes. "I'm glad you're able to talk to me about this."

Yes, it was comforting to be able to share about the accident, but the dynamics of our relationship were about to take a dramatic turn.

"I feel responsible, Cheryl," he said with a sigh.

And there it was, the elephant in the room. I had been dreading this moment. I was afraid that his guilt would create a chasm of separation and tear us apart. I could see the anguish behind his eyes and had mixed emotions myself, but I couldn't face the thought of losing him over this, not now. I felt too vulnerable to lose him now. So I took a deep breath and waded in. "But it's not your fault, Doug. I'm the one who slipped. I know that you tried to stop me. I know how steep and icy it was." Then I added more emphatically, "You're not to blame."

"That's what my friends say too," he said, gently shaking his head. "But I still feel responsible. I was the lead climber."

That was an important consideration, but I took no account of it at the time. My limited brain function, in fact, hadn't even considered it. I was consumed by the scene that had played in my own head at least a thousand times—I knew that I had slipped and fallen and I knew that if he took the blame for that, our relationship would crumble under its weight. I had to help him through this, so I tried a different approach.

"If you're going to feel responsible, then wear that mantle lightly. Please, Doug, don't let it eat you up."

I could see that he was still struggling with the concept. I somehow believed that if he heard *me* say that he wasn't responsible, it could make a difference.

***

Krista couldn't believe what she was hearing. "How could you let him off the hook when he told you he felt he was responsible?"

"What could I really do? Of course I wanted to explore those ideas more deeply, but in the moment, it was all too confusing." I explained. "I was feeling so vulnerable and didn't dare rock the boat or upset him at this point. I didn't feel like I had a choice. I would have to accept whatever he told me and let it be okay." My frustration came pouring out as I talked faster and louder.

"I felt like my life was crumbling around me; I couldn't lose Doug over this! He was my only connection to what had happened on the mountain. We were both there on the glacier, but our individual experiences were vastly different. At least he had witnessed how awful it was. It was hard for me to explain this whole experience to people who are accustomed to the comfort and ease of a suburban landscape when this took place on a terrain that most people couldn't even imagine. And I needed that understanding and appreciation almost as much as I needed help with food and getting around. Doug and I opened the door with this conversation, but I was not prepared to walk through it. Those were some really big issues, but at the moment, there were too many unknowns in my life. I was too vulnerable, too exhausted and too fogged for that."

"So what did you do?" she asked more cautiously after my tirade.

"I just tucked those thoughts away until I was stronger. I didn't know how long or when the right time would be, but I'd have to wait. I mean, given those circumstances, what would you do?"

***

As we lay there, I held Doug closer and stroked the worry lines across his forehead.

"We've both been through a lot," I said softly. "We've got to be gentle with ourselves around this."

He wrapped his arms around me and said, "It feels so good to have you back and to hold you," giving me a squeeze. "I've missed you so much."

All of my confusion melted away as I basked in how good it felt to be held and wanted. It had been three long weeks of feeling like I was a piece of meat on the hospital assembly line. The way he looked at me and kissed me made me feel like a desirable woman again, even if I did have long, angry scars and a lumbering splint on my leg. Most of the time I felt like I wanted to crawl out of my skin to avoid the pain. But as he held and kissed me, I dared to relax and let it feel good to be inside of my body again.

I was surprised when Doug started to caress me a little more intimately. With his hand underneath my shirt, I started to feel my tension slip away. I relaxed, laid back and welcomed his touch more openly. As his kisses became more passionate, I started to tingle in response.

I shifted my weight slightly and winced as my body reminded me of my limitations. Doug stopped when he felt me tighten up. He retracted his hand quickly and looked at me as if he had broken something in a boutique and was trying not to look like the guilty party.

I shook off his fear and relaxed back into a more comfortable position that would give him easier access to the parts of me that didn't hurt.

"Can I touch you like this?" he asked, reaching his arm around my hip.

I nodded my assent as we shared more verbal and non-verbal clues about what kind of positions my body would tolerate

He was very tender and worked to find a way to get closer that wouldn't hurt me. It was as if he had been asked to make love to a porcupine.

I emitted low "mmmmms" to reassure him that I wanted him to continue his cautious exploration.

"Does that hurt?" he asked, as he pressed against my hips. He was working hard to avoid rolling me onto my ravaged thigh or creating any motion down my splinted leg.

I was finally able to forget my leg and fully receive him. My body surrendered in the pleasure of our union and I reveled in the sweet ecstasy of release. If an orgasm is good for generating endorphins, then a flood of them went coursing in repeating waves all throughout my body. I drank deeply of this sweetness and savored the way it had effectively erased the memory of my weeks of pain.

As I lay there in his arms afterwards, basking in our achievement, a small smile crept across my face. I wonder what my surgeon would think of our little encounter? I took a deep breath, the likes of which I hadn't enjoyed for weeks. I felt as if my soul had just been welcomed home as I reminded my body that it was a good place to be. Lying there in his arms, I started to feel like a person again, which was a welcome contrast to the persistent feeling that I was just 120 pounds of somebody's problem to fix.

I Want to Walk Again

AFTER LIVING ON MY OWN for so many years, it was very hard for me to accept the radical shift I had to make from being free to do whatever I wish, to complete dependence.

I could not wash my own hair, take a shower, prepare my own food or drive a car without someone else having to help me — or do it for me.

From the moment I hit the rocks at the bottom of the glacier, I had been ported, carried and accommodated. I still felt like a cumbersome and fragile piece of cargo in cold storage. Still waiting for the swelling to go down before having the surgery to reconstruct my heel bone, I felt as if I was living in purgatory, a tormented soul, waiting to hear a verdict on my life.

I was grateful for the support, but I resented my need for it. My former life was gone and my future was uncertain — at best. When will I walk again? Will the pain ever go away? When will I be able to drive? Will I ever be able to hike or dance again? Whenever these thoughts began to fill my head, I'd blurt out, "I want my life back" in frustration. Over the next several months, I said these words repeatedly as a combined prayer, complaint and mantra.

I did my best to graciously accept the support that was offered from Doug and my family, but each kindness offered felt like a small blow to my soul. Unexpectedly going from being independent to utterly dependent was devastating. My sense of self became smaller as I was forced to give up control of even the simplest of tasks. It was necessary, given my condition, but it was slowly chipping away at my self-image. I could only hope that things would someday be better.

My hopes hung on the successful outcome of the surgery to reconstruct my heel. After three long weeks, I was finally going to the hospital. By the time the anesthesiologist came by to introduce himself, I had almost forgotten my plan. I rooted around in the blankets, found my notes, and said, "I know that I will hear whatever you and the other doctors say when I'm out. So please be positive." I looked at him to gauge his reaction to my request. He didn't balk, so I continued on. "Would you be willing to say these things to me while I'm under?" and I handed him my list with phrases such as, "You will recover quickly", and "Your foot will heal and you will dance again."

He took my list and nodded with a wry smile on his face.

"I'm a dancer and a hiker," I explained, trying to be more than just another body to him. "I want to walk again," I said emphatically, looking him in the eyes to make sure he took me seriously, and affirmed, "I want my life back."

And now a word from my sister:

Cheryl can't tell you about this because she is in surgery right now. So, I'll tell you what it was like for those of us who were languishing in the waiting room.

As Dad, Judi and I sat and waited for the surgeon, we agreed it was a miracle that Cheryl only suffered damage to her right foot and leg. We had all run the images of her falling down that glacier through our minds.

"She could have broken her hip, or had more internal and head injuries," Judi reminded us as we waited. "She could have been paralyzed when she hit those rocks." We all agreed that it was surprising that she had come back to us doing so well.

I looked at my watch and knew it couldn't be good that the surgery was taking hours longer than expected. Dr. Loomis finally came out of the operating room some time after nine o'clock. He looked so weary, like a man who had just suffered through a long ordeal. He looked at us with disappointment in his eyes. "I did the best I could," he said, shrugging his shoulders. "The x-rays didn't prepare me for how bad it was," he sighed, looking down and running his hands through his hair. "There were so many pieces," he continued on, shaking his head in disbelief. "I put in screws when I could find a piece of bone big enough to handle them. I tried to put all the pieces back in, but there were just so many." He paused, reflecting on his futile efforts. "I'm sorry," he said, dropping his head in defeat. "I just couldn't fit all the little pieces back in."

My heart dropped at his words. Poor Cheryl, I thought. Judi and I had been comparing notes on our Google searches on "shattered calcaneus." The prognosis for broken heel bones didn't look good. Many people have to undergo multiple surgeries and still can't walk properly after that. Cheryl loves to hike and dance so much. What will this mean for her life?

We followed her gurney when they rolled it to her hospital room, and I noticed that they had left her chart on the bedside table. There was an x-ray sticking out from the papers, so I opened the folder and glanced at the image.

Oh, wow.

I closed the folder quickly and looked over my shoulder again to make sure I hadn't been seen. Opening it slowly again, I saw a triangular plate with holes and a matrix of screws. It looked like that game where you stick all the needles through the tube. It was scary to see how much space there still was between the tiny pieces of bone. They seemed to be floating around inside of her foot, but not touching each other.

That's some piece of work in your foot, Cher, I thought. It's going to be a long haul for you. I looked at her lying there and thought I might cry. If the bones aren't even touching, it's going to take a long time for them to fuse back together. There was too much space! How could he leave pieces out? We're going to have to figure out how to keep her spirits up if she can't walk or needs to use a cane for the rest of her life.

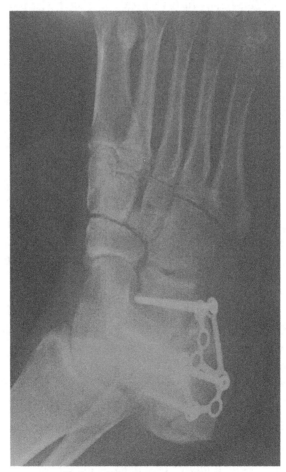

Plate and six screws in my foot

And who will be able to take care of her until she can function on her own?

The next morning, Dr. Loomis came to my room to give me an update on the surgery. "The x-rays didn't prepare me for how bad it was when I opened you up," he said with a sigh, shaking his head. "The calcaneus was in over a dozen pieces." He looked up from his paperwork. "I put in a plate and six screws to hold it together," with satisfaction before continuing. "I think I made it into a good shape." That was the whole goal of this surgery, so that seemed like good news. Maybe I could wear a matching pair of shoes again someday.

"Put no weight on it, keep it elevated and come back in a week," he said, "and I'll take off the cast."

I went back to my dad's house to recuperate from the surgery. I was in an even bigger fog after a second round of general anesthetic and taking a fresh round of pain pills. Doug wanted to keep in touch and asked me to call each day, but there wasn't much to share. My daily reports ended up sounding the same: "I'm tired, my leg aches and I'm bored."

My sister was the hero of the week when she picked me up to spend the afternoon at her house. It was great for the change of scenery and to have a little more company during the day. My sister's sofa became the most wonderful place in the world for me. There were big, soft pillows that I arranged around myself and placed under my leg to prop up my foot. I had both the TV and her kids for entertainment. And since it was summer, there was always someone around who was willing to get me water or bring over something to eat.

The kids were all curious to hear about my surgery and hardware, and to check out my new cast. "We could put racing stripes on your walker!" Luke enthused. "How about we let the dogs pull you around in your wheelchair?" At six years old, he was intrigued by anything with wheels, and wanted to maximize its performance options.

As I considered my new plaster cast and the swollen purple toes sticking out the end, I realized that I needed to get over the resentments that were building up whenever I looked at my foot. I knew that a negative attitude would impede my body's ability to heal, and I wanted to shift my focus to considering how this foot had saved me from further bodily damage. But it was a real stretch for me to generate any feelings of gratitude and thank it for saving me. Going from pain, humiliation and dependency to gratitude felt like an uphill battle. But all of the kids' creativity had given me an idea. Catherine, my eleven-year-old niece, had been admiring my plaster cast and the colorful bruising on my thigh, so I said, "Hey, Catherine, how would you like to decorate my cast?"

"Really?" her eyes lit up.

"Of course, Catherine. You're the artist in the family."

She fairly jumped up at the offer. "I'll go get my pens."

Marcia was watching, and said with a smile, "Oh, Cher, you just made her day."

"Well," I said, "She's doing me a favor. I look down at this thing and it reminds me of my pain and limitations. If Catherine can transfer her love and talent onto my cast, then maybe I can admire that, instead of resenting my foot pain so much."

Catherine returned with a whole set of colored markers. "So, what do you want me to draw?" she asked.

I thought about something cheery and hopeful. "How about flowers? Flowers and butterflies."

Catherine focuses on beautifying my cast

She started picking her colors and I settled in to give her easy access to her latest canvas. I delighted in watching her transform the ugly white plaster into a work of art full of green vines, colorful flowers and beautiful butterflies. I loved showing it off to people over the next week. It was my first step in a long road toward generating good will toward my *#!@*! foot.

Another afternoon at my sister's house found me alone with my nephew, Luke. He sat down on the sofa with his lunch and looked at me with great curiosity. He finally asked what was wrong with my foot. I did my best to explain the surgery for him, explaining the plate and screws that the doctor had put inside of my foot. He cocked his head, looked down at the big round lunch plate on his lap, and asked in all earnestness, "But. Auntie Cheryl, how did they fit a plate in your foot?"

I had hoped to save Catherine's artwork on my cast after my follow-up visit with Dr. Loomis. That thought was replaced by fear as the saw buzzed so close to my foot. The doctor peeled off the final layer of gauze. It was the first time I'd seen my leg in weeks. My foot was swollen like a purple football. I hardly recognized it as my own leg. My shin was thin and the inside of my calf was covered in brown, purple and green bruises.

Taking my foot in his hands, the doctor asked me to try to move it from side to side, then up and down. But as hard as I tried, it barely moved. "Okay, that's what I want you to start doing at home. Try to point your toe and flex your foot. Don't put any pressure on it with your hands. Just try to bend it using your foot muscles." This got me excited. Here was something I could do all by myself. After weeks of waiting, this felt like the first step on the road to recovery. He presented me with a grey plastic boot that looked like something pilfered from a storm trooper on the *Star Wars* set. Very hi-tech, I thought. "Wear this for protection, but don't put any weight on it. We'll think about that in another six weeks."

And now another word from my sister:

I was sitting right there in the exam room with Cheryl, but she didn't seem to even hear the doctor.

She asked him flat-out, "Will I be able to dance?" and "Will I be able to hike?" She didn't even flinch at his response. I knew that I wouldn't be able to deal with being told I couldn't walk without pain. I winced when I heard him say no to those joys in her life. Surprisingly, she seemed to blow him off, acting like everything was just fine.

I was waiting for a long list of caveats from the doctor. "If you do physical therapy" or "If you do these exercises properly." I've had four C-sections and the doctors ALWAYS give you a big list of things to do and then a whole bunch of "ifs" and "buts" about the outcome.

Yet Dr. Loomis didn't seem to believe that she'd be able to walk without significant pain. Either that, or she would have to use a cane for the rest of her life. He didn't give her any wiggle room, either. No hope. Just a flat no. Yikes.

I'd been preparing myself for this moment ever since she called me from Colorado and told me she had shattered her heel, and even more so when the doctor came out of surgery, deflated, after trying to put all the pieces of her foot back together. The entire family has been worried that we'd have to band together to pick Cheryl's spirits up when she realized how dramatically her life was going to change.

I didn't get it. Was she so spaced out from the anesthesia and pain meds? Couldn't she understand the implications of what he said? Didn't it sink in?

Well, I won't push it right now. She's having enough trouble simply getting to the bathroom and eating right now. I will have to tell Dad and Judi what the doctor said and give them a heads-up, because I don't think Cher got it, and we've all been concerned about her long-term prognosis.

I know one thing. I'm not going to be the one to remind her that she won't dance or hike again. That bitter truth will be evident soon enough. All I can do is love her through the pain. And make sure she takes that homeopathic remedy I gave her to help her bones heal. I'll remind her about that on the way home.

Second
and Last Conversation

THE LAST TIME DOUG and I had been together was before my heel surgery, over two weeks ago, and he missed being with me. He offered to drive to Davis and load me and my wheelchair up for another weekend together at his place.

On the second morning with him, I woke up and listened from my futon around the corner from his bed. I could hear that he wasn't up yet. I was happy to think that I could surprise him with an early-morning snuggle. Unfortunately, my walker made such a loud clunking noise, Doug was fully awake before I even got close to him. I scooted over the top of the bed and sidled up next to him. It felt good to be pressing up against his warm body. As he put his arms around me, we continued the awkward dance of "Is this position okay?" and "Can your foot go there?"

After I had settled back into that familiar place beside Doug, I had the feeling that something was off. When I had lain beside Doug before, I had felt something very different for him. *What's going on here?* I thought. I lay there for some time, trying to figure out what was happening. Then Doug started to caress me slowly and gently, and I must have stiffened, because he asked,

"Is something wrong?" He pulled back, afraid that he had inadvertently hurt me.

I froze. What could I say? "Something's wrong," or "I don't know myself here"?

I closed my eyes and tried to figure out why I couldn't feel anything for him.

"I'm not sure," I said, shaking my head slightly. "Something's different."

"What's different?" he asked.

How was I going to explain the conflicted thoughts I was having?

"I look at you and am used to feeling something." I paused, gathering my thoughts. "But now, I feel like there's something," I moved my hand in a circular motion in the space between us, "blocking me from feeling… for you." There it was, I said it.

Doug reflected for a minute. Then, ever the engineer, he asked, "What do you think is causing that?"

I sighed and dropped my head back on the pillow.

"Everything," I said exasperated. "I want to be here for you, but I'm a cripple and I'm in pain." I covered my eyes with my arm. "I can't do anything for myself. And I'm not even sure when I'll be able to. And now Dad and Judi are going on vacation and I don't know who will take care of me while they're gone. There are so many unknowns in my life." Then in a small, quiet voice, I confessed, "I'm really scared."

Doug rolled back onto his pillow without saying anything.

In the tide of fears that ebbed and flowed through my life, I had convinced myself that if I couldn't love Doug and give him what he wanted, then he would reject me, and I would be broken, helpless *and* alone. Judging from the look he had just given me, this seemed like the beginning of the end. My mind was still struggling through the fog of medications, so I was reduced to the simple fear that if I didn't give him the answers he wanted, he would boot me out onto the street.

Doug propped himself up on his pillow and gazed down at me with a look I couldn't read. Was he angry? Confused?

"I'll take care of you, Cheryl," he stated earnestly, then quickly glanced away. "You know," he started slowly, "it could have been a lot better. But it could have been a lot worse too," he paused as if seeing the scene all over again, "I mean, if you had turned sideways or rolled over on your stomach."

"I know," I said, starting to understand where he was coming from. I thought I was the only one who played the scene over and over in my mind. He was still deep in thought, so I let him talk it out.

"I saw you hit those rocks," he said, shaking his head slowly, "and then I saw the boulder move." A distant look came over his face. "I thought you were dead!" He dropped his head, and I saw a tear rolling down his cheek. Doug was not a man to show his emotions, so I knew that those memories were still having a powerful effect on him.

I reached out to pull him closer and marveled at this news of Doug's experience. I had no idea that he believed I had died after hitting the rocks. If I thought I was distressed by my own visions of the slide and hit, then Doug was certainly dealing with his own closetful of horrific memories.

I lay there holding him, allowing his words to sink in. Somewhere between my tearful confession and Doug's admission that he thought I had died, I felt my heart opening again. In the wake of all of the revelations, a burden had been lifted and I was able to feel my love for him again.

"Oh, sweetie, I do love you," I said, basking in the joy of rekindling my connection with him. I was spent from the intensity of the conversation, and grateful for the opportunity to share the emotions that were obviously weighing down both of us.

"You can come here," he repeated stoically. "I'll take care of you," his words were fully rooted in a strong sense of responsibility.

"I know that your dad is leaving town and you've got to go somewhere. You can come and stay here. I work from home so I can help you with things. I'll always be here for you, Cheryl."

I held him tightly as I drank in all that he had said. I had been feeling so untethered in my life; his words filled me with an incredible sense of relief. I wasn't alone. I wouldn't be stranded and helpless. Doug would be there for me. He would help. He still wanted me.

As I considered his offer, I still felt like I was a tremendous burden to my family. My sister had also offered to take me in when Dad and Judi went on vacation, but Doug continued to lobby hard to bring me to his house. He made my choice easier by reminding me that I could benefit from doing weightless therapy in his pool.

When I moved in, he set up a TV at the foot of my bed and my computer nearby, and did his best to make me comfortable in my new life as the reigning queen of the futon. Doug worked all day in his office on the other side of the house, and I slept. I didn't feel like I could handle visitors, since I was still so groggy from the anesthetic and exhausted so much of the day. He would bring me the newspaper, and I was starting to get better at being able to read and follow a news story. Often I would fall back asleep. Doug would come in to check on me and find that I had passed out, with the newspaper strewn all over my chest.

I knew that the weightlessness of movement in water was good for me, but getting to the pool was problematic. Even though Doug's bedroom opened out onto a deck near the pool, there were two steps leading from the deck to the ground. I noted the challenge and had devoted my time to developing a plan. I would take my walker as far as the door, dragging my crutches with me; then I'd leave the walker by the door and take the crutches over to the steps. My first attempt at using the walker on the steps didn't go well and I had come very close to falling over onto the cement.

"What are you doing out here? I thought you were going to call me?" Doug scolded me the first day he came out to find me already in the pool.

"I didn't want to bother you. You were working," I called back.

"I don't want you climbing these steps by yourself," he said pointing to the treacherous stairs.

"I did okay by myself," I said, knowing full well the risks I had taken to get to the pool on my own.

"I don't want you to hurt yourself out here," he said looking around the backyard.

I shrugged my shoulders. "I won't," I promised, giving him a Cheshire cat grin.

He just shook his head and went back in the house while I relished my independence and accomplishment for the rest of the afternoon.

But those few minutes in the pool were the highlight of my day. Though the water was a bit chilly this late in the summer, I loved the fact that in the water, I was free. I moved my body without pain, restriction or fear. I even tried out a modified breaststroke to test my thigh. I was able to stretch and exercise in ways that didn't hurt my foot. Being outside, dancing around in the water, it was absolute heaven for me.

Now that I was spending more time with Doug, I was surprised that we never broached the subject of what had happened in Colorado. Except for those two conversations we had when I was visiting him on the weekends, we never talked about what had happened on the mountain, or why. Doug was focused on his work and seemed distracted enough with making sure I had everything I needed.

I'd share something like, "I spoke to Donna Peters today," and he'd walk away or frown to show he wasn't interested in hearing about anything or anyone connected to the accident. It took only a few silent rebuffs from him before I learned not to make any references to what had happened in Colorado or on the glacier. Though I wanted to share more of my thoughts and feelings with him, I learned it was best not to upset him and keep them to myself.

One day, he was walking by the futon and stopped suddenly, looking down at the floor.

"You know," he said pensively, "when I look back at our other trips, I can see that something even worse could have happened."

I just nodded, recalling where I had balanced on a log over the raging creek or stood unroped on the edge of a cliff.

"When we were up on Cathedral or back in Desolation," he reminded me. "There were... situations... where something could have happened."

His eyes were distant, as if he were seeing a variety of disasters playing out. "Maybe we were just lucky up until..." he waved his hand so he wouldn't have to say it.

I didn't say anything, because I was both surprised and confused. Was this a confession, an apology, or something else? Was I supposed to agree that he had put me at risk many times before, or be glad that something "worse" hadn't happened? *I nearly died on the rocks*, I thought. *I'm now living the life of a cripple. What could have been worse?* flashed through my mind.

Then he walked away, leaving me puzzled about his reflections. I wasn't sure what he was getting at, but one thing was clear: I did not feel lucky at all.

Along with avoiding any mention of Colorado, I learned to have a ready smile for Doug whenever he'd come to check on me. If I said anything about being tired, in pain or frustrated, he would become agitated and try to fix the situation, which would just make us both frustrated, as there was nothing he could really do to hasten my healing process. I was discouraged at how slowly I was recovering and was plagued with doubts about what my future would hold. I couldn't think straight, and my short-term memory had more holes than a slice of Swiss cheese. All this, on top of my limited mobility, pain and sleeplessness was starting to wear me down.

One bright spot was the conversation I had with my angel family, the Peters. Even though they were back at their home in Michigan, talking with Donna was a delight. Feeling so removed from any connection to the mountain or my rescuers, it helped to connect with someone else who knew and understood what I had been through. It was much easier to talk to Donna than to Doug about that fateful night.

She told me of the rapt attention they garnered from friends when telling their experience with the injured hiker who crashed their backpacking trip.

"You say thank you to us, Cheryl," Donna said, "but we want you to know how much you gave to *us*."

"What do you mean, 'what I gave you'? I don't get it," I said.

"We give donations and volunteer time at the food bank and church, but we never really see the good it does in the community directly. It was a real gift to us that we could offer you our help, to really make a difference, and see those benefits immediately."

After all the help and support I had received from Donna and her family, I had trouble taking in the power of her statement that *I* had given *them* a gift. Donna was still surprising me, just like she did in the tent with her bottomless bag of clothes and equipment. But then, I guess it's an angel's prerogative to continually surprise you with unexpected blessings.

Coming Apart at the Seams

LYING THERE EXHAUSTED on Doug's futon week after interminable week, I started to feel as if someone had, both physically and metaphorically, dumped a whole truckload of lemons on me. With so much time on my hands, I searched around to find the opportunity in the situation so I could make myself some proverbial lemonade.

I decided to dust off an idea I had entertained a while ago about a home study course to get my own insurance license. I had been working in the insurance marketing field for several years, but never found time to study for the exam; maybe I could be productive with the time I had now. I was excited when the coursework arrived, but as I started to read, I quickly became overwhelmed. I thought it would make me feel better if were able to complete the home study course, but I could only concentrate on the material for a very short period of time. My brain felt like a sieve, and I would have to read a paragraph over and over again to understand it. Even then, I still could not remember the material well enough to answer the questions at the end.

One day, after an unsuccessful run at a new chapter, I tried to reach out and connect with someone on the telephone. No one was available to talk in the middle of the day, and Doug was out for a bike ride. This left me feeling isolated, desperate and lonely, so I decided it was high time for me to try driving again.

In my head, I had worked out how I could do this. I would scoot down to the garage, press the button to open the garage door, and get over to the car with my crutches. I had gotten halfway down the last section of stairs when Doug returned from his bike ride.

"What are you doing?" he asked, concerned to find me sitting on the stairs in his garage.

"I'm going for a drive," I explained. "I need to get out."

"You're doing what?" he asked incredulously.

"Going to drive my car. I've worked it out. I can get to the car, put my right leg over to the side, and drive with my left foot," I said confidently. My car had an automatic transmission, so I thought it was a perfectly reasonable plan.

"Where are you going to go?" he asked.

"Anywhere. Out. To the store. To the park," I said curtly. "I just need to get out."

"But I take you out and we get root beer floats together. We do get out."

"But I only see *you*, Doug. I need to see other people too."

"Are you saying you don't like it here?" he asked, extending his hands outward as if to remind me of all he had been offering me.

"No," I said, taking a deep breath. "Can't you understand?" my voice rising like the foreigner who thinks it helps to speak louder. "I need to interact with other people too."

"Well, it's not easy having you here, either."

"Oh, so now it's 'not easy,'" I shouted back, using air quotes. "Up to now it's all been 'everything's great.'"

"Well, you're so tired all the time. You don't want to do anything."

"Well, excuse me! I'm trying to recover here. Do you think I like being tired all the time, lying around day after day, wondering why I still feel like crap? My mind doesn't work; I have no energy. I need to do *something*. *That's* why I'm going out."

"No, you're not," he said calmly, but he might as well have slapped me in the face.

"You can't tell me what I can and can't do!" I screamed back at him. "It's my car, and I can drive it if I want to!" Then I collapsed onto the stairs, sobbing.

I couldn't believe that I had resorted to yelling at Doug. I never yell. What was going on?

I kept wiping at my nose as this senseless argument raged on. The acoustics of the garage made our argument sound even louder, so I'm sure the neighbors were getting an earful.

Finally, Doug threw me a bone.

"Look, if you want to drive, let me go along with you the first time, okay? I'll even go with you now. Is that what you want?"

"No," I said, feeling heavy, laid out there on the steps. "Now I'm exhausted. I just want to lie down."

He started helping me back up the stairs. "You're always tired, Cheryl. Are you sleeping okay?"

"Not really. I wake up a lot during the night when my leg hurts. What I'd give for a decent night's sleep."

"Maybe it's time for one of those sleeping pills you got from the doctor."

I don't like taking pills, but it really felt like my mind was coming unraveled. I couldn't remember things and I thought I was starting to go a little crazy. Ultimately my need for a good night's sleep overcame my aversion to taking yet another pill.

After I took it, I slept for most of the next 24 hours. I'd get up and Doug would fix me a little food, then I'd go back and sleep some more.

The following day I woke up and felt like an entirely new person.

"Wow, I'm sorry I got a little crazy these last few days," I said to Doug over breakfast the following morning.

"I'm just glad to see you smiling again," he said. "Let me take care of some things this morning, and then later we can go for that test drive."

But even going out in public had its challenges. Already weary from having to get around using the wheelchair, walker or crutches, I started to dread the inevitable "What happened?" question whenever I went out. My glacier experience was so foreign to people, they would ask lots of questions, starting with, "Why didn't you get a helicopter?' Someone I had just met in a store would ask why I hadn't been saved from the ordeal and plucked out of the canyon by a helicopter, like other people they had seen on television. After several times of explaining, I actually lied to someone.

That was during a trip to the dentist, soon after I could drive myself. I was already exhausted and nearly fell asleep in the waiting room chair, holding my crutches. The assistant leading me back to the exam room looked down at my walking cast and asked the perfunctory, "What happened?" Not wanting to go into the story, I simply said, "Car accident," as a private joke to myself. But she bit.

"Oh," she exclaimed, "I had a car accident not too long ago on 101...." and she was off, telling me all about her experience and not asking me about mine. *What a relief!*, I thought. She was doing all the talking, happy to tell her story to someone who would understand, who had ostensibly also been in a car accident. I just nodded as I crutched along and collapsed into the exam chair, grateful to have been saved from a near-miss.

After the success of my car accident lie, I was sorely tempted to continue, and mused with Doug about other plausible stories. "I could say I slipped and broke my foot in the toilet." Doug laughed. "Or what about being bitten by a brown recluse spider?"

"Ooh! I like that one," I said, as I crutched toward a restaurant with him.

The host greeted us. "What happened?" he asked, pointing to my casted foot.

I hesitated a half-beat, then said with a straight face, "Brown recluse spider."

"Oh," he said, "My sister got bit by one of those. They're nasty. Did it swell up really bad?"

"Um, yeah," I said, playing along.

He was so earnest in giving us advice on what had worked for his sister and asking about my healing protocol, I looked at Doug in a panic but he just shrugged his shoulders.

I finally broke down. "I'm sorry," I said, bowing my head in shame, "I wasn't bitten by a brown recluse. I shattered my heel falling down a glacier."

I guess the brown recluse bite was a more plausible explanation from a middle-aged woman, because we couldn't convince him that the glacier story was indeed the truth. He seemed genuinely upset at our little game of bait-and-switch.

Through all of these encounters, I learned that we ask, "How are you?" and tell our stories because we have a strong desire to understand those around us and, perhaps more importantly, be understood ourselves. We bond with each other and find common ground through the stories of our shared experiences. But sometimes the truth can get in the way.

In early September I was very proud to be able to drive myself the 90 miles from Doug's house to my foot surgeon in Sacramento. "Well, the bone looks good," he said after inspecting the x-rays. I'd say you're okay to put weight on it. But only when you're wearing the boot," he said, pointing to robo-foot on the floor. This was great news, coming two weeks earlier than he had originally predicted. He gave me no prescription for physical therapy, just encouraged me to do whatever I could and still tolerate the pain.

Later that night, when no one was watching, I cautiously tried out my foot. I stood with my hands on the walker, and then very slowly eased some of my weight onto my right leg. A rush of intense tingling sensations, but not pain, flooded my foot. I was excited; I could deal with intense, so the problem was with my weakened leg muscles. After two months of inactivity, the muscles had atrophied and could not support me. After a few days of putting weight on my foot, I regained enough strength and stamina to take a few steps. It was a slow process, and took incredible focus and my full attention on coordinating newly engaged muscles. And then I was able to identify no less than five different types of nerve pains coursing through my foot; this observation actually felt like an accomplishment. Such is the limited world of the invalid.

Ironically, my family and friends were upset when my nerves started to reconnect. I'd be talking with them when my leg would suddenly recoil, and I'd close my eyes and grimace in pain. It's hard to keep your focus on a conversation when it feels like a hot needle is being jabbed through your foot!

Since I could now drive, I gathered up my energy one afternoon and drove down to a local café for a change of scenery. I would sit and write in my journal, happy for the simple pleasure of being out in the world and watching people go by. I was still new at putting weight on my foot, so I used my crutches as makeshift canes in front of me. I had to concentrate on each step just to keep my balance. On my way out of the café, I was struggling with pain, keeping a close watch on where I was putting each foot.

I was tired from the effort and intent on my task. So I was surprised when an older woman said to me, "I just have to tell you how much I admire your courage," she said enthusiastically. *Courage?* I thought, confused. "I saw you walking across that floor," she continued, "and I know it's not easy for you."

All I was feeling at that moment was pain and the frustration of trying to coordinate my limbs to walk again, and yet she labeled that "courage."

I didn't know what else to say to her, so I mumbled a reflexive, "Thank you," hoping she wouldn't mind if I kept my focus on my feet.

I found myself fascinated by her reflection and realized that you don't feel anything like courage when you save a child from a fire, or persevere through pain. In the moment of an allegedly "courageous act," a person is likely to be feeling tremendous anxiety about the danger they're in. "Courageous" is only how it looks from the outside. Inside, there is trepidation, uncertainty and fear. I tried to accept the generous label that she had given me, but I can also tell you that in that moment I sure didn't *feel* courageous.

I was starting to get around on two feet, even if I was somewhat unsteady. When I told Doug that I was almost ready to return home, he found it hard to understand why I couldn't just continue living with him.

"If I'm going to come and live with you," I told him, "I need to do it on my own two feet. No pun intended."

"But I like having you here," he countered.

"I know," I said gently, "but I need to know that I'm coming here because I *want* to, not move in because I *have* to. I've got to prove to myself that I can be on my own again. I need to come from a place of wholeness before I can consider living with you. I haven't been home for three months. First I was with Dad and Judi, and now with you. Don't get me wrong, I'm grateful for all the help. I just need to feel like I can make it on my own again."

"I can understand that," he finally conceded, "I just don't like it."

Doug had an out-of-town business trip scheduled, so I ended up having to move out of his house a week before I felt truly ready to be on my own. I wasn't too steady on my feet yet, but at least I didn't have to use the crutches any more. He reluctantly helped me pack up my clothes and computer and moved me back to my house.

"You sure you'll be okay?" he asked after the last load had been returned to my room.

I smiled and nodded my head.

"Well," he paused, not knowing what else to do, "call me if you need anything," he said, and gave me a quick hug before he left.

Up until mid-September, I had been entirely focused on healing my body and regaining my mobility. Simple daily acts of eating, bathing and dressing had been such a struggle, as I had to juggle the cast, crutches and my walker. These inevitably turned even the simplest trip to the bathroom into a frustrating expedition. Now, able to move about with just the cast, I had free hands and a second leg to stand on, even if my early attempts might only have suggested the idea of walking. I was bipedal at last—and in my own house. These were tremendous steps and significant progress on the road to getting my life back.

I discovered that once I no longer had to show deference to my caretakers, something else started to shift within me. My body seemed to know that I was physically strong enough now to start dealing with the emotional side of my trauma. And now that there was no one around that I needed to protect from my feelings, they showed up. Big-time.

It started when I had to deal with all of the unused vacation gear that had been sitting in my bedroom for over two months. When I opened the door, it looked like a bomb had gone off in my suitcase: the unused backpack, torn-up socks, bloody hiking boots and climbing harness were strewn across the floor—artifacts of my former life and painful reminders of the things I couldn't do any more, like hiking, climbing and backpacking. I was haunted by memories of our past adventures, knowing that as I put these items away, I was saying goodbye to a whole part of my life. After all, walking was still painful, and the doctor couldn't promise me anything about my future. How could I think about backpacking when I could barely walk? How could I think about rock climbing when my foot was so swollen it wouldn't even fit into a shoe? And I still had no idea how my foot would behave with its newly installed hardware.

After putting away my climbing gear, I opened the plastic bag from the hospital. I reached in and pulled out my hiking pants.

237

I was totally transfixed by the sight of the crusty pant legs caked with my own blood. It tugged on a visceral memory and hit me like a blow to the chest. After two months, the emotional dam had finally ruptured and I started to cry uncontrollably, gasping for air between sobs. *This did happen to me. That's my blood!* I screamed in my head. These relics had triggered a fresh wave of memories of the pain and fear I had felt in the canyon. I continued to cry, clutching the pants to my chest, and rocking myself back and forth on the floor. "Oh God," I sobbed, alone in my room, "I did almost die!"

After several minutes, my tears subsided and my breathing began to return to normal. I was now able to take a closer look at the bloodied section of the pants. Geez, those are little bits of *my* flesh still stuck to the pants! And look, they weren't torn, that's why we didn't see the gash in my thigh. Upon very close inspection, I could see where the ice axe had pushed into my thigh and how it had only broken the outer stitching at the seam. There was only the slightest discoloration of the fabric where the steel tip of the ice axe had abraded the fabric on its way to slicing open my thigh.

I held the pants and wondered what I should do with them. I thought about washing them, but then decided against it—at least not yet. Those pants were a powerful symbol of what I had survived, and I held them like a treasured relic bearing an important message from a sacred time and place. I knew they had something more to teach me, and I knew there would be power in releasing that blood and washing them clean. I also knew that I wasn't ready to do that. Not yet.

Not long after Doug had returned from his business trip, his brother and sister-in-law came out from Michigan for his birthday. One night, over dinner, I heard Doug's brother John say that he had warned Doug about the icy conditions on Andrews

Glacier after having climbed there himself in June, just a few weeks before our trip. John's comment surprised me, and even more so when no none at the table seemed to react to this curious revelation. I was distracted for the rest of the evening by the thought that Doug had been warned about the conditions on what I now considered "my" glacier.

This new piece of information added to my growing storm of emotions and continued to fester while Doug went off with John and his wife to enjoy several days in Yosemite. As if John's revelation wasn't disturbing enough, I resented not being able to join them. After they had returned and Doug and I had the chance to be alone, I asked him about John's assertion. Doug believes I misunderstood what his brother had said that night, and denied having been warned about the ice before our trip. Doug had admitted to not having the greatest memory for conversations, so his denial did nothing to quench the fire that had already been stoked and smoldering for several days.

I thought talking to Doug would help calm my anger, but instead it just grew stronger. I had never experienced such a tide of anger as the one that had risen up to engulf me. I never yelled or said anything mean or vengeful to him. But as much as I tried to hide it, Doug told me he could still feel the anger, even if I wasn't saying anything directly.

"I'm sorry, Doug," I said, as I prepared to leave that night, "but these feelings seem like they're going to overwhelm me," I confessed.

"I don't want this to come between us, Cheryl," he said solemnly.

"Neither do I. And I don't want you to be affected, either," I said, staring at the ground. "But it feels so big, like it will crush me," I explained. "It's really kind of scary."

***

"Why didn't you tell me about this anger?" Krista asked.

"It came up kind of quickly and I was kind of embarrassed and overwhelmed," I replied.

"Do you think it was about more than the accident?"

"At the time, I couldn't see past it. But since then, I've learned a bit more about the power of emotion and how it can trigger old and unresolved feelings."

"What do you mean?"

"Well, take the time my aunt died. My response came out of left field. I hadn't seen her for many years, but I was a slobbering fool all night long and fragile through the rest of the weekend after I heard of her passing. I didn't really understand what was going on at first. Finally I figured out that I had tapped into the residual grief of my own mother's death over 20 years ago. Emotions are just that way; you get triggered and it touches off old wounds and feelings."

"So what do you think this dredged up?"

"Like so many women, I've experienced different forms of sexual abuse at the hands of men I trusted. Some experiences I can recall, but some were when I was really young. My anger at men for taking advantage of me is old stuff. But I guess it felt like an all-too-familiar emotional story from my life. I didn't know that this was what was at play at the time, but I'm sure it added to the intensity I felt. I was probably due to flush it out."

***

I asked Doug if we could spend a few days apart because his off-topic questions in the middle of our conversations would only make me angrier, and I was starting to lose sleep because of that. I was doing my best to deal with my overwhelm, and sent him an email telling him that I was searching for a therapist who could help me deal with my grief and anger. He replied and asked if he could come to see me on Saturday.

"It took some time," I told him when he came over, "but I've finally found a therapist who can help me deal with the trauma." I hoped that he would appreciate that I was taking such bold steps to deal with these powerful feelings.

He started telling me about his experience since the accident. "I've tried to make you happy, but you were always tired and didn't want to do anything." He then went off on a variety of related topics, and I was left trying to track just where this conversation was going. I knew something was coming, though, because Doug wasn't one to talk this much about his experiences or emotions.

"I feel like I'm walking on eggshells around you," he continued, cloaking any real feelings in long, meandering explanations that didn't seem relevant. What I did understand was that he was frustrated and at least was trying to explain the challenges he was facing. It was as if he had all the pieces to an emotional puzzle and was describing their shapes, but couldn't make them fit together in a coherent fashion.

I knew that my brain was still slow to process ideas, and that the drugs were still keeping me from playing with a full deck, so I remained silent and concentrated on where he was heading with this unexpected rush of words.

When he paused without having come to any specific request or conclusion, I had a moment to reflect. He continued to sit there and look at me; I thought I might have finally figured out what was going on.

So I took an intuitive leap and asked, "Are you breaking up with me?"

"Yes," he replied.

Stunned, I just sat there, staring at him. I couldn't believe he was doing this to me, especially now, after all we'd been through together. I had plenty of questions about his apparent acceptance of this decision to break up; and I was surprised. Even though I was playing with less than a deck, I felt capable of challenging him on his reasoning. But I also understood that, since he had gone to all this trouble to describe why he didn't want to be in a relationship with me, there was no point in my trying to dissuade him. I felt an odd pleasure in seeing that my brain was capable of such discernment and functionality.

His feelings about the accident had been impenetrable to me these past few months; we had only two brief conversations about it. Maybe he thought that he had done his duty by carrying me down to the Peters, going for help and then housing me for a while during my recovery. So the desire for a breakup was a shocking reversal from his recent request to have me stay with him and continue living together as a couple. Or maybe he just couldn't handle the thought of being responsible for causing me such incredible pain.

Doug's onslaught of words was focused solely on his skills, challenges and perceptions of the relationship. I had never seen him comfortable discussing the finer points of interpersonal relationships. In the years I had known him, he had often been puzzled by a friend's social expectations and would regularly ask me about it. My attempts to drill down to the "why" for him usually touched on what I considered the commonly held yet unspoken aspects of our social contract. He couldn't understand then, and he seemed to be overwhelmed with the burden and complexity of our unfolding relationship now.

Bewildered and not knowing what else to say in the face of his decision, I walked him to the door, shrouded in a thick fog of disbelief.

"Well, I guess this is goodbye, Doug," I said, distractedly. "Have a good life."

He turned and silently walked away.

Incredulous at this sudden turn of events, I walked around the house in a kind of daze, trying to understand the implications. I finally called a friend and asked if I could come over to try and sort things out.

"Doug broke up with *you*?" he asked incredulously. "I'd better get that boy on the phone and talk some sense into him!" Luckily, I was able to keep him from making the call, but it sure felt good to hear his wanting to take Doug to task. Now I knew that someone else was surprised at Doug's decision too.

After this, the fragile new life I had constructed suddenly collapsed. Doug had been my main support and social lifeline during my recovery. The outside world probably thought I was doing great, hobbling about in my walking cast. But in reality, my life was still a struggle, filled with pain and more than a little fear about what my future would hold.

I was in shock for a day or two, but then the truth started to sink in. I had lost my safety net, my friend, my only witness to the accident. I felt lost and sank into a weeklong depression that actually affected my healing, as the activities I had the strength or coordination to do earlier proved more difficult for me. I felt untethered, as if the fragile web of a life I had slowly been weaving had suddenly come unraveled. I floated through the week in a foggy haze, stripped of the comfort and support Doug had provided.

In addition to my physical challenges, my mind was still compromised by the onslaught of drugs that made navigating the world all the more daunting. The sudden loss of his support felt like a wet blanket, since all of the new demands of my recovery were now mine alone to shoulder.

***

The sessions with my new therapist focused on my coping both with the trauma and with the huge tide of anger I was drowning in. After I reported my final conversation with Doug, the therapist didn't take well to my characterization of the breakup.

"You're not a woman who gets dumped, Cheryl," she said adamantly.

"Well, from where I sit, that's what it feels like." Then in a singsong voice, I said, "'Cheryl's broken and too much of a bother,'" I mocked. In my normal voice, I added, "Dumped."

"You certainly have a lot going on right now. Are you comfortable writing about your feelings?" Yes, I decided, I was.

So I took her advice, sat down at my computer, and spewed it all out.

At our next meeting, I felt a little self-conscious as I shared with her what I had written with such abandon:

Doug, you lied. Yes, LIED to me, you did!

All those times you promised to "keep me safe" while we went out on our little adventures. Assuring me that you wouldn't allow anything to happen to me.

Well…you were WRONG! And in such a big way. You even admitted to looking back at the situation so many times when your judgment was off, and you've reflected on how much WORSE an accident I actually could have had under your tutelage.

How you sulked around with your guilt and your shame because you knew that you had caused me such pain. You know you led me into harm's way.

And now, it doesn't "feel right" to you. "We" don't work any more. So you dump me. You try to wash your hands of me, my injury, the pain, the repercussions of your mistake, and walk away free. Leaving me to struggle to rebuild my life, gain my strength and put my life back together — all by myself. You felt you had done your job — taking me in to assuage your guilt, fetching my water, buying me food, taking me out in the wheelchair. Always reminding me, "Be careful; we don't want to go through this again.!" Well, excuuuuuse ME for inconveniencing you so! You, who can walk and run and play. You, who can return to your life, knowing your body is strong. You, who have been able to enjoy getting out during the beautiful summer while I lay in pain, exhausted and isolated, save for your little trips for root beer floats. How much of this "care" was driven by your guilt and your hopes to "make it up" to me?

And now, it has become "too hard" for you to deal with me. You don't "feel good" being around me, and so you've dismissed me with the weakest of arguments.

Oh, how I would like to expose you for the coward that you are. To tell all of Petaluma that, yes, he carried me off the mountain, but as soon as I could function on my own, he decided that he'd had enough and didn't want to play any more.

But really, Doug, I pity you. You who will struggle with this guilt because you're so damned stubborn you won't seek help, and even if it is offered, you'd rebuke it. You'd stew; drink your beers; continue to lurk in the corners of the room because you're so damn scared to talk to people even if you venture out to a social gathering.

Yes, you're handsome and smart and fun to hike with, but for God's sake, Doug, grow UP! Get over yourself and get some help. Quit doing stupid yoga moves on the fountain and putting yourself at risk trying to entertain others because you think that's the only way they'll like you and be your friend.

245

"That's a good start, Cheryl," my therapist said, as we discussed some of the particular elements I had written. "I can see that this is a good way for you to get at your feelings. Keep it up."

"With everyone involved, from the Peters to the rangers to my family and Doug, I've been afraid to let my true feelings out for fear they wouldn't help me. My life and wellbeing depended on their liking me. I guess I needed permission to finally let it all out."

"And don't worry about protecting Doug from your feelings," she advised. "He's out of the picture now. It's time that you let yourself experience your emotions.

"Anger is a summary emotion," she continued, "I recommend that before I see you again, you look at the different components that make up your anger."

So I went home and churned out more and more venomous words into the computer. I blasted Doug unabashedly and blamed him for everything that was wrong with my body and life since the accident.

The sad thing about Doug is that he still just doesn't get it. He doesn't get that he broke up with me. And he's confused enough to make other people think that I'm the one who broke up with him!

I mean, it's bad enough that he left me when he did and I had to struggle to create a support network while I was feeling down. That set back my healing, no doubt.

They say that which doesn't kill you makes you stronger!! I've had to fight for my recovery every "step" of the way. Doug was there for me, but I guess all of his promises about loving me and being there for me and his telling me I was perfect for him, were all for show. Oh, he says he wants to be there for me, but it isn't true. He can't even ask, "How can I support you?"

And he certainly can't deal with anger. I tried to shield him from my anger since he said he was not happy being the recipient. But that didn't work, either.

That's the whole sad truth. Even when I broke up with him before, he didn't understand why because he had no clue about communication or how being understood about what I was feeling were commonly held guidelines for intimate communication. He just doesn't get the subtleties of intimate communication.

It's too bad, really. You're a pretty nice and decent guy. Well-intentioned, just lacking the emotional subtleties that I need to navigate a successful intimate relationship.

I felt so wicked writing those thoughts. It was easier, however, than speaking them aloud to someone. I was still nervous about this huge wave of anger that was surging through and over me. Letting it all out by writing down my feelings was safe for me. It seems that I was not just protecting Doug from my anger, but also protecting myself from being engulfed and obliterated by that overwhelming emotion.

Once I had released some of my anger through writing, I started thinking about what had happened on the mountain, daring to really examine those feelings. What was it like the moment I hit the rocks? I began to explore more of what I had experienced after being left alone and waiting in the wilderness. I would often cry myself through those sections as I wrote them. But I believed I was strong enough now to handle the fear and pain that the shock had protected me from. "Kissing the tiger on the nose," I called it. Going back to those scary places, and being willing to look at, feel and see and smell everything about them so that the anger and trauma could be shaken loose and released.

It was hard to revisit the terror I had felt, let alone piece together the words that could convey the depth of my experience. But I had been a writer for years, and journaling had always been a way for me to process. I was already familiar with the practice of writing out my thoughts and feelings as a way to help me gain insight into a situation. It was a familiar, yet odd, comfort for me to be at the computer late at night, when the memories would keep me from sleeping. I would sit there, typing away, taking a break every once in a while to wipe my nose. I let everything pour out — tears and all.

As I revisited my time on the mountain, I was interested in exploring the creative potential of all that pain. I recalled something I had read when I was studying comedy, an explanation of why we laugh when someone on screen falls down. It seems that the biggest tragedies produce the greatest comedy. *Well, this is the biggest tragedy I've ever had,* I told myself, *so it should make for some really great stand-up material.* I dug in and started making notes on the funnier aspects of my fall and the rescue.

I told a friend of my plans to do stand-up. She said, "Cheryl, you're still too angry to do that." I assured her that I was not going to rip Doug apart in public, and kept gathering ideas for an open mic at the end of October. I thought that it would be very healing to work with humor. I was fascinated as I watched my emotional healing progress. My ability to joke about the experience slowly crept its way back up the mountain. First I could joke about the rangers on the trip down, then my time in the tent, then finally I could touch on the material about butt-scooting over the rocks. Black humor has been a valuable coping mechanism for me ever since my sister and I cracked awful jokes to each other years ago about our mother's ALS symptoms. Black humor is a relief valve that could help me with all the powerful emotions I was feeling now.

I wanted to lighten things up a bit with the stand-up. Get another handle on the story, a new perspective on it. After all, there's no support group for "I almost died at 12,000 feet" survivors.

After a third friend told me that I was still too angry to do stand-up, I finally conceded defeat. My glacier comedy routine would have to wait until the anger had abated. I shelved my notes for now.

Halloween Healing

By MID-OCTOBER I WAS given the okay to put weight on my foot without using the cast. My foot was still very swollen, so I had to find slippers that might pass for shoes. I didn't want to look like I had just rolled out of bed or was already suffering from a senior moment. My stamina was slowly returning. I could get out of the house and go to the store more easily. My surgeon still wanted to see me one more time before he gave me his approval to go back to work.

Halloween was coming up and represented yet another opportunity to help me move to the other side of the trauma. I was glad for the holiday and something more positive for me to focus on. As a kid, my dad's Halloween fun was about "scaring the little bastards" of the neighborhood with his elaborate displays. One year he went so far so to acquire a used casket that had been used to transfer a body from where a person had died to where they would be buried.

It was just a simple pine box covered with grey cloth, with a hinged lid split in half. We arranged stuffed fishing boots and pants in the bottom half of the casket, so the kids had to come into the garage, walk around the casket and reach inside where the "legs" were right next to a bucket of candy. Dad's hands and face were painted to glow in the dark and he would jump out at the kids as they came into the darkened garage. Some kids were so scared that Dad had to throw the candy out onto the driveway for them. I share this so you can have a better understanding as to how I come by my rather dark sense of humor.

October in Petaluma is full of preparations leading up to the Day of the Dead. You'll find traditional Mexican altars and sugar skulls all around town that commemorate the dead, and giant skull puppets in a parade down Petaluma Boulevard. The skulls and skeletons everywhere in these dioramas are to remind us that death is close at hand, and to give us time to remember the loved ones who have already passed.

I was already hearing the repeated refrain, "You could have died!" from people who heard my story. So with all of those skulls floating around the city in October, it seemed inevitable that my inspired costume for Halloween would be as a "skeleton hiker." I'd just have to paint a skull on my face, and go as an alternate version of my glacier-climbing self. It was a good creative outlet for me in the wake of the breakup with Doug, and I was happy for the distraction as I planned my costume. Between my frequent naps, I found a pair of pants at the thrift store, and purchased some face paint, fake blood and a big plastic bone.

At first, it was fun to plan and gather everything. But when Halloween arrived, I started to get nervous. I had hoped for some resolution of my feelings after coming so close to death, but instead, I found myself feeling very anxious. I started by painting my face with white and then adding black accents to the eyes, nose and mouth to replicate the skull-like image on the package. As I darkened my eyes, I knew that this had the potential to be a healing ritual, yet at the same time I was growing uneasy about my costume. My attempt to creatively confront my accident in the spirit of Halloween fun had instead become an increasingly painful reminder of how close I had come to death. My hand started to shake as I applied the makeup, yet I pressed on. I was on a mission to overcome my anger, and Halloween seemed like as good a time as any to acknowledge the true horror of it.

After taping the fake leg bone in place, I poured the fake blood over my thigh. I let it soak into the pants and drip in thin rivers of red down my leg. *This is what I looked like,* I thought, *with my own blood soaking through my pants and dripping down my leg.* An eerie sense of déjà vu swept over me, and I swooned a bit at the memory of standing at the tent site while Doug and the Peters inspected my gaping thigh.

I turned to look at myself in the mirror and stood there for a long time, taking in the sight of my bloodied leg. The blood-stain, though now in front, was as big as the original. The bone sticking out was a sign that I had broken bones. My eyes widened in disbelief as I stepped back to consider the overall transformation. I was looking into the mirror, but I saw someone unrecognizable staring back. The real Cheryl was hidden behind a mask of death. I couldn't identify with the image confronting me in the mirror. I hadn't discussed the "coming back" aspect of my experience with anyone, so it struck a raw nerve to confront it so dramatically now. My stomach was starting to twist in my gut and I feared that I would be overwhelmed by the anxiety that was creeping through my body. I shook my head and quickly rationalized the anxiety that was building up in me. "Maybe this will help me get on with my life," I said, trying to convince the skeleton in the mirror. Then I shot up a silent prayer: *Could I please embrace the fact that I almost died, so I can move on with my life?*

Careful not to smudge the heavy makeup on my face, I drove downtown and hobbled along in my slippers, admiring the kids parading by in their costumes.

I saw a few people I knew, but most didn't recognize me. The one who did stopped, looked me up and down, and said, "Is that you, Cheryl?"

Me as "skeleton hiker"

"Yes, it is."

"Wow, this is a great costume. Great job with all that blood."

"Well, that's how big my bloodstain was. This is how I looked as they pulled me off the mountain."

I saw a wide-eyed look of sudden recognition. I was glad that I had finally gotten through to someone here at home who could understand exactly how bad it had been.

Then I went to show off my costume to my friend.

"Wow, Cheryl, you look amazing," Aliza said. "That sure is a lot of blood."

"Well, I did lose two units. This is no exaggeration," I said, pointing to the stain on my leg.

I had shared more deeply from my experience with her than anyone else, and yet even she stood there shaking her head slowly, with greater understanding. I had described my injury to people over and over, attempting to explain exactly what it was like. "A picture's worth a thousand words," I thought, finally understanding that mere words might never be enough.

Solstice Cleansing

FOLLOWING MY THREE-MONTH post-op visit to my orthopedic surgeon, I touched base with my friend Carol and gave her an update on my progress with walking, as well as describing the break-up with Doug. "The doctor says I can go back to work on November 19," I sighed, adding, "This is taking so long."

"Well, be patient," she advised, "your body has been through a lot."

"You know, Carol, a while ago a friend asked me what I had learned from this whole thing. It seemed like a reasonable question, yet my mind couldn't handle it. I was so focused on just getting my body to heal. I still feel like I'm just struggling to get by."

"It could take 30 years for you to figure out why this happened, Cheryl. God has His reasons, but sometimes we don't understand them right away."

Carol's words came to me as if God was speaking through her with a message I needed to hear. It shook me out of my small-minded, everyday thinking and made me realize that things are not always as they appear to us in the physical realm. I was speechless: When a truth smacks you upside the head, you don't dissect it, you don't argue with it, you just let it be. I wanted to see if that divine message could give me some desperately needed perspective to wake me up out of my depressed funk. I was humbled by her words and the wisdom they contained, and carefully tucked them into my heart where they helped to ease my discomfort. Somewhere in my mind, I set a timer to check in after another 30 years to see what God had in store for me.

Thirty years is a long time, though, and her suggestion gave me some much-needed perspective in my rush toward normalcy. Maybe I *could* use a bigger dose of patience with my healing process. I understood that this accident had cast a long shadow on my life and I had been wrestling with its meaning. My biggest preoccupations now were about gimping around in my cast, struggling to carry groceries in from the car and grieving the end of the relationship with Doug. For now, the bigger questions of meaning would just have to wait.

Throughout that fall, my anger seemed to subside in proportion to my ability to do more and more things for myself. I remember the supreme joy I felt when I was able to fit my still-swollen foot back inside one of my sneakers (if I pulled the sole out to make enough room), and the first time I was able to walk through a store like a normal person. I was relieved to no longer attract inquisitive looks and questions about my cast, crutches — or more importantly — the "Why didn't you get a helicopter?" question. After months of explaining my situation to curious onlookers, I would be happy never to hear the word "helicopter" again.

By December I was back at work, but only had the stamina to work part-time. I felt like a homeless Imelda Marcos, as I had to carry a big bag with shoes, the robo-foot and slippers for whatever mood my foot might be in during the day. My stepmom Judi, ever on the ball, made sure that I had a temporary "Handicapped" sign for my car. This made a big difference when I was going back to the office, because on the days my foot hurt and I was back in the cast, my exposed sock would get wet in the rain. These more mundane concerns were a wonderful indication that I was returning to a more normal life.

Now that the swelling had gone down, I was experiencing what my foot's normal placement in my shoes would be, but the continuing pain worried me. I called the surgeon's office, but only got as far as the office manager. "My foot still hurts, now that I'm wearing normal shoes. I'd like to get a prescription for an orthotic."

"Foot pain is normal after your kind of surgery," she advised me. "The doctor doesn't believe in orthotics. He doesn't want his patients to waste their money."

This sounded like a perfunctory speech that I'm sure she had delivered to countless patients who continue to struggle with foot pain. She and the doctor had dismissed both my request for pain relief and for the benefits of custom foot support. But I knew my own body and how the pain had increased as the swelling went down and the angle of my foot had changed.

I was convinced that I could make my foot happier, so I set out to make the necessary adjustments for myself. I found pieces of cardboard and cut out shims to place inside of my tennis shoes, trying different placements, layers and shapes to get my foot position just right. After all, as I was walking around a lot more, I ended up placing more demands on my foot. But pain-free walking was still an elusive goal. So I would get the scissors out each night and try yet another configuration for the next day.

I hoped that with the passage of time, and my success in walking and returning to work, I would finally feel like I was ready to wash my bloodied hiking pants. I looked ahead to the shift in energies represented by the winter solstice as the day I would perform the ritual. The ancients recognized the powerful transition from the lengthening darkness into light, and the likes of Stonehenge were built to identify and celebrate the very day that the light returned. We moderns only acknowledge the original intent of this time of year with the time-adjusted dates for both Christmas and New Year's, depending upon which papal calendar you've chosen to follow. Today, liturgical churches celebrate Advent as the season of expectant waiting. It is characterized by lighting advent candles in preparation for the return of the light represented by Jesus' incarnation.

The natural turn from the shortest day of the year to the return of sunlight at the winter solstice was important to me, and I hoped that I could ride this energetic wave by washing the blood out of my pants, thus more fully integrating that return of light into my own life. I was all too ready to leave the darkness of my year behind and believed that now that I was walking again, I was strong enough to release that poignant reminder.

As I picked them up, the pants were limp, except for the stiffness of the crusty brown patch that laid flat over my hand. They gave off the sick, sweet, coppery smell of dried blood that crinkled and cracked with the nylon. Before washing them, I first checked the inside pockets. I was surprised to find my little spiral notebook; it was bloodstained around the edges. *My blood*, I thought, fingering the crusty brown pages. I also found a forgotten lip balm, two bloodied quarters and some tampons. I stared in awe at the tiny time capsule in the palm of my hand. I was mesmerized. These objects hooked into my memory bank and took me back to scenes by the tent, on the mountain, all the fear I experienced. They became sacred relics because they were there with me, touchstones of a life-changing event. I set the bloodstained quarters by my sink as a tiny reminder of what I had survived.

The pants were not only proof of my ordeal, but a gruesome reminder of my harrowing escape from death. I hoped the act of washing my blood out of them would allow me to return to a world that was normal and safe. But would that finally sever me from my connection to the mountains? Would it tame the angry fire that continued to burn within me? The pants were a stinging reminder that I might never be able to return to the mountains. There were good reasons to hang on, and equally good reasons to let go. But as much as I soaked and scrubbed it, the bloodstain only faded. I could not make it go away entirely.

***

"A pretty good metaphor for how this accident has landed in your life," Krista interjected.

I gave her a questioning look, and she continued on.

"Well, you've tried hard to work through your anger and your brush with death. But you bear the scars and harbor metal inside your body. As much as you want to "get over" this, you will never get beyond it. You can scrub at the memories and soak in the feelings, but you will never erase the stain of that experience from your life."

It was true. I was on a mission, doing everything I could think of to put this behind me, but she was right. I would never be able to forget. The bloodstain on the pants would continue to hold lessons for me, some I wouldn't learn for a few more years.

After all my efforts with soap and elbow grease, I had to content myself with the fact that the stain was much less visible, and that the pants were still usable. I thought of Donna wanting to throw them out, and felt a certain satisfaction that they weren't all brown and crusty anymore and that I could still wear them.

Getting Back in the Dance

ALTHOUGH I WAS MAKING PROGRESS toward walking like a normal person, the prospect of dancing again was still a big unknown. The November 3rd dance that I had held as a goal came and went, as I continued to struggle with foot pain. My daily struggle now was recovering my stamina after returning to work part-time and juggling footwear. After Thanksgiving I set my sites on the Waltzapalooza on December 13th, but my foot wasn't ready yet. Everyone else was swept up in the holiday season with parties and shopping, while I was obsessed with getting my feet into my dance shoes. Finally, by Christmas, I was able to show up at my family gathering without crutches, without robo-foot and wearing normal, inconspicuous shoes.

Finally, as the weeks went by, I felt like I might be ready to try contra dancing at the end of the month. I went to my first contra dance on December 28th, only because that was the first time I could fit into my dance shoes. I was surprised that I could really dance and make it through most of the evening.

Everyone was glad to see me, and wondered where I had been for the past six months. I tried not to get too much into my story. But the biggest question of the evening was, "Did you get your ticket to the New Year's Eve dance?"

My foot was hurting as I danced that night, and I didn't know if it was worth betting $20 on going to the event if my foot was acting up and I couldn't dance. But I was so thrilled to be back with my contra dance family after the many months of isolation during my recovery. I was also ready to leave a painful 2007 behind and dance into the New Year with joy.

So I bought the ticket.

My foot had hurt somewhat while I had danced that first night, but it protested much more loudly the next day when I woke up. I was back to gimping around, and strapped myself back into robo-foot because the support helped ease the pain. I guess I had pushed my foot farther than I should have, because it was still hurting several days after that first night of dancing.

New Year's Eve was upon us, and I was searching around for options for how I could still go to the dance and not just sit on the sidelines. I was upset at being back in the walking cast, but robo-foot was the only thing that minimized the pain of walking. I knew that it would be too painful to dance in my regular shoes. As crazy as it sounds, I started to consider the possibility of dancing in robo-foot. I asked my then roommate Ron to do a test run with some dance moves while I wore the cast. He spun me around in the kitchen and the rubberized sole, though thick and clunky, spun very easily on the smooth tile floor. It also did a great job of keeping my foot stable, supported and free of pain. I made the decision to go to the dance, and wore the bulky cast underneath a dress and its long flowing skirt. My center of gravity was off a bit with the extra weight on my leg, but otherwise I could swing around and do-si-do just fine.

"I may need to step out of the line if my foot hurts too much," I advised my partner as I showed him my walking cast. But we did just fine. As I stood in line waiting for the next dance to start, other dancers who happened to glance down would gasp, point and say, "You're wearing a cast!" as if somehow I hadn't noticed.

Contra is a very energetic dance form and I didn't want to wear myself out too soon. I chose to pace myself and sat down to rest after only a dance or two, just to be safe. A fellow dancer came over to sit with me. Shaking his head incredulously as he inspected my leg, he asked, "Why are you dancing in a cast?"

I searched around for words that could explain the depths of despair I had felt since July. How could I make him understand the endless weeks where I had been stranded on a bed and could only *dream* about ever dancing again?

The joy at finally being able to dance again was nearly exploding out of my pores. I sat there, marveling at my triumphal return. I searched for words but was unable to articulate the reasons. My desperation to express the thrill was building up like pressure inside my body until I looked at him and exploded, "I'm a crazy f@*k!" Then I started laughing, surprised by my own inarticulate expression, until tears rolled down my cheeks.

My endorphins kicked in around 11 p.m., and I couldn't tell my pain from my bliss. I waltzed at the stroke of midnight and was flooded with relief to put this *annus horribilis* behind me.

At my final doctor visit in January, my foot surgeon told me that the dancing couldn't hurt me, even with all the metal in my foot. It was only a question of how much pain I was willing to bear. As with so much of my healing trajectory, it was two steps forward and one step back. Over the next few months I would go to a contra dance, only to be sidelined by intense stabbing pains in my foot. My frustration was supreme, having my foot pain kick in and negate all of my fun. I stayed away from the dance floor for several months, finding it too hard to get so close to my joy, only to have the pain pull me off the dance floor and disappoint me once again.

In the New Year, I continued to test my foot in other situations. I was able to finally leave robo-foot behind for good at the end

265

of January, when I could continue walking comfortably in normal shoes. In the spring, I was thrilled to feel confident enough to put on my hiking boots and tackle a gentle hill after work. "Are you sure you're ready to do that, Cheryl?" my friends would ask. I was never sure if pushing myself like that was a good idea, but still I had to try. If I had not continued trying to push myself at every turn, I would probably still be on crutches and spread out on the futon, listless. And now that it was spring and the wildflowers were calling me from the hillside, I wanted to get back outside.

Actually wearing my bloodstained hiking pants again affected me more strongly than I had expected. The first time I put them on, the memories started coming back until I was curled up, trying to explain myself through my tears and sobbing on my hiking partner's shoulder. I was unprepared for the powerful emotions the pants evoked in me, as I was forced to relive the last time I had worn them. I had looked at them for so long as a symbol of what I had survived. Somehow I believed that after I cleaned them, I could put the experience behind me. Then I became more respectful of the power of those memories, even so long after the accident. It took half a box of tissues, but I was able to move beyond the intense vulnerability the memories had evoked and continued on with our hike. After that first time, I was able to feel proud of what I had survived and pointed out the bloodstains to my hiker friends. Their eyes would get wide when they realized how much blood I had lost to create such a huge stain.

When my foot swelling had decreased even further, I was able to get the custom orthotics I had wanted. My foot surgeon told me they wouldn't help, but I knew that if my foot tilted off at a weird new angle (which it frequently did because I had lost some nerve function on the right side of the foot and in my pinky toe), my knee, hips and everything else in my body would be off-kilter too. I was able to go hiking with more confidence, knowing my feet were more properly aligned.

And each time I felt a painful setback, I would rail at Doug and blame him for my latest round of pain and frustration. He had been out of my life since October, but I was still easily provoked to anger about "what he had done to me." So, whether it was after any problem with walking or if I had to leave the dance floor early because of my throbbing foot, I would automatically blame Doug for the painful injustices I continued to endure.

It was nine months after the accident before someone finally came out and said that Doug was, indeed, responsible.

"He was the lead climber, right?"

"Yes, I was following along as the novice."

"Any lead climber knows they're responsible for the people in their group."

My climbing friend was insistent that this is the natural order of things in the world of leading an expedition. I was resistant to this new line of thinking., I had taken a protective stance to Doug early on in order to keep the relationship together—as well as fighting against my family's animosity towards him. Doug had actually claimed responsibility himself right after the accident. Yet, I had been too afraid and vulnerable to let in that truth at the time.

Although I had railed at him in anger through the months of recovery, it now felt odd to have someone else agree, and assign responsibility and blame for the accident to him. I often felt like I needed to defend my choice to follow Doug up the mountain, and people looked at me strangely when I told them I had injured myself on a glacier. It was almost refreshing to have someone point the finger at Doug for a change. As I sat with this new perspective, it opened a door and gave me even more permission to grind away in my anger at Doug.

New Horizons— Yosemite Hike

LATE IN THE SPRING, my friend Carol had invited me to join her for another week's stay at her home in Yosemite. The thought of going back was all too bittersweet for me. I was still so limited with how far I could walk and thought it might be a cruel trick to play on myself. *Go back, but you only get to drool about the mountains you used to climb. Look, but don't touch.* I didn't know if it would hurt too much to get so close and not get off the tourist trails and back into the high country mountains I had grown to love. I didn't want a vacation that reminded me of all the things I couldn't do any more.

I eventually agreed to go, but decided to take a lot of books— just in case. Carol really looked after me with an eye toward protecting my foot. Our first day's hike was on a relaxed, flat path chock full of wildflowers. My foot hurt so much when I woke up the next day that reading by the river was starting to sound pretty good. I quickly learned that if I just sat and rested every so often, my foot wouldn't hurt too much. That's how we did our hikes over the next few days.

Then Carol got "the call." Her mom had fallen and broken her hip; Carol had to go to Fresno the next day. I would have to go to the valley all alone. As much as I was concerned for Carol and her mother, I was distracted about what might happen to me if I hiked alone. I didn't want to have to call in rangers if I had a problem on the trail. Carol helped me sort out my best options and suggested a few trails she thought I could handle.

The next day, as I approached the Four Mile Trail alone, I was encouraged to see that it was paved. I had my hiking poles for extra support and walked slowly, always monitoring how my foot and knee were feeling. Carol had suggested this trail because it was nice and smooth, with a gentle, sloping climb. I was delighted at how well it was going. I had been so focused on my foot as I slowly climbed, it was a surprise when I looked up and saw the massive granite wall and the Royal Arches through the trees.

Upon seeing them again, I was struck with a sudden rush of awe. I stood there sobbing tears of relief at the side of the trail, marveling that I truly was here. I became a sniveling drippy mess, wiping my nose on my sleeve and drying my eyes with my T-shirt. I was sidelined for so long, I had to wave on other hikers who stopped to see if I was okay. After collecting myself, I continued to bask in the unbelievable reality of being back on the trail in Yosemite Valley. I continued on up the trail. Soon Half Dome came into view. As I was afraid of getting too far up, I made the difficult decision to turn around and go back. My foot was still a concern, and I heard Carol's voice telling me to be careful.

After lunch, since it was still early in the afternoon, I thought I might try the Yosemite Falls Trail that Carol had also suggested. Dare I attempt it? I felt like I was getting away with something for *even thinking* of making a second hike that day. But nobody was there to tell me not to, so I decided to go for it.

As I approached this trailhead, I could see that this was my kind of trail—exposed granite, with a few trees thrown in for shade. The trail zigzagged back and forth up the mountain, and

I had to stop regularly to catch my breath. I almost missed the fact that I was actually climbing through the rocks on a steep trail! I'm doing it! I'm back! Hiking this way seemed so familiar; I almost took it for granted.

I was working hard to get up the trail and thought, *What am I doing? Should I be climbing a trail like this? Well,* I wondered, *what else would I rather do here in the valley?* I stood still, right there in the middle of the trail, and paused a moment to think. *There is nothing else I would rather do in the Valley than climb on this rocky trail.* So, I continued on, muttering to myself, "I must be crazy," then every few steps affirming, "yeah, this is the crazy part of my afternoon."

As I was going up the trail, other hikers were coming down. I sat down for a rest next to a woman who had stopped to wipe her brow. She was catching her breath, her face was red from the heat and she looked more as if she belonged inside a minivan rather than on the trail.

"I forgot mine in the car," I said, pointing to her trekking poles.

"Yeah, they're good for my knees," she said as we both looked at the industrial mix of neoprene, stainless steel and Velcro. "My family thinks I'm crazy," she said wryly.

"I thought I was the only crazy one here today," I laughed. "I've got screws and a plate." I pointed to my knee and foot.

"Yeah, well, my knees hurt whether I'm sitting home or hiking out here. So," she added with a self-satisfied grin, "if I'm going to hurt, I might as well be doing something I love. I've got to take my time when I hike," she said, lifting up her poles in explanation, "but I'd rather be here on the trail than sitting at home on the couch."

Sweet sister on the trail! She understood! She knew what it's like to overcome the odds. She continued down the trail and I thought to myself, I may not be fast, and I may not last long. But at least I was back on the mountain!

Two screws in tibia: $6,914

Plate and screws in foot: $41,500

Climbing Yosemite Falls Trail after only 11 months: Priceless

Now that I was high enough to see above the trees, a beautiful view of the valley opened up. I saw how far I had come. *Wow, I* thought, *no one is going to believe I climbed all the way up here.* So I pulled out my camera and asked a young man who was hiking there, "Could you take a picture with me in it, that shows how far up I am from the valley? This one is for my orthopedic surgeons," I said, smiling. *Look at me, Dr. Monroe,* I thought.

My foot works, my knee works! No one else hiking on the trail could possibly appreciate the incredible triumph I felt — or how far I'd come in the past year. I could hardly believe that I had scaled the mountains on two hikes that very day. I couldn't wait to get back to Carol's cabin and tell her about my success.

Only eleven months after my accident, and I'm back on the mountain!

The Anniversary

AFTER I RETURNED from my triumph in Yosemite, Carol encouraged me to continue the writing I had started back in the fall. I had stopped writing to focus my energies on returning to life rather than looking back at my brush with death. But the "high" after Yosemite had given way to a sense of foreboding as June came to a close. I was confronted by a rush of images and emotions that started to bear down on me as the July anniversary of the accident approached. Just by turning the page on the calendar, I felt as if a giant wave was looming over me, waiting to crush me with the weight of those memories. That heavy feeling grew stronger each day as we drew closer to July ninth.

At work, I regularly had to press my hands flat on my desk and take a deep breath, willing my hands to stop shaking. As the date grew closer, I turned too fast and banged my eye on the edge of my cubicle wall. What was going on? Why couldn't I control my body? Why was it suddenly so hard to navigate through the world?

"Are you okay?" a coworker would ask, watching my hands shake. *What could I say? I'm confronting my brush with death a year ago?* I couldn't exactly explain that July ninth jumps off the calendar and slaps me around. I got tired of explaining why I was distracted and hadn't really heard what someone had just said.

So I decided the best thing to do would be to take that day off. Stay home. Be safe.

When I woke up that morning, I was already in flashback mode. I curled up in a ball underneath my covers and would have been happy to stay there in bed all day. And I would have, if it weren't for my bladder's demand for relief.

I took my time as I prepared my breakfast, feeling the burden of the day's momentous anniversary. That made me move more slowly and cautiously.

I sat down and rocked in the glider, knees pulled up to my chest, trying to comfort myself as emotions and memories coursed through me. I thought I could manage my emotions, but then the energy would build. I'd think that what I really needed to do was dive in and work my way through to the other side. Avoiding them would only leave the feelings trapped inside me. The only way through this was to purge the trauma.

I called my sister, hoping she might understand. "Anniversaries help us process what we couldn't handle at the time," she offered. *How true*, I thought. "Reactions to the memory have been coming out of me all week," I told her. "The shakes are the worst."

"I remember getting the call from you last year," she said, referring to how she learned of the accident. "I Googled 'shattered calcaneus' after you called me from the hospital. None of it was good, Cher."

How strange, I thought. Here it is a year later, and I am still learning things about that time.

"I was reading about people who had undergone multiple surgeries," she continued, "and others who were still not walking after three years." She added gravely, "We weren't sure if you would ever walk again."

"I never heard you talk about this, Mar," I said, stunned at these revelations. I was grateful that she hadn't shared this depressing information while I was still struggling to walk again.

"No, you were dealing with so much at the time, it didn't seem helpful."

Like I'm dealing so well with it now, I thought. But still, there was something magical about the anniversary and what it was pulling out of me. It was as if my body could finally relax, knowing that after a full year, I wasn't at risk of dying anymore. I was now safe and strong enough to know fully what I had avoided last year, when part of my soul left my body to avoid the pain and trauma. The last week had been proof that I was processing a big emotional download. On the outside I was shaking because on the inside I was falling apart. Today, on the actual anniversary, I was simply trying to hold myself together and get through the day.

Some time later that day, a friend from the dance community called me to find a good time for us to go for a hike.

"What are you doing today?" he asked.

"I'm...um...." What could I say? I wasn't even sure. What won't sound too weird? I eventually collected my thoughts and stated, "It's my anniversary, and I've taken the day off."

"Anniversary of what?"

Oh, God, I thought, *don't make me explain my accident.* I don't want to have to explain why I wasn't roped up and why I didn't get a helicopter. Not again. Not today. Maybe I should just not answer my phone.

As the afternoon wore on, I decided to try going for a short walk. Once outside, I could see the street, houses and trees, but I still felt like my body was in two different dimensions. One was in Petaluma, and the other was still in Colorado, trying to make my way safely down the mountain. I walked slowly and purposefully, as if to remind myself that I was walking on a street and not stranded alone in a canyon. I felt so exposed and vulnerable. Did my walking appear to be unsteady to anyone else? I thought that if I moved slowly and walked in the middle of the street, I was less likely to bump into things and hurt myself.

After I had hit my eye in the office, I really felt like I was losing it, whatever "it" was that made me able to negotiate my body safely around objects. Some part of me believed that I was going to do serious harm to my body again. So staying home was my attempt at keeping myself safe.

What I wanted to do most that day was reconnect with Tim and Donna Peters, back in Michigan. They understood what had happened; they had shared in my uncertainty. Would they remember the date I crashed into their lives? When I called, Donna answered. She was delighted to hear from me and learn of my progress with both hiking and dancing.

"I've also continued to write about the accident as I continue to process the trauma. Although I had just been thinking of writing a 'thank you' to my 'rescue rangers.' A friend said this sounded like a good book to her."

"Oh, yes, Cheryl!" Donna chimed in. "Whenever you finish it, send me 20 copies. People don't believe me when I tell them the story. I need the book as proof. 'See here, I told you this actually happened!'" she enthused. "Yes, finish it soon, so people will believe we were really there to help you."

We both laughed at how, in our own ways, each of us had a hard time making people believe what had happened.

"You know," she said, "we still have your messages on our answering machine."

What messages? I thought.

"Whenever we check the machine, we hear your wonderful 'thank yous' from last summer. I guess neither Tim nor I have had the heart to erase them. We get to hear them nearly every day. I guess we like hearing over and over again that we made a difference."

I was speechless. It had been a year, and I had not yet found a gift to send the Peters family that would express my gratitude. But a phone message I couldn't even remember leaving was a constant reminder to them of my appreciation.

After a day of struggle, Donna had finally given me something positive I could reflect on. I marveled that somehow my desire that the Peters knew how much they meant to me was being delivered daily as a heartfelt message of gratitude.

Thank you, my angels, for getting me through this day. And for delivering a gift to Tim and Donna so much more beautiful than anything I might have tried to fit into a box.

Insights Unfolding

SOON AFTER THAT FIRST ANNIVERSARY, my foot had stabilized enough that I was successfully back on the dance floor again. Contra dances are a joyous affair for me, and with over a hundred people in attendance, it is a pleasure to greet old friends and continue to make new ones. I was especially glad that I was able to dance almost all evening long, just a year after my heel surgery.

As we paired up with another couple in the line and took "hands four" for the next dance, I caught people looking to see if I was still wearing my walking cast. My new dance partner was curious about it, so I had to explain to Michael, a visitor from Portland, about my shattered heel and new bionic parts.

The music started and as the dance began, my conversation with Michael continued. Between swings, courtesy turns and petronella twirls, I learned that he had been an ice climber up on Mt. Rainier, "before and after Mount St. Helens blew."

Talking during a dance is not unusual, but it can distract from the intricate moves we dancers weave together as we progress across the dance floor. I was enjoying these snippets of conversation, especially since I had never before known anyone (besides Doug) who had done technical climbs on a glacier.

The conversation came in short bursts, whenever we came back together to the same side of the set. On our next turn, I said, "I've been on a glacier in the Rockies," before going back across the set.

"How many in your party?" he asked. When we came back together, I answered, "There were just two of us on that climb."

It was getting harder to keep up with the dance, especially when he started asking questions that threw me back in time. Luckily, his next two questions were more perfunctory, and I answered them easily: "titanium" and "last July." Then he casually observed, "For a glacier descent, there should always be at least four people — for safety."

When that new safety factoid arrived, it absolutely exploded inside my head. If I hadn't been dancing, I would have been stopped stone cold. My whole perception of the accident shifted under the weight of this startling new piece of knowledge. I stumbled a bit and fell out of sync with the other dancers, but was guided back to my partner's arms and continued on.

It was as though I became a zombie for the rest of the dance. I was wide-eyed and totally distracted, trying to make sense of Doug's decision to take me out on the glaciers in the first place. What the hell was he thinking? My anger sprang forth with a renewed vigor as I compared this new information on proper hiking protocol with Doug's behavior and the choices he made for us that were supposed to "keep me safe."

I staggered away at the end of the dance, having just had my whole view of last year turned upside down. I sat out the next dance to let my head cool down, waiting to talk to Michael again so I could unravel this swirl of new information and fresh rage that was moving through me.

I searched through the crowd of people and caught Michael's eye before I approached him during the break. I started asking him questions; he seemed to be quite knowledgeable. I was intrigued—I hadn't been able to talk glaciers or high-altitude climbing with anyone since leaving Colorado.

I explained my limited experience of climbing and the dynamics of our day on the glaciers. He outlined the considerations involved in making a glacial ascent. "I've stood at the base of any number of glaciers, only to make the call, 'Not today,' and then sat down to enjoy the view over lunch. The snow can change day to day," he said, "It's never the same."

Michael shook his head when he reflected on Doug's leadership skills. "It's always easier to go down the glacier than to climb down the rocks on the side," he said, raising his eyebrows warily. "But...." he said, shrugging his shoulders and cocking his head knowingly toward my foot.

Michael understood well the dangers, conditions and technical implications of our trip, and offered an even-handed appraisal. "Doug didn't train you enough, he didn't have enough people on the climb and he hadn't read the snow properly." The indictments kept adding up. "He didn't rope you up, and he didn't take your shallow skill base into account before telling you to walk down that steep glacier face." These were stunningly potent condemnations, seeming like huge blocks stacked one on top of another. I couldn't embrace them all at once.

I was slightly shocked at his assessment, but he just continued sharing his love of climbing. Hearing my love of the mountains, he said, "You know, there are guides in Washington who will take you up on the glaciers." I shot him a puzzled look. It's true that I loved to climb, but did I even dare to think about going back yet?

"*They* know what they're doing," he continued. "*They* would rope you and do what's necessary to keep you safe," he added pointedly.

283

I was intrigued by the idea of going back on a climb. But ropes or no ropes, I would probably never make it onto a glacier again. I thanked Michael for the information and walked away with conflicting thoughts and a belly that was starting to tighten up again.

Michael's insights brought sudden clarity to my anger, as compared to the vagaries that had been rolling around the edges of my consciousness for almost a year. At different times in my recovery, I would become frustrated whenever I encountered a big "I can't" because of my injury. Unfortunately, shaking my fist at God offered no satisfaction. And of course I was slow to accept that I had been the one who chose to trust and follow Doug, based on all of his "I'll keep you safe on the mountain" speeches. Michael's insights had given me an odd sort of peace, as if my anger had found its rightful home.

Over the past year it had become increasingly difficult for me not to verbally eviscerate Doug when people asked why we didn't go around the ice that day. "He misjudged the snow," I would say to them, shrugging my shoulders, meekly feigning acceptance. What did they know of proper protocol for a safe descent at elevation?

Then I met Michael, a trained and expert ice climber, who shared his stories and adventures about this mountain or that ice bridge. He rocked my world with his matter-of-fact statements about how many climbers should be on a glacier and how proper safety techniques are drilled into climbers so that the proper self-arrest techniques become second nature. What should have been done before I had even set foot on a glacier was all very obvious to him.

Here, in an unexpected turn on the dance floor, an experienced lead climber found Doug guilty of negligence, endangerment and dereliction of duty.

Learning to Forgive

IT HAD BEEN OVER A YEAR since the accident, and I was still trying to heal the resulting emotional trauma. By this time, I was dancing more regularly and able to go on short hikes. But there would inevitably be someone who would ask why there were only two of us on the glacier if I was a novice, or why Doug hadn't roped me up. These conversations would trigger a fresh burst of anger within me that I had to rationalize away. I was concerned about how that continual provocation of anger was affecting my body. The biggest impact was that I lost sleep as I'd lay there at night, stewing in my own juices. That would continue to wreak havoc on my body's biochemistry. I wanted out of the vicious cycle of anger that kicked in whenever someone asked about the accident.

I knew that forgiveness was the key to unwinding that knot of anger, but I was still stymied as to how to do it. Growing up in the Lutheran church, I was familiar with Jesus' exhortations on the subject. Yes, it was important, but how does one achieve it? Simply saying, "I forgive Doug" didn't make it so, and certainly hadn't abated my anger.

Then one morning I was stretching, folded up on the floor in the child's pose. I was bent over and my forehead was touching the floor. Then it struck me. Seventy times seven. That's what Jesus had said. I knew that in Hebrew terms, seven was the number of completion and wholeness, as in it took seven days to create the world. So seventy times seven means completely and utterly forgiven. How in the world could I do that?

The answer came later that day in a book I was reading. The section on forgiveness gave an example about how a woman didn't think it was humanly possible for her to forgive the person who had wronged her. Boy, could I relate! But she reflected that God had already forgiven him, so she asked God's forgiveness to work through her so she could forgive this man. That's it, I thought excitedly. Let God's forgiveness move through me, since I couldn't do it myself.

I immediately sat down, closed my eyes, and visualized God pouring a huge bucket of forgiveness into the top of my head, filling my entire body. The forgiveness was a white light, so my body was filling up with a white glow. Then I visualized Doug standing in front of me. "God," I said in my mind, "I don't have it in me to forgive Doug, but you do. Please move your forgiveness through me so I can forgive Doug."

And as God kept pouring that forgiveness into me, it overflowed through my heart and filled the space between Doug and me. Then the white light filled Doug. God kept pouring until forgiveness filled and surrounded both of us.

It felt so good to bask in the flow and energy of forgiveness. As I sat there and made sure that every little space between us and inside us was filled, I kept saying, "God, you have to do this, because I can't. Thanks for moving your forgiveness through me."

Then I thought about the love I still felt for Doug at the time and prayed, "God, fill me with divine love for Doug." Suddenly pink light started pouring into me from above, filled me and flowed into the spaces in and around Doug and me.

I felt so much more peaceful as I sat there, and then the images of other people who were also in need of my forgiveness began to appear before me. So I kept having God pour in forgiveness and love that flowed out to other men who had hurt me. I thought this would be a good time to clean up any old unresolved anger with men that might stand in the way of my attracting a wonderful husband.

After this parade of forgiveness, I was so relaxed and happy that my mind opened up to all kinds of creative thoughts. Inspiration flowed in. It's as if my angels were guiding me on a path to my future, now that I had entered into a more forgiving space. I was so grateful that I had found a way to offer Doug forgiveness. I decided to flow this forgiveness energy from God to Doug every day for several minutes, to make sure that I had worked the anger out of me — utterly and completely.

Still More Anger

ONLY A FEW DAYS after that forgiveness meditation, I was out having dinner with some friends who were new to my glacier story. One of the men at the table asked a simple question: "Did he help pay?" in reference to my medical bills. I shook my head, "No."

"He didn't give you anything?" the other man asked, his voice rising with indignation.

It seemed that they looked at me and saw a woman who had survived a life-threatening trauma and deserved some justice.

"Didn't he have ropes?"

"Yes," I answered, suddenly feeling like I was under interrogation on the witness stand.

"Why didn't he use them?" the other asked innocently. If they only knew how that question had burned within me for over a year. "You'd have to ask him," I said through gritted teeth and with a steely smile.

"Didn't he do anything?"

"He did reach out to try and stop me on the way down. But I was going too fast."

"Well, how steep was it?"

How do you explain a steep pitch? I held my forearm out at an angle, trying to approximate the slope. "About 45°. Pretty steep."

Both sets of eyes widened, slightly stunned as this academic exercise in responsibility showed its lethal edge.

"He watched me hit the rocks," I added coolly. "He thought for sure I had died," I added, hoping that this would end yet another uncomfortable conversation about the dynamics of my fall. But instead, they were captivated. "Then what happened?"

Oh, no. Not again. I didn't want to have to keep telling the story over and over. I sighed and gave the briefest of synopses. "Took them 24 hours to get me off the mountain. I was off my foot for two and half months. Took me a long time to walk again." The pain of the memory washed over my face. I looked up furtively, then back down at my salad.

But they were not satisfied at the resolution.

"You weren't a 'Class A' climber?"

"No."

"And he took you up there?"

Now I was back to having to defend myself. "He said he had taken his young nephew on this glacier before."

"Weren't you using crampons?"

How many times would I have to go through this? I thought, before I explained once again. "We used them going up the first glacier, but not on the way down."

"And he had ropes, but he didn't use them?" one recoiled, puzzled by this seemingly foolish decision. "That's like manslaughter," he concluded.

I was alarmed at this sudden uptick in the conversation.

"Or 'reckless endangerment,'" the other added.

"Negligence," I stated flatly, once again, hoping this would stop the onslaught.

Finally they noticed how uncomfortable they'd made me with their line of questions, so the conversation veered off in another direction. I sat there, totally wrung out from yet another emotionally charged conversation about what Doug had done and why. The rest of the evening was pleasant enough, but not until I got home did the full impact of the conversation hit me. It's not the first time that a man had reviewed the circumstances of my injury and prescribed some remedy, albeit retroactively. Unable to save me with their well-intentioned helicopters, these two men now obliquely suggested I take the legal route for justice.

I was supremely frustrated that this issue just wouldn't go away. Whenever questions came around to the fact that Doug was the lead climber and I was the novice, he had ropes, there were only two of us; that's when *their* anger erupts. *They* are upset that I hadn't been better cared for — up on the mountain or since.

I had been focused on forgiving Doug, doing what I could to move the anger out of my body. So why am I still so easily provoked? I spent yet another night lying in bed, churning away with angry thoughts, unable to sleep. Would I ever be able to get beyond this? Hasn't my forgiveness work done anything? Why am I still so angry? Why does this idea of holding Doug responsible keep coming up?

But this time I was compelled to try out a new idea: a legal solution. Someone suggested that Doug should share some of the financial responsibility for my injuries and the subsequent costs of the surgeries and rehabilitation. After the incident, I had worked hard to protect Doug from his own responsibility and my anger. Then I had a disquieting thought: am I still protecting him from the true cost of the incident?

My dinner companions' questions and charges haunted me through the night. "Reckless endangerment" had a satisfying ring to it. I loathed the idea of a lawsuit. But I needed to know if there was some way I could put a stop to the nagging questions.

I was talking with my friend Aliza the next day, and was rather nervous about bringing up my anger. I didn't know if it was fair to share my anger with her, since she knows Doug. After giving her the highlights of the previous evening's conversation and my subsequent lack of sleep, I laid out my plan.

"I'm going to make two calls tomorrow, one to the Colorado Climbing School. I've been wanting to call them for some time to learn just how far I did hike and what their opinion is on taking a novice up a glacier. The second call," I said, taking a deep breath to summon up the courage to tell her, "is to a lawyer." Then I rushed to explain, "I want to know once and for all what my legal recourse is."

She looked stunned, but I continued on. "Intelligent people listen to my story and are shocked that Doug didn't pay for any of my medical expenses. Then I feel like a dupe for letting him get away with that. They see quite clearly the reckless endangerment and negligence involved here, and quite frankly," I said, my voice rising in frustration, "I'm sick of having this thrown in my face time and time again. I can't keep allowing a simple question to trigger such anger in me that it keeps me up at night while my mind tries to sort through my options."

Aliza looked at me and weighed in carefully. "Do you really think calling a lawyer is the answer?" She held up her hand so I would let her finish. "Just think a minute about where that will lead. A lawyer will ask questions and you'll have to go over this again and again, Cheryl. Do you really want that?"

I dropped my head, shaking it slowly. "No," I conceded, "I don't. But I've got to do something about it when people keep asking these obvious questions. What can I say?" I pleaded. "'Yep, he's a jerk'?"

"Yes, Cheryl, you could say that."

Her answer surprised me, and I stopped for a moment to consider that as my resolution. But it wasn't enough.

"So, tell me, what's wrong with this picture? I get busted up," I started counting on my fingers, "nearly die, and get to deal with pain and limitations for the rest of my life," I concluded, pointing to my foot. "And Doug? He decides he's had enough and walks away scot-free. You know," I paused and a wicked smile curled across my lips, "I was even writing him a check before my second surgery to cover my half of the frigging rental car, because even on all those drugs, I knew enough to be responsible. But Doug didn't."

"Why do you think he didn't?" she asked.

"Oh, Doug, he was never great with those kinds of social conventions."

"Well, what do you think a lawyer would say?"

"That Doug was wrong. But it probably wouldn't be worth it to sue him," I mused. Then I thought, what does Doug really have? His house? I flashed on what it would be like to sue Doug and I didn't like what I saw. *How could my life have come to this?* I thought. Then, as if to counter the thought of letting him off the hook, "But he led me into harm's way. He was the lead climber," I said vehemently. "I was supposed to be able to trust him. Lord knows he told me to trust him often enough."

I was on a roll and it felt good to finally let this all out.

"Negligence," I continued. "That's what it was. He took me up on that glacier. It's like placing a kid in the middle of the freeway and saying, 'You've got eyes, you've got legs, so be careful on your way home.' Remember that ice climber I met? Michael? The one who told me there should always be at least four people on a glacier." I held out four fingers to her for emphasis. "Four, not two. And me a rank beginner," I said with disgust.

Aliza had a look of steely determination on her face, the likes of which I had never seen.

"Cheryl," she said slowly, "I want to caution you about what's going on now that we're in Scorpio. There's a lot of anger in the air because of the economy and if you let it, your anger will just keep coming and coming." She continued in a calm voice. "I just say this so you'll understand why emotions seem so much more intense right now."

I heard her words, but I was out for blood. Michael had given me reason to realize that Doug had broken the rules of climbing, and I had been the one who paid for that. It felt good to finally be able to express my anger, and I didn't want to stop.

"Well, I've done my forgiveness work. I'm still doing it. But this anger is so big. I don't know if the work will be enough. I mean, here I am just talking about it, and I'll probably have to take another sleeping pill tonight to knock me out. I just can't take this anymore!"

Aliza looked at me for a few moments before responding very calmly and deliberately to my verbal tirade. "Cheryl, we can concede that Doug was negligent. Yes, he was wrong. And so you bury Doug," she paused. "Then what? Where does that leave you?"

"At least I'll have something to say to people when they ask."

"But there will always be something else. People are like that. They'll find some new angle." That was true. People used to be fixated on the helicopter that didn't rescue me, and now it was Doug's negligence. Aliza's steady voice and line of reasoning were finally having an effect on me. I was breathing more normally now and speaking in a more normal tone of voice.

"Well, you see, Aliza," I said calmly, "it's not quite that simple. See, I'm not only angry at Doug," I paused and looked down, "I'm angry at me."

It felt good to finally share this new revelation with someone I trusted.

"I mean, was I so stupid to let Doug convince me to go to Colorado? He said it would be fun, that I could handle it. Was I wrong to go on such a long hike at altitude? I did my best to push back when we were planning our trek in the coffee shop. I wanted to go down one of those earlier glaciers to shorten our hike. Was I wrong for not questioning the glacier surface? Doug was walking down it just fine. Was it wrong to agree to even go on a glacier? He said he'd taken his teenage nephew on it. I made all those choices and let Doug set me in the middle of that freeway called Andrews Glacier. So, sure, I'm angry at him, but I don't know if I can forgive myself for choosing to trust him."

Aliza was stunned at this turn in the conversation. I hadn't spoken about this since I took a swing at my anger over a year ago with a therapist. "I don't know what I'm supposed to do here," I said, running my fingers through my hair, "I don't want to be blindsided by my anger every time someone dares to suggest that Doug should have helped me financially. Maybe

I should just ask him straight out," I said, surprising myself. I wondered if such a simple and direct approach would work.

"Maybe you could," she replied.

"Or, let a lawyer do that for me." I said, as my eyes lit up with wicked intent.

"Cheryl," Aliza cautioned again, "just remember that everything seems much more intense right now. Be careful where you put your attention."

"I know, I hear you," I said, finally feeling like my anger was spent. "I just don't know how to resolve this. I want to take the 'high road,'" I said, flashing air quotes for emphasis, but my inner warrior disdained the thought. "I *am* trying to work it out through forgiveness," I explained in frustration, "but God is going to have to root way down deep inside of me to quench *this* fire."

She let me sit with the power of that thought.

"I'm going to have to meditate on this and figure out what to do next," I said. Maybe calling the lawyer wouldn't be so helpful right now.

"Cheryl, you have a good heart. I know you'll figure out something."

"Argh," I growled. "It's not easy, let me tell you. My anger is right there," I said putting my hand in front of my face. Then I sank back into the sofa. I felt thwarted from my quest to slay Doug in my attempt to release my anger.

"I know it's not easy," she said, "but you don't really want to hurt Doug, do you?"

"Well," my eyes lit up again, ready for the fight, but then I sank back down, "I guess not."

Darn, I thought, I was really up for a good fight.

In the days after that angry outburst, I continued doing my forgiveness meditations. I thought a lot about my option of going through life with my righteous anger as the victim of a horrible accident, or living a life where I got to experience the peace of wellbeing. You can say it's a no-brainer, but I can tell you that there was a very real choice point where I had to consciously choose to let go of my "angry victim" story and give up its satisfying thrill.

I figured that if I were truly to own my anger, embrace it, dissolve it in a sea of forgiveness and love it, then I could stop people from being angry *for* me. At that point, I believed that when people heard my story, they were only reflecting my unresolved anger back to me until I got so sick of it that I would finally do something about it.

I saw it as a public service too. I would cease to provoke other people with my unhealed anger, and stop promoting the idea that being angry is the natural state of affairs after such a trauma.

At this point, I'm willing to bet my life on love and forgiveness. After all, I'd much rather tell people about how I healed through forgiveness than about why I felt compelled to take Doug to court.

What's This Talk About Miracles?

BY TWO MONTHS after the surgery, I had sought the help of a psychologist when my anger finally surfaced and coursed through my body. But now, after having done all of those forgiveness meditations, I thought I had completed the emotional work necessary to process the trauma of my fall. What I didn't realize was that there were still aspects of the event hidden throughout my consciousness. I didn't understand they were there until they had been ferreted out during various conversations with friends and family.

The first of these conversations was with my sister Marcia. I had just regaled her with my success, going dancing two nights in a row without major foot pain sidelining me.

"My bodyworker was working on my foot the other day, and he said that my progress in healing and the ability to dance was a miracle. I don't feel like a miracle," I complained to her on the phone, "I've worked hard to get my foot back!"

This seemed to surprise my sister.

"Cheryl, don't you remember what the doctor said?" she asked.

"I'm not sure I know what you're talking about," I said.

"He said you wouldn't walk or dance or hike again." She had been there in the doctor's office with me, so she should know. "Don't you remember that?"

"I guess not. My brain was like a sieve after two surgeries."

"I remember being surprised that you didn't have any reaction when he told you that."

I don't know if I had blocked it out, forgot, or just chose not to believe him, but his verdict on my future didn't impact my vision and desire to dance and hike again.

I realized that the special November 3rd Contra Dance figured very prominently in my path to recovery. Whenever I heard a new projection for how many weeks it would be before I could put weight on my foot, or how many more weeks I would be in the walking cast, I'd mentally calculate that I could still go to that November 3rd dance. When my foot was too swollen and tender to even consider dancing in early November, my love of dancing pulled at me to set my sights on a night of waltzing on December 13th. Ultimately, I ended up dancing at the end of that month and on New Year's, only five months after the surgery to reconstruct my shattered heel.

The point is, I was always counting on being able to dance again and at an unconscious level, I just didn't allow myself to hear the foot surgeon tell me otherwise. I say "unconscious" because it wasn't as if I told myself to ignore his prognosis, I just wanted to dance again and couldn't wait to join my Contra community on the dance floor.

"And that's why it's a miracle, Cheryl," Marcia continued. "You weren't even supposed to walk without pain."

Now I could understand why the secretary at the surgeon's office didn't want me to "waste my money" on custom orthotics to correct my foot pain. Apparently the doctor just expected me to accept that I would always have pain and that I would need to learn to live with it.

"I've been delighted to hear of your progress through the year, Cher," my sister continued. "First it was hiking, then starting to dance, and then getting through an entire night of dancing without pain. And I couldn't quite believe it when you went rock-climbing again."

"Yeah," I agreed, "I thought hiking and rock-climbing would be hard on my foot, but dancing has turned out to be the final frontier."

"I still remember the night after your surgery when I saw the x-ray with all those tiny pieces of bone, Cher. It *is* a miracle that you can walk," she added emphatically. "So Jim's right," she said, referencing my bodyworker, "you really are a miracle."

That conversation rattled around in my brain for many days as I tried to allow the "miracle" label to stick. I'm grateful—don't get me wrong—but miracles are something that are supposed to happen to others. I didn't feel comfortable applying that label to myself. So I found this new perception a bit distracting every time I approached the stairs. Being able to climb stairs again had been a real triumph on my road to recovery. But even as I walked around pain-free, I continued to resist the idea that I harbored a miracle in my foot.

It felt as though whoever or whatever bestowed the miracle could just as easily take it away. Miracles seemed capricious in nature and I didn't want to have mine revoked. I wanted my foot to stay whole and healthy, even if I did have a drawerful of hardware shoved inside it.

The "miracle" story had marinated inside of me for a month or so before I started to notice that my foot was actually starting to hurt more. I was concerned that calling my foot a miracle was causing me to lose faith in its recovery and made my healing somehow more tenuous. There was more pain because I was asking more of my foot at the dances. The reality is that I was and continue to manage some kind of equilibrium as I challenged my foot more. But that has been the rule from the beginning: two steps forward, one step back—excitement in the progress of increased ability and then disappointment in the limitations of pain.

Greater ease with my foot was one thing, but then the prospect of seeing Doug again was something else entirely.

Giving Thanks

I HAD BEEN BACK on the dance floor for many months before I ran into Doug again.

It was at a monthly brunch we used to attend together as a couple, before and right after the accident. When he came in, I smiled a hello and hugged him. He seemed stiff, almost wary of me, and I didn't really interact with him the rest of the morning. Maybe he was concerned I would bring up the issue of financial compensation again. Granted, the last time he had heard from me I had mailed him, asking for money to cover some of my ongoing medical expenses. I composed it after the two men had made the suggestion, but the letter just sat around for several weeks before one of my friends encouraged, "Just send it."

Either way, this was my first encounter with Doug since the break-up, and I had been open and friendly. So much had happened since the sleepless nights where I had stewed in my anger the previous fall. I dreamed of some fitting closure, but didn't feel comfortable inviting Doug to talk about the whole ordeal. He never struck me as a man who wanted to process it, nor did he possess the ability to grasp the finer points of a relationship. It just didn't seem worth pursuing.

Then I ran into him at a community party. The Art Crawl was moving through different galleries in town, so there were lots of people milling around, reflecting on the art and having a good time. Since I didn't want to feel like I had to avoid him, I took a deep breath, stood tall, and smiled as I approached him.

"Hi, Doug. How's it going with you?"

He seemed pinched, even uncomfortable, by my very presence.

"Okay," he said, but his tone said, "I don't want to talk to you."

I felt unwelcome, while his male friend shot daggers at me. So I bade him a good evening and walked away, disappointed at the apparent wall that was forming between us. It seemed that my hopes for a peaceful or friendly coexistence had been dashed. I melted back into the crowd and rejoined my friends, distracting myself by critiquing the artwork and chatting about my favorites.

The Crawl's final destination ended at the Petaluma Art Center with a dance party. I was perusing this last gallery and waiting for DJ Val to finish setting up the music. As I wandered around the art installations, I felt my stomach catch when I saw Doug again. Only this time he was standing very close to a woman.

This is exactly what I had wanted to avoid, I thought to myself. I wanted clarity and closure, directly with him, BEFORE I had to involve a second person. After all, she might not even know about the accident. I didn't need the extra weirdness of being the one to inform her of how he nearly got me killed. I didn't want to be spooked every time I saw him, either. We had unfinished business, as far as I was concerned, and I would feel its prickly reminder whenever I saw him. *I've GOT to do something*, I told myself.

I shared my dilemma with my friends and new acquaintances at the party. They were sharing their relationship histories with me and I explained my unresolved business with the tall, bearded gentleman standing across the room.

"Do you want me to distract his girlfriend so you can talk to him alone?" one of the men asked. I appreciated the offer, but feared that any plotting on our part could turn my efforts into a bad episode of *Laverne and Shirley*. Besides, I wasn't sure exactly what I was going to say to him.

My friends and I moved outside to where the music was now playing, and I tried to shake off my concerns about Doug by dancing. There were only a handful of us on the dance floor when he came outside to watch, all by himself. I figured that it was the first time Doug had seen me dance since the accident, and I felt a renewed desire to talk with him. But soon he was sitting with his date at the edge of the dance floor.

As I continued to dance, I prayed for guidance. How can I approach him? What will I say? It was really weighing heavily on my heart, and it seemed all the more daunting with his girlfriend at his side. I know that I had harbored some vengeful scenarios, like "Has Doug ever mentioned that he nearly killed me on a glacier?" or "Has Doug offered to teach you mountain climbing?" But I was well beyond the need to needle or humiliate him in public or provoke his girlfriend. I was committed to clearing away any discomfort and give him some reassurance that I was doing well.

"What can I say? What can I say?" I pleaded with God as I continued my dance. I wanted to thank him for the experience, but how would I express that without sounding trite or forced.

Then it came to me. The last time he had seen my foot it was all purple and swollen. Now I was dancing barefoot, so it would be easy to show him my vastly improved foot. But what will I say? "See my foot, Doug. I can dance...!" Then what? I had dreamed of being able to say just the right thing to him. I wrestled with that, dancing through my fear, literally shaking the fear away.

Finally, tired of trying to prepare the perfect speech, I stopped right in the middle of a dance and told myself, "Just do it!" I walked over and stood in front of Doug, put my feet next to each other and bent down, saying, "Doug, I wanted to show you how good my foot looks now. I can dance and even do a whole night of contra dancing. It has taken a while to build up to that, but now I can last the entire night."

I then turned to his girlfriend. "We've never met. My name is Cheryl," I said, offering her my hand, "and you are?"

"Janette," she said, taking my hand.

"Nice to meet you, Janette." Then I turned back to Doug. "I also wanted to thank you, Doug." I held his eyes so he would know I was sincere.

"This has been such a transformative experience for me. I've learned so much. It's really been amazing." He didn't say anything, so I just plowed ahead. "I had to process the whole thing somehow, so I just started writing. Did you know I'm writing a book?"

"No," he said, "I didn't know that."

"Oh," I said, surprised, "I mentioned it to your friends, Hank and Mark. They didn't tell you about it?"

"No," he said, "Do you have any pictures?"

"Just the one I asked you to take of me, at the bottom of the mountain with the rescue rangers."

"I didn't think to take pictures at the time," he added, matter-of-factly.

My mind lurched back to the canyon and the absurdity of taking pictures in the midst of such chaos.

"We were both in shock," I offered. "It was a traumatic experience for both of us. The only pictures I have are the one at the bottom with the rangers and then one of Catherine decorating my cast."

"So, are they going to take the plate out?" he asked, looking down at my foot.

"No, the doctor said it would be best to leave it in. It's moody sometimes, but I do okay."

"Can you tell the weather yet?" he said with a smile.

"No," I laughed, "not yet. And hopefully, not for some time."

I recounted the doctor's prognosis and my sister's verdict on my status as a walking miracle. I was delighted at the relative ease of the conversation. I had said what I wanted to say.

I thanked him one more time before I said goodbye, and returned to the dance floor, jubilant at the success of my conversation.

I was confident that I could put my past to rest and dance into the next chapter of my life.

The Initiation

IT WAS NEARLY A YEAR after that conversation with Doug that I was sharing a movie night with my girlfriend Audrey. After the movie, she felt my angels talking to her.

"They have a message for you, Cheryl. Would you like to hear it?"

As a professionally trained Angel Reader, this was not a surprising occurrence with Audrey. I was always pleased to get their guidance, so I agreed to hear them out.

"It's time for you to release the objects that remind you of the fall," she said, "That energy is holding you back and it's time to move on."

I sat quietly as I received this surprising news.

Then she asked, "Which objects are you holding onto?"

I said the first thing that came to mind. "The map to the Peters' campsite that Donna gave me."

"Yes, Cheryl, get rid of it," she said, authoritatively.

I was stunned at the idea. That map was my only connection to the Peters, the lone relic of my night with them on the mountain. It had become a sacred object to me in the absence of any other touchstone to this life-altering event.

"What else?" she asked.

I searched through my bedroom in my mind's eye for any other items that remained.

"The quarters?" I asked. These had been in my pocket when I slid down the ice and were still covered with my blood. I had placed them by my sink, hoping they would be a symbol to remind me of my strength in adversity.

"Yes. Anything that reminds you of the fall," she confirmed.

I searched my memory and my room's contents in my mind for any other objects that still had my blood on them. I thought of my hiking pants next. I had worn them so proudly, sometimes showing off what remained of the large bloodstain. Even though it was faint, the stain was still visible. I had been able to show my friends the two abrasions in the fabric where the ice axe had pushed through and into my thigh.

"My pants?" I offered up, reluctantly.

"Yes."

Oh, no, I thought. If I have to get rid of the pants, then I'd also have to get rid of my nice Marmot fleece and jacket.

"My Marmot jacket too?"

"Yes," she persisted, "if it makes you remember the accident, then you need to let it go."

I knew that I still looked at the cuff and showed that bloodstain to people. "Look here," I'd say, "That's my blood." It was an easy way to bring the fuller impact of my experience to people who hadn't understood the extent of my injuries. Of course the coat was a reminder. No matter that it was still a perfectly good jacket and the pants were still in good shape, they were tainted goods for me and filled with the energy of my painful past. Apparently it was time to release them.

"You're going to honor those items, Cheryl," Audrey continued, sharing the instructions she was hearing from my angels. "Go to a sacred, secret place, somewhere private and special to you. Dig a hole, wrap them in beautiful paper. Cover and place something special, a marker, like a crystal, on top. You want to thank them, Cheryl. Thank them, honor them and release them. You want to do that with anything else you were wearing."

"My boots?" I said, stunned. "I paid $200 for those boots," I protested.

"I don't care how much they cost, Cheryl. How do they make you feel?" she continued. "See yourself putting them on. How does that feel?"

I envisioned wearing the boots and felt a horrible sinking feeling. "Like death," I admitted. Suddenly, I knew that I would have to get rid of them too.

"You're getting ready to move into your own place and into a new chapter of your life, Cheryl. It's time to let them go."

It was going to have to be a big hole to hold all of that clothing. And there were other items like the shower stool and my raised toilet seat to consider.

"Give those things away to someone who needs them. Someone whom you don't know," she advised. "Someone who doesn't know the story."

As hard as it was to hear, I knew my angels were right. I would have to release these items if I wanted to move on.

We continued talking, even after my angels had finished their message for me. Audrey was then reflecting on a powerful experience that she had seen as her initiation. And that's when it struck me.

"I've been initiated through the accident," I interjected to her surprise.

"How has your life been changed, Cheryl?" Audrey asked.

"It got me to write my book, it inspired me to pursue my dream of public speaking. And it showed me my mettle, how strong and resilient I am."

I had dipped into my own inner well of strength and courage. That inner power had helped me withstand the life-threatening challenges I faced in the canyon. And I had already seen how so many people had been inspired by my story.

Reflecting quietly on those gifts of the initiation, I heard a voice inside of me say, "Your life matters." Surprised to hear such direct inner guidance, I burst out in tears at the realization, stunning Audrey, who couldn't understand why I had suddenly started to cry.

She hadn't known me through those long years of depression. I was crying too hard in the moment to explain all the years when I had contemplated ending my life. But those kinds of thoughts were nowhere present for me on the mountain, after I had realized that I was still alive. Sitting on the rocks just beyond the glacier's edge, I had been given a chance to let the circumstances deliver me into death's embrace. I could have given up hope, refused food, water and help, and chosen to stay in the canyon to die. It was an excruciatingly painful trek down the mountain and a long night of trepidation in the tent. But in fact, I didn't choose death. It was a rather revolutionary thought that some deeper part of me was still choosing life.

For all of the scraping around I had done, trying to find the meaning of this "life-changing accident," it had just been laid out for me quite simply: my life matters. For someone who had held onto life a little too capriciously at times, that was a powerful statement that my being on the planet was important. In the moment, the why or how didn't matter. It was almost as if my angels decided to talk directly to me to disabuse me of any notion that I might still harbor about checking out prematurely.

And the funny thing? It was my beloved rocks that initiated me. Sliding down the ice, I had feared a painful death. But it was as if the boulders had given me a big NO when I crashed into them. They gave me a taste of what leaving this life would be like, and as a result forced me to be grateful for being alive. I developed an intense lust for life after the crash, and was driven to get myself down to safety. The other gifts have been unfolding more slowly over time, and have been harder to see. I had to pay closer attention to see the shift towards more gratitude, offering forgiveness, and inner strength that now permeated my life. I could only hope that my hard-won lessons could now inspire others to find the gifts hidden in their pain, and be led to greater peace on their own path to forgiveness.

The Ritual

ARRIVING HOME AFTER my conversation with Audrey, I immediately started gathering the objects I needed to release. I needed to ride the wave of confidence I had gained from our conversation, and took the first steps. I needed to show myself that I could indeed release any energy, object or story that had the power to hold me back. Soon I had all the items in the box: my hiking pants, blue shirt and hiking boots, the map Donna had given me with their address and the bloody quarters that had been in my pocket. I thought that if I didn't segregate these items now, I might not be willing to let them go.

The box sat there for several weeks. I looked upon it as a tiny prison cell, safely sequestering all the negative energy from the accident. I became more comfortable with the idea of letting the items go, so when I made a trip to the thrift store, it was fairly easy to say goodbye to them and bless them on their way to someone else.

I had already pulled out the smaller items, like the map and the quarters, and set them aside for the release ritual.

As I packed up to move, I put them in my toiletries bag so they would not get lost in the sea of boxes. It was several weeks after my move to my new apartment before I screwed up the courage for the final ritual. I was heading out for a hike in Putnam Park when I remembered at the last minute to take those items with me. I had chosen to release the items in Putnam because it was a large park with lots of trees that would offer me some measure of privacy for the ritual.

Trying to imagine what it would be like to do the burial, I saw myself kneeling by a small hole and placing the objects inside it. That was a peaceful image, a still life. The reality of doing the ritual, however, would prove very different.

I had gathered all the objects and a small crystal and handed them to my hiking partner, Ken, as we headed out. I asked if he had a shovel in his car. He suggested that a few screwdrivers would work, and I agreed they would be able to open the earth to receive my items.

We chatted easily as we climbed the trail, but I had my eye out for an appropriate site to dig. Luckily, there were only a few hikers out, as it was near dusk. I was glad because that meant a lower risk of my being seen. I didn't want to have to answer any passersby's questions about my curious undertaking.

We veered up a new trail towards a thick grove of trees. The gnarled oak branches interlaced above the trail as if they were creating an entryway into another world. I have loved these trees for a long time and thought they were old enough and strong enough to handle the energy I would be releasing. I sent up a silent prayer of thanks to them, as they would be helping me bury the pain from my past.

Entering into the grove, I motioned to Ken and we stepped off the trail. My feet crunched through the dried leaves and I slowed down as they softly sank into the deep, spongy carpet with each step.

I knelt down and asked Ken for the screwdriver. He took a second one out and started to work the ground with me.

"Please," I said, placing my hand over his screwdriver, "let me do this by myself." He sat back on his heels and watched me as I pierced the mat of leaves and pulled up. A whole clump of leaves lifted off, just like a lid, exposing the bare reddish earth below. I stabbed repeatedly at the earth, enjoying the physical release of tension that had been building in my body. My heart was pounding as I loosened the soil, and my hands were shaking a little bit as I brushed away the loosened dirt with my hands.

Once the hole was a few inches deep, I asked Ken for the items, then nervously placed the map and quarters inside, and the crystal on top. I've done it, I thought with relief.

My mind started searching around, trying to remember what else I was supposed to do. I sat back on my heels looking at my objects, which were clearly out of place. The bright white square of paper and the perfect round of the quarters were at odds with the irregular brown of the matted leaves and the rusted red earth. I had to trust that this improbable pairing of the elements could somehow transmute the energy and release me from the negative connection I had to them, and to the painful events they represented.

Staring at the hole, I couldn't think of anything else to add. My breathing was quick and shallow and my mind was in overdrive, jumping around, trying to make sure I had incorporated all of the right elements for this to actually work. In my nervousness to get it done I had rushed out, and now I was trying to figure out if I had forgotten anything.

Suddenly, I realized that I needed to state my intention to complete the release. I had been so caught up in the physical logistics that I hadn't given any thought as to what I would say. So I blurted out a simple request. "I release all the anger and pain from the accident," I said quickly. Then I added, "I forgive Doug and release this energy back into the earth to transmute it." I was slowly patting my hands over the hole as I spoke, as if I was packing these intentions in the hole to make sure they would fit, along with the objects.

I then covered everything with the loose dirt and placed the leafy mat back on top. You could barely see that anything had been disturbed. I stood up, still unsteady on my feet and shaking slightly, then looked back at the spot. "Archangels Michael, Gabriel and Raphael, seal this spot," I called out. "Clear any cords to these items," I continued, moving my hands as if I were brushing unwanted dust off my body. "Cleanse me from any negative energy." When I was done, I looked around and said, "Thank you, trees."

Ken had been silently watching me go through my gyrations. I finally looked at him a little nervously. "Anything else?" he asked.

"No," I said. "I'm done. Let's go."

It happened so quickly that I wondered if the ritual had done any good. I kicked myself for not being more prepared and having something more elegant to say. *Oh, well,* I thought, *I covered the basics, so it would have to be good enough.* I was just relieved it was over so I could focus on moving forward with my life.

As with so many things, you have to give it your best shot and trust that your angels can take care of the rest.

An Invitation

IT WAS THE EVENING of June 12, 2011, almost four years since my trip to Colorado, when I received a note on Facebook from my angel on the mountain, Tim Peters. "Donna, Anna, Allison, Chris and I are headed out to Yosemite in July. I would very much like to see you while we are on the west coast."

I received the note rather late in the evening and thoughts about a visit plagued me the whole night through.

My thinking went along the lines of, "I owed them something extra special for having saved my life." Somehow I felt that I had to do something more extraordinary with my remaining time, to make it up to them for their efforts on my behalf. If my life was worth saving, then what had I done with it since then? Sure, I could walk and dance again, but it had been four years and I hadn't even finished writing my book.

These ideas were piling up inside of me until I started to feel my apprehension of their visit like a physical weight.

It took me a few days to reply to Tim and agree to meet with them again. They were coming all the way from Michigan to vacation in Yosemite. Why did they want to see me?

I was feeling the added weight of the Peters' visit as the fourth anniversary of the accident rolled around. I had to explain to new co-workers that I might be a little edgy in the upcoming week, and I got tired of explaining that my body still remembers "the anniversary of the day I nearly died." In the past few years, I've seen the power of the anniversary enough to respect the impact it had on me. Once again, I found it best to just simply take the day off.

But after a week of apologizing for being edgy and explaining the story to people who "had no idea" about the accident, I was truly weary of it and ready for a new story.

Luckily, I remembered that twenty years ago, I had the inspiration to reframe the first anniversary of my mother's death as "the day she met her Lord." It had taken the negative spin off the painful memory and allowed me to get through that powerful anniversary with much less drama and grief. So when I took a fresh look at my glacier experience, I chose to declare this anniversary as "the day my angels tossed me back."

I had only recently dared to mention to anyone that I had passed through the subtle energetic gateway after hitting the rocks and losing consciousness. I was now more open to the idea that I had actually "come back." This understanding had been informed by the sentimental storylines in some made-for-TV movies. You know, the ones where an angelic being explains to some bewildered soul that they need to return to earth for some important reason.

I have no memory of what happened on the other side — I only know that I came back from some other dimension. Finally embracing this reality, I decided that it was my angels that had tossed me back. "Not your time," they probably said. "Get back down there!" as they wagged their fingers at me like a petulant child. I enjoyed envisioning that kind of conversation with them. So I started using that phrase with people. It really helped lighten my mood when I said it. Along the way, I developed a deeper sense of curiosity and wonder about what my angels had in store for me since they had sent me back for this, my second chance at life.

The Peters' Visit

I SPENT THE WEEK BEFORE the visit in nervous anticipation of seeing the Peters again.

As their visit drew closer, it prompted me to make a deeper evaluation of what I'd done with my life and this second chance I had been given. Here the Peters had gone to the trouble of saving me, but I was now asking myself, "What did I have to show for it?" I wasn't getting anywhere with that question rolling around between my ears. I needed to get out of my head to sort these feelings out, so I tried laying it all out to my friend Audrey.

"I keep telling myself that because I'm not married and have not procreated, somehow I've not measured up."

"That's just society's standards. You're unique, Cheryl," she implored. "Don't you see how you've transformed over these years?"

"No," I said through my tears, "I guess I don't."

"You are one of the most compassionate people I know. If someone is hurting or in recovery from surgery, you're there — helping. You really understand and you are so supportive. I've seen it time and time again."

I listened with curious disbelief. I hadn't seen the shift myself, or maybe I had just taken it for granted that this is who I am.

"I've seen you grow into it, Cheryl. You *have* changed. Your life has tremendous value," she affirmed. "Do you know how many people you've touched? You light up a room when you enter it." Audrey continued on, doing her best to convince me. "You know, you could have ended up bitter, crippled and cynical about life after the accident. But you haven't. Look at you!"

I guess she had a point. I could not only walk, but was able to hike and dance again. Not bad for the woman the doctor said would need a cane or be in pain for the rest of her life.

"And the Peters," she continued, "they'll probably be delighted to see you again."

"Yeah, it will be the first time they will have seen me walk." Though it was an odd thought, it was true. I had been carried both into and out of their life. "I can show them how well my thigh healed."

This family was all the more important to me because they were part of the select few who had actually seen deep into my bloodied thigh. I had a hard time communicating the severity of my injury to people once I got home. But they knew, and had seen just how bad my injuries had been.

As the Peters' visit loomed, I had to look more closely at the fact that I hadn't been able to process the experience with Doug, visit the site where I fell or talk to anyone who was there. I was trying to explain this to Audrey too.

"The Peters' visit is like a piece of my painful past coming back for a visit. Shining a light on a still-dark corner of my experience," then I continued on sarcastically, "offering up *yet another* layer to be peeled back for healing."

"You're feeling these things now, Cheryl, because it's safe." Tears were streaming down my face by now, and she reached out and patted me on the knee. "The rest of the world sees you as a shining light. You smile and dance and touch a lot of people. It's okay. You can cry with a good friend. You'll get it out and return to dancing and laughing soon enough. It's okay, Cheryl. This will pass."

"How many layers will I have to peel through?" I sniffled, still frustrated to be dogged by the lingering pain of the fall.

"It was a very deep trauma and you are a very tender person," she offered, sweetly. "Seeing the Peters will be a kind of closure for you."

Having bounced back from death after the accident, I had come to expect some big shift in my perspective on life over the long term — to somehow be more excited about my life or feel a more dramatic uptick in my sense of purpose. But life continued to be challenging, and I was still subject to disappointment. I had heard enough stories about other near-death survivors and the reports on how their lives had been totally transformed after coming back. Hearing of these revelations, I was still a bit disappointed that I hadn't been the recipient of some big watershed experience.

These deeper reflections had started in earnest after a Sunday service when a breast cancer survivor spoke about her experience. "My Spirit Guides were pretty clear," she said. "'We didn't want to have to do this cancer to you, but you left us no choice,'" she said quoting them. "I got my lesson," she reported elaborating on the specific things she had learned through her chemo and radiation treatments, "and I've changed my life accordingly."

I wondered how much my angels were laughing among themselves now. About how they had been somehow forced to send me down that glacier. Her experience felt a little too much like my own story, and I wondered what lessons my angels wanted me to get.

That I have indeed chosen life over death?

That forgiveness is a powerful act, not just an abstract concept?

The importance of support and friends?

That independence is overrated?

I had explained my reaction to the cancer survivor's talk to Audrey, and she reflected, "Don't you feel more excited about your life?"

"Problem is, you see, I'm not. I'm not up here," I said, holding my hand up above my head. "I'm about here," I added, lowering my hand to chest level. Then I thought a moment and added, "But at least I'm not down here," moving my hand down to the chair.

"Well, see, Cheryl. That is a big change. Sometimes I think you're too close to it to see. You know how you can be too hard on yourself sometimes," she added knowingly with a smile.

So, there really has been an improvement in my appreciation of life. And a newfound wonder and curiosity that lifts me up whenever I consider that I was "tossed back" by my angels. I can't help but be amused when I even consider what they may have sent me back for.

I was pondering all of these thoughts and shedding even more tears in the days leading up to the arrival of the entire Peters clan. But on Friday morning, waiting for them to actually arrive, I was a bundle of nerves, pacing around my apartment. My biggest fear was that I would be a slobbering fool with them all day long.

When I heard them in the courtyard below my door, I rushed outside to welcome them. Seeing them at the bottom of the stairs, I did start to cry. As much as I had anticipated their visit, the first sight of all of them triggered a profound wave of disbelief as my angel family came ambling around and up the stairs to greet me.

There were five Peters family members filling up the stairwell. Tim and Donna were all smiles, with their children, Anna, Allison and Christopher. Sorting through my memories from the tent, I matched them with the faces now before me. I was reminded how tall Anna was when I hugged her, remembering how she held me up on my one good leg and allowed me my tears. Her hair had been up in a ponytail then, but now it was beautiful brown hair falling over her shoulders. Allison was the one who had changed the most. She was only 11 when I met her in the tent, and she was now a beautiful 16-year-old with her long hair, expertly applied makeup and slightly shy demeanor. As more hugs were shared and tears were wiped away, I also met their eldest child Christopher, the son who hadn't been on the Colorado trip. You could see the family resemblance as he had Anna's eyes and dark hair, and Tim's smile and lean, athletic build. After the first round of hugs, I ushered them into my apartment.

Overwhelmed with emotion and having them all now standing in my living room, I didn't quite know what to say or do. Then I remembered that the last time they had seen me, I was lying on the side of the trail after falling off the horse. So first I gave them a demonstration of how well my foot worked, flexing it and standing up high on my toes. Then, remembering their intimate care of me, I dismissed any thoughts of modesty and dropped my pants to show them how well my lacerated thigh had healed. They had seen how deep and open my thigh had been, so I was thrilled to show them how well it had healed. I twisted around to show them and was delighted at their appreciation of how nice and clean the scar was. It gave me such joy to show these people who had shared my fear and uncertainties back at their campsite that they could now see me not only standing and walking, but how beautifully functional my leg was now.

Christopher led with the questions about my leg and the accident, since he hadn't been there that fateful night. It dawned on me that none of them knew what had happened to me as I was carried down the mountain. As his questions poured out, I realized that answering them all could take some time, so I suggested, "Let's get into the car before it gets too late; that way I can answer more of your questions on the drive."

As I had planned the day of their visit, Tim had told me that Donna was interested in redwoods and in seeing a winery. I had chosen to take them to the Armstrong Redwood Reserve and the Korbel Champagne Cellars for a tour. I was intent on being a good hostess and making sure they had a good time by showing off the best that Sonoma County had to offer.

Once we were all together in their rental van and on the road, I continued to answer some of their more basic questions.

"What about Doug?" Allison asked excitedly, as soon as we were settled.

I took a deep breath and searched for what I could say to bring them up to date. "Well, he broke up with me partway through my recovery and we haven't really spoken since." I paused, then remembered to add, "And I heard he got married last year. Looks like he took his fiancée up on the glaciers too."

"No!" Donna exclaimed in disbelief. "He didn't!"

"Yes, he did. It was even in the local paper. There was an article featuring him as an interesting person in the community. Doug told the interviewer that she had balked at going up Ptarmigan Glacier—that's the one he and I had climbed earlier in the day — and that it nearly ended their relationship. A girlfriend of mine spotted the article in the paper and said she nearly fell off her chair when she read it. I couldn't quite believe it myself."

"So, he took another woman up the glacier AFTER he took you and you fell?" Anna asked incredulously.

"Yes, he did," I said as impassively as I could.

"I can't believe he'd do that!" Christopher chimed in. Everyone in the van shared some variation on how stupid Doug or that idea was.

"Some people never learn," Donna opined slowly.

Having worked through my anger at Doug, I wasn't interested in renewing any Doug-bashing habits at this point, so I continued on with my update.

"But for two brief conversations," I continued, "Doug and I never discussed the accident. It was clear to me that he didn't want to talk about it. If I ever broached the subject with him, he would just leave the room. I didn't want to upset him while I was staying at his house during my recovery, so I didn't push him to talk about it. That's one of the reasons I started writing. I had no one to process this incredible experience with."

Maybe this is a good time, I thought. My heart beat faster as I spoke. "I brought some chapters from the book about our time together in the tent....I could read them to you while we drive." Then I added quickly, "But only if you want me to."

"Yes," "Please do," "Oh, we'd love to hear you," they all said at once.

Breathe, Cheryl! I'd been nervous when I had my friends read the manuscript, but to read it to people into whose mouths you've put words? That would be intense. But I was wildly curious about their response. I wanted them to know how much they meant to me and how much I appreciated their support in my desperate hour of need. I also wanted their blessing and approval on how I had captured them for the book. So I pulled out some pages and began to read.

I started with the section where Tim and Doug came back up the canyon to find me alone and waiting. Tim interjected that they had heard Doug calling out just before they were to have their dinner. "This big tall guy comes into camp," Donna added. "At first, I was scared because he had blood all over his arms." *My blood*, I thought. "Then he told us what happened and we had to figure out what we could do."

I had revisited my side of the story alone for so long, it was fantastic for me to finally hear their side of the story.

"We sent Tim to help," Donna continued, "then tried to figure out what we could do in the tent to prepare to help you."

What a revelation! After years of working it through on my own, I was now really sharing it directly with the people who were there!

As I continued to read, they laughed along and Anna commented, "That's how Mom talks!" and "I remember Dad doing that," when I mentioned using the duct tape from his water bottle to cover my wound. Donna added, "That's right, Allison's nose did bleed a lot back then."

I was so relieved that they had liked the words I had put into their mouths. I was also nervous because they were getting to hear what I was thinking and feeling about them back at the tent. I also wanted them to like what I had written. It was a very complicated cocktail of desires from this writer to her listeners.

By the time we arrived at the Korbel Winery, it was time for lunch. As we sat down for the meal, I was once again welcomed into the family as we broke bread together. I enjoyed the joy and comfort of easy banter with them as we finished lunch and moved on towards the tour. I had to stop and reflect on the wonder of this incredible reunion. I was struck still with a wave of disbelief that they were actually here with me. I felt such a rush of love rising up from within me, and a pouring out of appreciation for them and their presence in my life. It felt like a bubble rising from inside, then expanding outward. I could not contain the joy that was left in its wake. It seemed like such a marvel to me, and all that I could do was bask in the fact that they were here, seemingly enjoying themselves, and that I was privileged enough to see them again.

Me with my Angel Family: Tim, Donna, Allison and Anna

I was watching Allison, who looked a little distracted, and I checked in with Donna after the tour. I wanted to make sure they were enjoying the winery. "We just spent ten days on the road and four days backpacking in Yosemite. Allison is ready to go home."

Christopher overheard us, and my concern as their tour guide, before stating very matter-of-factly, "This day is all about seeing *you*."

His comment took me aback. Here I was trying to be a good hostess and show them a nice time, and he's telling me that I was the reason for their visit. It seems that I hadn't yet come to understand how my accident and appearance at their tent had affected them.

As we drove on, I continued to read them the next chapters that covered my night in the tent, the rangers' late-night arrival and the morning send-off, complete with bears.

"I've told your story so many times," Tim said with a big smile, before adding with melodramatic flair, "AND there were BEARS!" Everyone laughed and Donna added, "He loves telling that part! I've told your story many times too, Cheryl."

"And I've even written a paper on it," Anna interjected.

"Really?" I asked, amazed.

"Yes," Anna affirmed.

"You really changed our lives," Donna said.

It was quite a story they had to tell, after all: heeding Doug's call for help in the wilderness, then sending Tim ahead to help me come down the mountain. At their tent, they took me in, covered my open wound and gave me two sleeping bags plus their cooking pot to keep my body warm and my bladder empty. They had even endured an eviction from their tent in the middle of the night when the rangers came to evaluate me.

Their enthusiasm for telling the story over and over made it clear to me how important my appearance in their lives was to them. After all, how many times in our life do we get to really make a difference or to save someone's life? I had given them the opportunity to step up, and in the process I had unknowingly transformed each one of them into a hero. They each had their individual perspective and had been telling their own story about the part they had each played in helping me make it through the night.

Along the way I had become a player in their family's history — a source of shared pride and triumph as well as a tangible example of how they had been able to make a very real difference in the world.

The irony of these curious insights took over a year for me to comprehend. Through the years I had agonized over what token, words or gift could express the depth of appreciation I had for their outpouring of generous support. Yet what they were clearly showing me was how happy they were to have been able to help me.

That's the funny thing about heroes. They are very humble about the extraordinary acts they have performed.

Donna had repeatedly mentioned that she felt "we had been guided there [to the campsite] to help you." She had easily sidestepped their choice in the matter by relegating themselves to being humble participants in a grander plan for good. And against my protestations that I was using too many of their precious resources, they brushed me off and continued to reach again into their backpacks and their hearts to offer me even more.

Another hallmark of a true hero is that they would simply explain that they couldn't have done anything different under the circumstances, often with an imploring look of, "I'm not special," and, "You would have done the very same thing if you were there." And this is exactly what Tim, Donna and the whole family had been doing for four years, shrugging their collective shoulders and saying, "I'm just glad we were there for you."

All of this flew in the face of my furtive attempts to give them some *thing* to acknowledge the power of their gift to me. Ultimately, it was taken out of my hands, for I could never have conceived of the actual gift I had given them. I never imagined that I could turn them into heroes; I simply saw them as my angel family. But just as being able to save me had echoed loudly through their lives, their profound acts of hospitality continued to echo through mine.

As we all walked along the trail among the redwoods, the rest of the family was out ahead of us, so Tim and I were sharing a quiet moment, standing still, soaking up the beauty of the grove. That's when he pulled himself out of his thoughts, shook his head in disbelief and finally spoke. "It was your *attitude,* Cheryl." His statement stood alone and held such a potent combination of amazement and conviction that I had to take notice.

My attitude?

And what a surprising proclamation this was, from Tim, *my* guardian, the man who had come to save *me*. The man whose smile was a shining declaration that I wouldn't die. Tim, the unbiased witness to some of my darkest moments, when I was barely clinging to life. This man was now telling me that I had inspired *him* with my attitude?

After a day full of revelations, his quiet statement was still powerful enough that I had to stop a moment to open my mind and my heart to receive it.

I finally realized that it was true. My attitude said I would not stay on the mountain and that I would get down to safety. My attitude said I will dance again, against the doctor's best prognosis. My attitude continues to say I will not let the trauma — or anger — rule my life.

All of these surprising revelations eventually backed me up against the big "Why?" of this accident that I had posed to Carol when I was impatiently recovering from the surgeries.

"You may not know why this happened for 30 years," she had wisely replied.

As I write this after only five years, I can see that the gifts and mysteries continue to be revealed to me and will unfold over time.

As I bade farewell to the Peters, I had the sense that I would see them again. Tim was clearly enchanted with the beauty of the redwoods, the coast and the proximity to Yosemite as well as the Sierras.

"This might be a nice place to retire," he said, seeing the possibility of coming back to stay. This story continues to have surprising twists and turns.

And if Carol is correct in her assertion, I have at least another 25 years to look forward to as my glacier experience reveals even more of its mysteries and blessings.

*** The End ***

About the Author

Cheryl Berry has had a lifelong love affair with rocks and adventure as well as spending 25 years in marketing, publishing and editing. She graduated Phi Beta Kappa from Wayne State University with a degree in French language and literature.

Cheryl is an award-winning Toastmaster and member of the Bay Area Independent Publishers Association. She now delights in the continued exploration of the hills and mountains of Northern California in search of the season's best wildflowers.

Cheryl Berry lives in Petaluma, California. This is her first book.

You can learn more about Cheryl at CherylBerryPresents.com.

Cheryl Berry Presents

Cheryl is very engaging as a motivational
and inspirational speaker and trainer.

Speaking topics or workshops include:

Practical Forgiveness

Breakup Recovery

Let Your Loves Lead You — Goal Setting and Dream Fulfillment

Change your Story — Change your Life

Power and Practice of Conscious Touch

Or let Cheryl know what your group needs and she can
tailor a presentation or workshop to inspire and empower
your attendees.

You can reach her at Cheryl@cherylberrypresents.com.

Made in the USA
Coppell, TX
23 September 2020